THE ORGANIZATION OF KNOWLEDGE IN LIBRARIES

THE ORGANIZATION OF KNOWLEDGE IN LIBRARIES

AND THE SUBJECT-APPROACH TO BOOKS

BY

HENRY EVELYN BLISS

GYAN

Published by

Gyan Publishing House
5, Ansari Road
Daryaganj, New Delhi-110002
Phone: 011-47034999, 9811692060
E-mail: books@gyanbooks.com

Distribution Network
gyanbooks.com
India, USA, Canada, UK, Australia, France

ISBN : 978-81-212-6250-7 (PB)
First Published, 1933

2nd Impression 2022

Printed at: Gyan Press, Delhi.

THE ORGANIZATION OF KNOWLEDGE IN LIBRARIES
Author: HENRY EVELYN BLISS

THE ORGANIZATION OF KNOWLEDGE IN LIBRARIES

AND THE
SUBJECT-APPROACH TO BOOKS

BY
HENRY EVELYN BLISS

To the librarian
who is organizer and educator
this study is dedicated
earnestly

"It must be clearly borne in mind, however, that the classification of knowledge should be the basis of the classification of books; that the latter obeys in general the same laws, follows the same sequence."

". . . . A book classification, I cannot repeat too strongly, is a classification of knowledge; . . . .

W. C. Berwick Sayers

". . . . in general the closer a classification can get to the true order of the sciences and the closer it can keep to it, the better the system will be and the longer it will last."

Ernest Cushing Richardson

"I believe, however, that the maker of a scheme for book arrangement is most likely to produce a work of permanent value if he keeps always before his mind a classification of knowledge."

Charles A. Cutter

PREFACE TO THE SECOND EDITION

After six years of "tumult and shouting," of doubting and challenge, the economic situation into which this book has fitted has changed so much that a new edition has become requisite. Floods of print, theories, news, and propaganda, archives and documents, towering collections and overflowing storage, crowded and cumbersome catalogs, confused and inefficient classifications, statistical investigations and drastic proposals—a multitude of questions have thronged into the arena of professional discussions. Microphotography now to the fore! We have divided our catalog into subjects on the one side and authors and titles on the other, announces the Library of the University of California. Yes, our catalogs are too complicated; but our classifications are less efficient, challenges our old friend, Grace Kelley, in a partly statistical investigation, backed by a large experience and a course of study. We thank her for the corroboration. And not only books but documents and catalogs can be photographed, minified, stored in tiny spaces, reproduced and distributed by mail, then magnified and projected on screens and in reading machines. A millionaire union catalog can be made in a year by machines so employed and by hands and eyes otherwise unemployed. Paul Vanderbilt has done it for Philadelphia, and he has merited the award bestowed. Why not elsewhere? Why not add subject-catalogs? Why not classify the subjects in them? The International Federation for Documentation has undertaken an inquiry and has divulged that a radical revision, or reconstruction, of *La Classification Décimale* is contemplated for the near future.

It is a live situation, and it is kicking. The burdens are becoming too great to bear with a "horse-and-buggy" economy, or even with the auto-truck resources of a mechanized movement. Our book-stacks are crowded with dead books and those soon to die. Our catalogs are encumbered with their cards in complicated arrangements. In a few decades much of this material will be in decay; much of it will be useless. Yet most of it should be stored somewhere. Some of it may be precious some day. Some of it, never precious, will have occasional readers. Some of it may be reprinted. Shall we still classify and catalog all of it; or shall we select and separate? How shall we coöperate for these purposes? These questions persist. They have urged us to this new edition.

This second edition has been largely rewritten. Over two hundred, or about two thirds, of its pages have been altered more or less. About a quarter of these have been entirely reset, some of them being wholly new, as are three whole sections, those on "Consistent and Competent Classifying," on Microphotography, and on the Colon Classification of Ranganathan, and also the Appendix, and several bibliographic paragraphs.

Acknowledgements are due to the friends who have advised and encouraged, and to the reviewers of the first edition.

Henry Evelyn Bliss

The College of the City of New York,
January 26, 1939.

PREFACE TO THE FIRST EDITION

(With omissions)

Any librarian who has considered books with regard to their contents, and the seekers of books with respect to their quests, must have learned, whether selector, classifier, or adviser, that to define, specify, and relate the countless subjects and interests is the most complicated and difficult problem in the service of libraries. Selection of books may be hardly less so and of course comes first actually. Judicious selection from the bibliographic multitudes is indeed the prime test of librarianship. Then how to meet the multifarious demands, urgent or gentle, of the reader's direct approach from the author's mere name or fame may be the most pressing of the economic problems that have absorbed the interests of librarians during the extensive development of their services. But this immense "author-approach" is easy for reader and for librarian, compared with the veiled and hesitant "subject-approach" to the bibliothecal mazes thru the subject-catalog and the classification. Here the organization of services involves the organization of collections, of subject-matters, of knowledge.

That this difficult, repressed, yet pervasive problem is real and inevitable is shown in the first chapter of this book. It is likely to become more so in the changing world of libraries. Problems now are more than men or women, and subjects more than authors. Studies are less for culture and more for emergent questions. When these have been answered, readers with more leisure will return to educational and intellectual interests. These too they will approach as subjects.

That the organization of society and of industry depends on the organization of purposes and interests, and these on the organization of knowledge and thought was the purport of the first part of the author's preceding book. The relation of these actualities to the organization of libraries was broached in the fifth chapter of that book, and in its Introduction by Dr. John Dewey.

The supposition that for a changing world this ever-developing problem of the subject-approach to books was tentatively solved by an undergraduate in 1873, or definitively in 1900 by an international institute, or effectually since then by a national library, for all libraries and for all nationalities, has been edifying and comforting to many American librarians and to a few European bibliographers, but it has been an illusory assurance. For evidently two or three "systems" have been accepted as standards, tho these must be adapted to special requirements and tho they have not attained to the status of "tentative standards," as maintained by associations for scientific standardization. Then there is the discomforting pessimistic negation that the immense problem is inherently and practically insoluble, that librarians and users of libraries should get along with what they have in the way of classifications or else give up the whole undertaking to classify books on the shelves. To that negation this book is a considered and positive answer.

The opinion that imperfect or confusing classifications can be rendered efficient by means of a correlative alphabetic index to their notations the writer has called "the subject-index illusion." Notation and index are but correlative to classification; they serve it, they locate groups of books, but they do not organize subjects on book-shelves. That is classification, that is our problem.

Moreover it is a problem not only for book-shelves but for card-catalogs. Collections increase beyond capacity, and catalogs beyond convenience. This situation must be faced, and it should be earnestly studied. The undertaking to organize subjects in an alphabetic catalog by means of heading-references thru all the complications of terminologies has proved as expensive as it is cumbersome and as dispersive as it is roundabout. But cards too may clearly be classified by subjects; and by means of notation, *if this be simple and concise,* such a classified catalog may be conveniently served by an alphabetic index.

Librarians have been so preoccupied with the organization of their services and the economics of their profession that they have had scant time to study this problem of the organization of their collections. Nor have the schools for their training treated this interest educatively on broad grounds with expansive views. Where much else must be provided, the courses are necessarily meager. Beyond those confines the texts and the literature have seldom ventured. The associations and their committees have proceeded little further than their constituencies. "The historical situation" has been pervaded by a threadbare tradition and myopic conservatism or complacency. Moreover the economic aspect has predominated. But now the economic situation is changing. Libraries should be organized with more adequate regard to the subject-approach.

From these considerations we submit that this book should interest not only classifiers and catalogers but all librarians and bibliographers. It is intended to furnish a foundation to the study of the problem, and to propose a solution. It has grown out of many years of purposeful study, grounded on long experience in classing many thousands of books and classifying thousands of classes for them under conditions permitting of tentatives and readjustments such as have availed in few other libraries.

The need for such a study as this has been expressed by leaders in published statements and in unpublished letters of advice and commendation. It is pleasant to thank some of them here. Several I have thanked personally for more especial services.

For the phrase "the subject-approach to books" I am indebted to Miss Grace Osgood Kelley, who originally used it as the title of a thoughtful paper, read at the Conference at Los Angeles, and published in the *Catalogers' and Classifiers' Yearbook* for 1930. The phrase implies that readers in libraries approach the subjects of books not only thru subject-catalogs but thru classification.

Especial acknowledgement is due to those in The College of the City of New York who have permitted me for many years to give so much of my time to these interests. To the Librarian, Professor Francis L. D. Goodrich, I am furthermore indebted for much wise and friendly advice.

The critical chapters seemed requisite to complete the study. Destructive criticism is hardly less unpleasant to the writer than to the persons whose work is criticised. The unpleasant facts have been delivered as fairly and fully as the limits of space have permitted, with a minimum of argument, and this without controversial emphasis.

July 12, 1933.

CONTENTS

PART III: CRITICISMS OF HISTORIC LIBRARY CLASSIFICATIONS

PART I

THE PROBLEM, THE PRINCIPLES, STRUCTURE AND SYSTEM

"Ainsi la classification doit être fondamentale dans l'esprit et il est plus nécessaire encore de ranger les connaissances dans notre intelligence que de classer les livres dans notre bibliothèque et les notes dans notre répertoire."

Paul Otlet, *Manuel de la bibliothèque*.

"And, if we classify for persons interested in subjects, why separate allied topics generally of interest to the same group of persons by such wide digressions and intrusions as those we have noted?"

William Warner Bishop.

CHAPTER I

THE PROBLEM OF CLASSIFICATION FOR LIBRARIES

1. Some Preliminary Reflections

A book is an embodiment of knowledge and thought. In a sense and in some measure the knowledge and thought are "organized." This is true even of fiction and of juvenile books — using all the terms broadly. A book is also a form of expression — or virtual expression — of some personality or purpose, plea or passion, in life or in art.

The knowledge in a book, as organized by its author, is partly a product of his mind and partly drawn from sources beyond. The thought in which this knowledge is given meaning and life, purpose and interest, is more individually the author's own, tho it may indeed be partly, or mostly, reproduced from other thinkers, or quoted from their writings, or even plagiarized.

Books and their sources, and their writers and readers, constitute an intellectual community of manifold reciprocative influences. Libraries are not merely repositories of books, or organizations of knowledge, they are virtual and influential centers of such intellectual communities.

Books of knowledge, great or small, may be educational or scientific, they may be books of information or description or record or matter of fact, — but the distinctions are not clear. Some books, however, are valuable for their influences, purposes, or powers rather than for any content of knowledge. The "literature of power" was De Quincey's term antithetic to the literature of knowledge. Bacon long before had similarly contradistinguished "luciferous" studies from "fructiferous." Underlying all this is the qualified truth of the adage, *Knowledge is power*.

Knowledge and thought are so inherently related that in language and in literature they are wholly inseparable. Thought is but a linkage of data of knowledge, or of experience. Influences avail most effectually and most beneficially when they flow from the truths of valid thought springing from verified knowledge. The books of best influence, the best books of all, are the books that embody the higher wisdom, not of the ages — the dead ages — nor of the sages — dead too — but of the organized knowledge and thought of living science and philosophy, sifted by the sages thru the ages, illumined by the torch handed on, vital now, current and clarified in masterly literature.

But in libraries the general distinction between books of knowledge and thought on the one hand and books of influence and entertainment appears, tho vaguely, in the separateness of science, philosophy, and history from literature, fiction, and art. There was some truth in Bacon's otherwise inadequate and fallacious division of intellectual products into History, Poetry, and Philosophy, referred to three mental "faculties," memory, imagination, and reason. Philosophy there anticipated science, and poetry, in the Aristotelian sense, implied both art and literature.

History, Science, Philosophy, Philology, and Art, these are the most general classes of higher studies — so general that they tend to become all-comprehensive, and no longer distinct. History comprises a science and a philosophy of history as well as a history of science and of philosophy. Science involves history not merely of its own developments but of all social applications of science. Moreover, on scientific knowledge philosophy should ground its conceptual and rational systems of thought and belief. Science on the other hand has sprung from philosophy and has not wholly outgrown some of the misconceptions of past philosophy. Both science and philosophy are qualified by true criticism of their historical and logical grounds, while history and criticism themselves become more scientific and philosophic. Valid literature expresses thought informed by scientific and philosophic education as well as by intelligent experience. Literary expression furthermore enhances the human interest and the intellectual value of the best scientific and philosophic literature. In brief, while the best literature is philosophic as well as humanistic, the best scientific and philosophic writings are humanized and clarified by the qualities of good literature. In this sense a well selected library is all literature and at the same time all science and philosophy, all well written thought arising from well organized knowledge.

By *art* is meant here of course the *literature* of art, the books about art. A similar distinction obtains between books about history (historiology) and books *of* history, written history (historiography). The distinctions considered here are so often overlooked that it seems desirable to indicate them. *Historiography* might by good analogy mean, not the descriptive account of historical events (like geography and biography), but the enumerative account of written histories (like bibliography), that is, the history and bibliography of history. Written history, as record, description, and narrative, is distinct from *actual* history, the course of events viewed sequentially and in relations of dependence. It is these relations and the verity of historical data that are subject to scientific and methodic study. And it was to this investigation that the term *history* was first (in the 6th century B. C.) given by the ancient Ionians. Two centuries later the reciter of stories (*historikos*) was distinguished from the investigator of facts (*historeōn*). Aristotle distinctly used the term history (in the original Greek) for the literary story. Indeed this word *story* is but history minus the first two letters. A vestige of the other ancient meaning persisted until recently in the term *natural history,* which connoted specific and concrete description and investigation rather than historical succession.

Books about science are likewise distinct from books of scientific knowledge and thought. And the same is true of philosophy, save that philosophic thought and system are involved with philosophic method and criticism so that the distinction sometimes becomes difficult to apply to the literature. All thru the sciences there recurs the distinction between books containing subject-matter of special sciences and books discussing the sciences, as sciences, regarding their scope, relations, methods, histories, bibliographies, etc.

One purpose of our touching upon these matters at the very outset of our study is to show the importance of considering distinctions in bibliographic classification. Despite the indistinct outlines, the changing contents, the merging forms, of the composite subject-matters, and despite the interrelatedness of studies, distinctions must be drawn and classes defined in classifying books, in organizing knowledge in libraries. The studies, tho free, should be defined, the subjects denoted, and the books should be classified, for convenience and for efficiency, and moreover to reduce confusion.

The undertaking issues in absurdity, said years ago an authoritative logician in an often quoted passage.[1] But to pronounce so upon this practical problem from the logical point of view was itself illogical. A good reply has been given by the librarian, Mr. Berwick Sayers.[2]

There have been other negatives. Indeed the leading American library classification may be regarded as an elaborate and persistent negation of the feasibility of logical and systematic classification for libraries. This problem, however, can not be solved adequately by merely practical considerations, without logical principles and systematic organization; and this is the main reason why it has not yet been solved, tho there has been a growing recognition of its increasing gravity and burden.

2. The Value of Classification for Libraries

Books differ in manifold diversity, in matter and in manner, in infinite variety and in complicated relations. They retrace worn paths; they blaze new trails; they run wild over frequented fields or in regions hitherto unexplored; they climb the heights; they plumb the deeps; they delve; they discover *bonanza* mines; they take winged flight into the empyrean. How can the librarian bring such wayward creatures into the bonds of organization? How shall he bind these intertwining vines to the trellis of classification?

[1] Jevons, *Principles of Science*, London, 1874, v. 2, p. 402-3. In the edition of 1892 this is on p. 715.

[2] *Manual of Classification*, 1st ed., 1926, p. 72-4.

Yet this must be done, the librarian says. The educator and the scientist agree that data and subject-matters must be classified; each study and every book must organize its subject-matter. There must be organization of knowledge, thought, and purpose. It must be functional, but it must first be structural. It should be as free as possible, but it must be coherent and stable; else our whole scientific and educational undertaking would crumble in confusion.

When we librarians have recourse to a library with a strange classification, we feel frustrated and confused. How much more confusing must the "system" be to untrained readers and students? This stricture affects not only the arrangements of books but the files of cards in catalogs, whether classified or alphabetic or "dictionary." The confusion indeed may be inherent in the very system; it may be unsystematic, or unclear.

One argument for alphabetic arrangement is that it is immediately recognized and is psychologically the simplest; everybody can work it — if it be not too elaborate. This sounds paradoxical, but alphabetic arrangements of great extent and detail have their own special kinds of elaboration and complexity, and some of these are very troublesome. The main objection to alphabetic arrangements, however, is that they are illogical and unsystematic, everywhere dispersing related subject-matters; they are the very antithesis of classification. To arrange an entire library alphabetically by authors' names and titles is difficult too; then to keep them so arranged, and to find them when disarranged. As Justin Winsor said long ago, an unclassified library is a mob of books. Alphabetic order may serve for card-catalogs, dictionaries, indexes, and "encyclopedias," but for books in libraries, and in bookstores, some grouping by subjects is requisite for convenience and is an essential economy.

Arrangement by accession-numbers would be subject to the complexities of accession. The resulting meaningless confusion would be wholly unjustifiable by any practical purposes. Yes, libraries are classified by subjects because they should be.

Classification by subjects should indeed subordinate the more special subjects to the respective general subjects. There results a more consistent collocation of closely related subjects for convenience in reference and research. Books arranged in small groups in some order can be located more readily than in extensive arrangement, provided the groups have correlative notation and an alphabetic index to that order. Individual books can more easily be placed and replaced; and several books listed may be selected and regrouped for various purposes. Lists for readers may with facility be compiled by librarians. Then classification, together with a corresponding classified catalog or a *shelf-list,* may afford readers a more comprehensive survey of the resources of the library. Librarians may by comparison with other catalogs or bibliographies strengthen their collections by selection and acquisition. Mr. Berwick Sayers summarizes this very well: "As classification is applied in libraries: it brings like books together; it saves time in finding them; it reveals the weakness or strength of the collection; it makes systematic revision of and addition to the stock possible. In fact, it is the foundation of all successful modern library work."[8] Yes, classification is an essential economy to readers and to librarians.

But there are librarians and educators who depreciate the value of bibliothecal classification. They argue that, knowledge being relative, while interests and studies are various and intricate, structural classifications are likewise relative and transitory, and that the requisite

[8] *Op. cit.*, p. 71.

groupings of books are occasional. Most users of libraries, they say, have little regard for classification, and most public libraries have little need for it. Classifying in conformity with scientific and educational systems, and reclassifying, involve more expense than is justified. What is true in these arguments we admit. But most libraries *are* classified, because most librarians *do* believe in classification. Unsatisfactory tho these makeshifts be, they *do* serve needs. Scientists continue to classify their scientific matter; students partition their fields of research; and general readers want groups of books on groups of subjects. Librarians, serving these interests, envisage a problem that calls for their best efforts toward a workable solution.

Then why not combine the utilities of classification with the simplicity of alphabetic order? The advocates of alphabetic order in subject-catalogs have tried this in the past with very unsatisfactory results. The truth is that alphabetic order is not a logical order, and classification is, or should be. The two orders may, however, be combined in several ways. As regards subject-catalogs, we shall consider this question more fully in a subsequent chapter.

A recent study[4] questions the efficiency of specification in subject-classification, as compared with the alphabetic subject-catalog, indicating negative, if not pessimistic implications. The inefficiency is said to result from thirteen factors, six being inherent in all classification and seven arising "from present methods of operation," that is, conditions of application and use. Two of these factors only (the third and the sixth) were investigated statistically. For the third only three subjects were chosen and these were investi-

[4] Grace O. Kelley, *The Classification of Books*, New York, H. W. Wilson Co., 1937.

gated in only one library. If a larger number and less specific subjects had been taken, the statistics would have been less averse and more significant, and the conclusions more valid. The other eleven factors are merely inferential and still matters of opinion and argument. They have been implicitly anticipated or answered in these and in subsequent pages. The second investigation was valid from an adequate sample. In the "Bibliographical Notes," on p. 323, Dr. Kelley's book is criticised more definitely.

It needs no statistical investigation to show this writer that subject-catalogs and classifications are less efficient than they should be. Statistics are but cross-sections of experience, present or past. The *sequential* course of experience in time is often equivalent to a cross-section. Ten facts in one day may equal ten similar facts in ten days. The writer has experienced the inefficiency in question for over forty years, and he has argued adversely for nearly thirty years. But Dr. Kelley's experience is long too, and her opinions should likewise be considered. Her opinion here is averse to specific classification, as her statistics are, and comparatively favorable to the dictionary catalog. Her "inquiry" is not proffered as a thoro investigation, but it calls for one. Her argument has been spoken of as a "challenge." If so, the challenge is taken up here — on the point of an unexcited pencil.

The writer has shown more extensively why these subject-catalogs and classifications are inefficient, and he has given more facts and more reasons than Miss Kelley has, tho some of these are the same. She reasons that specific classification is inefficient because it separates related subject-matters. We thereupon invoke the fundamental principle of *subordination*. The specific subject-matters will not be separated, or will be less so, if they are properly brought together as sub-classes of a more comprehensive class. Miss Kelley argues that specific subject-matters are less dispersed in an alphabetic subject-catalog because, for one reason among others, cross-references serve to relate them. That is what we call "the subject-index illusion." Cross-references and indexes relate only terms and notations; they do not bring subject-matters together. Cross-references could serve as well too in systematic classification. To bring the closely related sub-classes or subdivisions together under the relevant comprehensive class unifies them by the principle we call *collocation.* The combination of logical subordination and practical collocation effects a *maximal efficiency* in use.

In classifications thus rendered efficient, if subjects for which many books are requisite in a library, for instance, Methods of Teaching, Wild-flowers, and Photography, were tested by similar statistical methods, the efficiency of classification would be much higher, the comparison with alphabetic subject-cataloging would be fair, and the results would be, not negative, but quite positive. But, if special subjects such as Miss Kelley chose for her first investigation, the Beaver, the Buffalo, and the Cormorant, hidden in *those* classifications behind the terms for more inclusive taxonomic orders, *Rodentia, Ruminantia,* and *Steganopodes,* happen to have very few books in those libraries, the statistical results are insignificant.[5] From very little one can infer very little. The subject-catalog, however, lets these subjects in by their common names, and the "analyticals" follow with their references to other books and pages. Thus the negative comparison is unfair and the pessimistic inference is invalid.

For philosophical and for literary studies classification may be less important, less effectual, than cataloging,

[5] *Op. cit.*, p. 84-5, 88, 92, 96, and especially 98.

and more baffling for the students, while more difficult for the classifiers. Classification of abstract and philosophical subjects and of indefinite literary topics becomes, as the elder Cutter remarked many years ago, increasingly burdensome where carried out in special detail; and for such studies general classes (broad classification) may be not only more economical but more satisfactory. On the other hand, specific or *close* classification is usually more requisite for concrete, descriptive, scientific, and historical subjects. These considerations should be applied in systems for libraries. The confusions of close classification *without proper subordination and collocation* should not mislead us to discredit specific classification in science and history, where *proper subordination and collocation may serve with maximal efficiency.*

3. Types of Approach and Use In Libraries

Readers and students come to libraries in such diversity of interests and needs that it is difficult to generalize regarding them or to typify them. Yet certain types that are familiar to librarians may be distinguished, and valid conclusions may be drawn regarding these types.

(A) The simplest, most direct, most frequent call is for an individual book, the author and title of which the applicant knows more or less precisely. This may be called "the author-approach to books." The author-catalog indicates whether the library has the book, and shows the call-mark, by which to designate or locate it. The librarians know the locations of the classes and usually go directly to the shelves, without consulting the catalog. In collections classified for the most part in comparatively small groups it may be a little less easy to find the group, but, when this is found, it is much easier to find the book. If small groups are labeled on the shelves, books may readily be found or replaced in them, even if strict alphabetic arrangement by authors within the classes be not maintained. Free access of readers usually results in considerable disarray on the shelves. But for most specific subjects the advantages of having the smaller groups outweigh the disadvantages. Classification is an economy in this fundamental utility.

(B) Akin to the foregoing type is that of the reader who wants some book of a certain author. The catalog again may suffice; but, if the author has specialized and his most important books are together, access to the group may allow a better choice than could be made from a catalog. This type avails of classification more positively than type A.

(C) A third simple type desires any good book on a certain subject. This is the elementary "subject-approach to books." A subject-catalog is primarily purposed to serve this need. But to accept *any* good book seems too simple and undiscriminating. What the unadvised or uncertain applicant needs is access to a group in a classified collection; that is, he approaches to the next higher type.

(D) If advised or provided with a list of cited or recommended books, the student already has a selective class. He may need only to choose from a select group of books. For this classification serves.

(E) In similar standing is the type that comes provided with a list selective from related special classes. If the related classes are dispersed thruout an extensive book-stack, or even in separate rooms or buildings, there would be lack indeed of library economy. Here the principles of collocation and synthesis affect not only the reader but also the reference librarian and the lending assistants. This is the higher, more important, and more difficult stage of the general problem.

(F) In this type culminates the need of research for systematic subject-cataloging and for systematic bibliothecal classification, for subordination of special to general classes, and for references to related classes. Research takes various forms and may grade from the elementary inquiry of the undergraduate to the expert investigation of the scientist or the scholarly research of the historian. In this type the quest is both definite and purposive; in the most advanced stages it is thoro and may be exhaustive. All the resources, not only in the one library but perhaps in several libraries, not solely in the special subject but also in those that are closely related to it, are to be examined and mastered. Access to the shelves is prerequisite, but this may need to be supplemented by the completer shelf-list and by reference to the subject-catalog, extending to a wider range of classes; and special bibliography may prove extensively serviceable. This is one of the more important modes of the organization of knowledge in libraries.

We have seen that type A represents the majority of calls for books and is that for which the alphabetic author-catalog principally serves; that type C is that for which the alphabetic subject-catalog is intended; and that types E and F involve systematic organization of classes on the shelves and in the catalogs. Some libraries serve only the simpler types A, B, C, and D, having neither need nor resources for types E and F, while in other libraries these research types are regarded as of the highest importance. Even in these libraries, however, the simpler types may be in the majority, and there should be provision for all the types; there should be alphabetic catalogs and indexes to the classifications. How to combine these and economize their compilation and use, and to standardize and coöperate for these purposes, are special branches of the complex problem we are studying. A library that elaborates a cumbersome classification with a complex notation and develops a catalog too complicated for ready reference is hardly a happy hunting-ground for the simpler types of use.

4. The Problem Stated and Considered

Subject-classification has been established in library economy and its value is generally recognized. The question now is, what shall we do to improve and develop library classifications, and to adapt and economize them?

A problem arises in any undertaking to solve or control a complex situation of facts and events, forces, motives, and relations. A valid answer is a theory. An adequate answer is a solution. A difficult problem seldom has a solution without a theory. A theory is a generalized statement of basic facts, relations, and principles. The problem should usually be stated first, and then the theory may be derived from the applicable principles involved. An unsolved problem of importance needs an applicable theory.

This problem of classification for libraries has been discussed for over half a century, yet it has not been considered adequately. So baffling has it been and so deterrent the posted warnings, that one may indeed hesitate to undertake it. Still, in other views, the thing seems comparatively simple.

The problem comprises four general questions: (1) What kinds or classes of books are there? (2) What books are in these classes? (3) In what order shall these classes be classified? (4) To what classes in the classification adopted are the books in a collection severally to be assigned? Let us consider these four questions.

(1) What kinds, or classes, of books are there? This is the question of likening, differentiating, defining, and naming the classes of books. It especially concerns librarians and bibliographers.

(2) What books are in these classes? This second question arises directly from the first and is its obverse, brought to *subject-catalogs,* and to *bibliographies* in manifold forms by readers and students. If the classes are not definite and orderly, the queries may run into labyrinthine confusion.

(3) In what order shall these classes be classified and systemized? This is the question of *classification,* of structural organization. It involves a structural plan, a synopsis, and schedules, with correlative notation, with alternative locations, with cross-references, and with a complementary index. These may render effectual the functional organization requisite for meeting the first and second questions. This third question is one to which our third volume purposes to furnish an answer.

(4) To what classes in the classification adopted are the books of a concrete collection severally to be assigned? This is the question of *classing.* It involves *classifying* too, for it assumes an adaptive system.

We should here distinguish four correlatives: (1) a classification of *subjects* of knowledge or of studies;

(2) a system, or *schedule,* of *terms* for such classes, with correlative notation and index; (3) a classification of *books* correlative to the schedule; (4) the *shelf-list* correlative to that classification.

A bibliography, whether national, special, or subject, selective or enumerative, may also be classified, but the term *bibliographic classification,* sometimes restricted to such classified bibliography, is usually extended to such classifications of books as we distinguish here, and also to subject-catalogs that involve some form of classification, whether of main headings or of sub-headings.

All these forms of classification, however, are comprised in our problem, the solution, or investigation, of which therefore concerns not only catalogers and classifiers but all librarians and bibliographers, and furthermore all users of libraries and their catalogs.

The relations of subject-catalogs and subject-bibliographies to classification will be treated in subsequent chapters. Here our statement and discussion will have regard chiefly to the relations of classification of books to classification of knowledge and to library economies.

Let us now outline some of the well recognized features of the problem. The books and pamphlets are to be classified by subjects, general and special, by aspects, and topics, by languages, by historical periods, by nationalities, by geographical regions or localities, etc. The forms of literature are to be classified distinctively, and the several forms of arranging or compiling subject-matter in books of information (by librarians termed "classification by forms"). Then books of larger size are to be shelved separately, and probably pamphlets. Historic antiquated books are to be segregated, and "dead" books stored apart, or discarded. Within the classes the more recent books may well be brought together, or all may be arranged by date, or period, or by evaluation, or for convenience; or they may stand as usual in alphabetic order of the authors' surnames.

This familiar recital shows that our problem presents, even thus far, complexity enough to enlist the abilities of the expert and the talents of the artistic. But our adventures have just begun. It is not enough to provide a classification; we must keep it moving and growing. No static structure can satisfy the needs of these dynamic vital interests; a plastic system, adaptive as well as expansible, is requisite for the ever changing developments. To set up a rigid structure, however adequate at the time, and to maintain that it is permanent, is the ponderous blunder of the conservative.

The groups of books must be adjustable to the shelves, and the shelves must of course be adjustable to the size of the books and of the growing classes. Even the plan of the building should have some regard for the probable requirements of the increasing collections and their classification. New classes must be provided for everywhere. The schedules will need revision and alteration. The notation in the schedules and wherever placed on books, catalog-cards, shelf-labels, and elsewhere, will have to be altered correspondingly.

The classification of the books on the shelves is the organized, objective product, dependent on the schedules and notation and correlative to the shelf-list. If the notation is applied permanently to the books, the difficulty and cost of alterations is thereby increased, comparatively more than on the cards of the catalogs and the charging-system. Economies of funds and of hours must be considered; but let us also consider the mental economies of the users of libraries.

Abilities must be considered too — the capabilities of catalogers and classifiers to classify books by schedule and index, and to adapt their classifications to external standard classifications; and the abilities and willingness of readers and students to follow the complexities of classification, notation, and cataloging. These modes of library economy, so complicated to librarians, should be as simple and clear as possible to the familiar public and to the unfamiliar scholar with his special point of view.

One recognized economy is coöperative cataloging and classifying, which we will treat later as a special problem. This would depend on standardizing adaptive classifications for the several types, or classes, of libraries, general or special.

In the preceding paragraphs the ground has been prepared for a summarized statement of the problem: how shall a system of classification for libraries be provided to serve most uses and best interests with maximal convenience and efficiency, with requisite economies, and within the capabilities of the classifiers and of the users of the libraries? Aspects of this problem have in its halting history been outlined and discussed, but no satisfactory solution has so far been found.

Answers to the questions comprised in this problem will be presented in the following chapters, treating of the principles of classification for libraries, the relations of the classification of books to the classification of knowledge, the methods of schedulizing, of devising and economizing notation, of classifying and reclassifying collections, grouping and re-grouping books for various uses, and of coöperation for economy and efficiency.

CHAPTER II

THE PRINCIPLES OF CLASSIFICATION FOR LIBRARIES

1. What We Mean By Principles

Principles in science and principles in conduct, however different, are fundamental, like the keel and timbers of an oaken ship. In various or unprecise usage *principles* range from elements and generalizations to theories and laws.[1] In the study of classification for libraries we should speak of principles rather than *theory*. Such "principles" as have been put forth by the several writers appear to be deductive echoes from texts of logic, lacking especial applicability, not derived from inductive studies and validified by adaptation to the problem.[2]

Principles are generalizations, or generalized statements, of *constant essential relations in definite recurrent actions or conformities in processes and methods.* But principles do not imply ultimate dependence on determinative relations or highly probable necessity or "causality," as do *natural laws,* nor *compulsion,* as do "canons" and laws of government. They are more general and comprehensive than *rules* or *precepts.* They are *derivative* from the respective bodies of fact and experience rather than *determinative* of facts or of conduct. Briefly, they are concise descriptive and prescriptive statements of modes of relation and action, but they are not rules of conduct or practice, tho they are applicable to these or may lead to them.

[1] The relation of theories and laws to principles is implicit, as appears in three paragraphs (p. 194 and 176-8) of the writer's preceding book.

[2] A trenchant yet courteous criticism by Mr. L. A. Burgess appeared in *The Library World,* July, 1931, v. 34, p. 3-6.

In our preceding study of classification we derived fourteen principles, logical and scientific.[3] These are general and fundamental, and with adaptations they are applicable to classification for libraries; but they must be supplemented with others especially relevant to this field. Before essaying to state them let us go over some of the ground with regard to the purposes in view. It is obvious that, whether the whole conduct of libraries be termed *economy*, and the study of this economy *science*, such a fundamental economy and science as classification for libraries should no longer lack principles consistently derived and stated.

2. Classing and Classifying for Libraries

A *class* consists of all the things comprised by its definition and denoted by its name. The class is the correlate of a concept comprehensive of the essentials of the class and similarly defined. A class of real things is real, other classes conceptual. If real, it is the reality to which that concept corresponds. The concept develops from the likeness, the like properties or characteristics of the things so classed, their individual differences being disregarded. This is the principle of the *Correlation of Classes to Class-concepts,* numbered III in our list cited above. The name of the class is also correlative to the class and to the concept.

Classes may be *relative* to all kinds of definite likeness in all kinds of relations, local, temporal, mental or personal. Classes in a library may have regard especially to uses or services, and such classes may be determined by or affected by the interests, or distorted by the

[3] *Op. cit.*, p. 156-7, there listed with references.

idiosyncracies, of those who use or those who classify the books.

It is the same as in other walks of life. "Pigs is pigs," said the Hibernian express-office agent in Ellis Parker Butler's amusing little story of that title. "No, these are guinea-pigs, and they are pets, not domestic animals, and should be charged at the lower rate": so expostulated the consignee. It is a question of classing and naming the little animals. To the Irishman "Guinea-pigs be dago pigs," and "pigs is pigs," whether pigs of *dagos* or of other aliens.

Books may be likened and classed and the classes defined and named by any distinct *characteristics,* contents, or subjects, aspects or topics, qualities or relations, internal (intrinsic) or external (extrinsic); or the likeness may be in the scope or method, value or utility, language or age, date or place of publication, typography or binding, size or condition, authorship or ownership. The class may be defined by any of these *specifications,* or by any combination of them. Some of the particulars may, however, be temporary or *accidental* and not significant or relevant to the purpose or interest. As studies, aspects, and uses may differ with persons, places, and times, there may be several different ways of classing the books and of classifying the classes.[4] Here are implied the principles of the *Relativity of Classes* and the *Relativity of Classifications,* numbered IV and IX in the list cited.

There may be several books by an individual author within a definite class. Logically, these in themselves form a class, or sub-class. Again logically, all the copies

[4] The distinction between *classing* and *classifying* is stated on p. 142-3 of our preceding book.

of an individual book form a class. At the other extreme, all the books in the library of the Grolier Club of New York, or those in The White House at Washington, may be said to form a class by virtue of that illustrious ownership.

The characters or the relations of a class may *change,* its definition changing accordingly, tho its name may not change. Classes may change because the things classed may in themselves change without passing into another class. Or the aspects in which they are to be regarded may change, or the things may enter into different relations; or they may be variously likened from different view-points. Classes are thus relative in that the things classed may exist in manifold relations, in that they may be regarded in many different aspects, and in that they may change in themselves or develop. This is a more concise statement of the principle of the Relativity of Classes. Its corollary is the Adaptiveness of Classes. In library practice relativity is especially manifest in classifying, or arranging classes, and adaptiveness is especially requisite to developing classes, to which books somewhat different in their individualities and hardly fitting the definitions may contingently be assigned. These matters will be stated concretely in Chapter IV.

A class may have several names, in one or in several languages, and a name may have two or more *terms.* The name may be changed without distinct change in the characters or relations of the class. But in any distinct classification the classes may have distinctive names and terms, which should be used consistently thruout that classification.

But books are usually classed by their inherent and permanent *characters,* and especially by their *subjects* (definite contents), their purposes, and their authors.

We speak generally of libraries having *subject-classification,* with arrangement by authors within the classes.

The class of books named Community Organization may be defined as treating of the sociological principles and methods of organizing a community. Those books that treat of methods rather than principles may then be differentiated; and those that give organization-charts or diagrams may furthermore be specified. We may further have a series of sub-classes specified thus: Community organization, methods, with organization-charts, printed in English, not specially bound, not over-size. Here we have an order from the general to the more and more specific, each sub-class being *subordinate* to the preceding. The class specified may accordingly be defined: Sociological books on community organization methods, showing charts, printed in English, not larger than octavo and not specially bound. From the logical process of subdivision and specification, which is implied in definition, derives the important principle of *Subordination* to generic classes of specific classes, and successively more and more specific (numbered VII in our list).

In the last and most particular specification within a class we may come to the individual book, in which characteristics, accidentals, and relations are unique, as, for instance, in your priceless copy of Tennyson's *Maud,* first edition, in crimson levant, with the poet's autograph on the fly-leaf and with the seventh page unhappily torn.

A class of books comprises *all* the books that may be so defined and classed, and all copies of them. If its definition does not limit the class as to time and space, it may, or does, comprise all books so defined, those out of print, those not yet published, and all copies of them that have existed and may exist. This applies the principle of the *Inclusiveness of Classes,* numbered V in our list. It may, however, be more precise to define the class so that the past, the future, the distant and the contingent are not to be included in it; or they may be regarded as definite sub-classes that were, will be, or may be included in the class. These distinctions are stated here to obviate such confusion as that by which *groups* of books on shelves in libraries are loosely called classes. We shall return to this in the next section of this chapter.

When a book is found by a classifier to come under the definition of a certain bibliographical class, fitting into it, as we say, and when that book, that copy, is placed with the others of that class in that library, then it actually comes into its bibliothecal classified group.

There are countless classes and any number of ways of classifying them. There are many kinds, or classes, of classes; and there are grades of division and subordination from the most general, or comprehensive, or *synthetic,* to the most special, or specific, or *analytic.* Those of the same order of division are termed *coördinate,* whether they are together subordinate to a single general class or to several related special coördinate classes. From these relations derives the principle (numbered VIII in the list) that *Subordination and Coördination are Relative and Complementary.*

The term *class* is properly applied to *all* definite classes, whether general or specific; but in natural science the terms *class* and *sub-class* are used distinctively, tho somewhat variously, for certain divisions more comprehensive than the taxonomic genera, families, and orders. In library usage the term *class* should not be restricted, as it usually is, to one grade of classes only, the major general subjects, such as Physics and Sociology. For these the term *main classes* would indeed be appropriate.

The term *sub-class* might then be applied distinctively to such branches, or divisions, of main classes as Ethnology, and Applied Sociology.

For similar reasons the term *division* should not be restricted to divisions of a main class, nor subdivisions to divisions of the second order. Such uses, current in the literature of library classification, are unprecise and confusing. Any class may be successively divided and there may be many orders of divisions and subdivisions. Since, however, there is need for some conventional terminology the term *main division* may conveniently be applied to the broadest divisions of knowledge, such as the Physical Sciences, the Social Sciences, History, and the Arts. The terms division and subdivision may then be used freely for any class, for any stage of division. The divisions of a main class may conventionally be termed *sections,* and divisions of sections may accordingly be termed sub-sections. So we should have five orders of division, of subordination, or of "expansion," as it is termed in library parlance; and the conventional terms would be: *main divisions* (for groups of sciences, etc.), *main classes* (for principal sciences or studies), *sub-classes* (for sub-sciences, etc.), *sections* and *sub-sections.*

Classes of books may be regarded as defined implicitly by their successive specifications and subordinations in graded schedules of classification; and they may be classed and classified according to these subordinations and marked according to the corresponding notation. For instance, a book on the Matriarchal Family may be classed under Social Sciences in main class Sociology, sub-class Ethnology, section Ethnic Sociology, sub-section Primitive Institutions, and there, under the caption Primitive Family, in a subdivision for Matriarchal Family. The systematic definition of this class of books with reference to this classification would thus be: the ethnic-sociological primitive institution of the matriarchal family. For convenience, however, the class is named more briefly, and is still more briefly designated by a mark combining factors standing for certain of the successively subordinate classes.

3. Grouping Books for Library Services

The location, ownership, condition, temporal or other accidental relations of books may change without the books being regarded as changed to other classes. For it is by their more intrinsic characters that books are usually classed. When individual books are placed together for the time being on a shelf or table, they form a *group*. Others may be added to the group; some may be taken away; yet the group remains there, tho it is not the same in all its components. The books may have come from one or from several classes. A group of books is concrete, composite, localized and temporary, selective and enumerative, not comprehensive or definable, nor relatively permanent, as a class of books usually is, tho relative and adaptive (principles VI and IV of the list cited).

Books may be grouped and re-grouped by the selective interests of some individual librarian or reader, for some purpose or study. On the shelf at my elbow there happens to be a group of seven books, a treatise on Logic, volume II of Jevons' *Principles of Science*, Pearson's *Grammar of Science*, Giddings' *Scientific Study of Human Society*, Berwick Sayers' *Manual of Classification*, Richardson's *Classification*, Roget's *Thesaurus*. This is an objective concrete group. Tomorrow it may be there, but different in having other components. In my memorandum-book there is a list of books I desire to read in the coming months. I may add a title there today; I may cross out one finished or no longer desired. That list stands in a sense for a selected group of books, tho the books will never be brought together physically in time and place. This kind of group is virtual, *selective*, or *enumerative*; it is not concrete, objective, or localized. The Arthurian romances named by a critic as sources to Tennyson's *Idylls of the King* may likewise be termed a selected group; or the books referred to by a judge in chambers in considering a case of contested censure for immorality. The list of Arthurian romances may be far from complete, and so may the references of the judge.

The books on Community Organization in the Suburbia Public Library are a selected group. Let us suppose that other libraries acquire other copies of those books to form similar groups. The selection might become as famous almost as President Eliot's shelf of recommended classics. This in any reader's room is a select localized group; but in general it is a *selective class*. In either instance there is a class of such localized groups. Temporary groups may be recurrent, and, if so, they would form a class of *recurrent* like groups.

In a classified library the books of a definite class that at any time stand together on a shelf or table are a *group* of that class, not, as so often miscalled, the class itself, not the whole, the inclusive class. This is true even if every book belonging to the library and so classed is present there — unless the class should for some reason be defined as identical with that group in place, time, and composition. Certain books may be loaned or temporarily transferred to other shelves or rooms; but by lending books we do not change their definite classes, tho we may regard them for the time as being in another class of *books lent.* The same may be said of *books lost,* or *books misplaced,* or *books not yet cataloged.* A group of new novels may be grouped with other new books on a shelf for *New Books*; these at any time are a group of new books; but all the temporary groups of new books may be regarded as belonging to the changing class defined as *books newly acquired for the library.*

These distinctions between classes and groups are important in the discussion of library services and economies. The most general and most important distinctions are that groups are *selective* or *composite,* whereas classes are *inclusive* or *comprehensive*; groups are *localized* and enumerative, whereas classes are usually neither; and groups are relatively *temporary,* while classes are relatively *permanent.*

From the various bibliographical classes of books librarians have made selection for their several libraries. From these bibliothecal groups many readers may choose lesser groups in the multiplicity of their occasional interests. One reader may pick out certain books that seem easy to read; another may be looking for designs or charts; another may desire only those in French; another may need only those that are technical. It would be impractical to *classify* books for all these diverse personal and temporary interests and purposes. From the groups selected by the librarians to stand for the respective classes the readers and students may select more temporary groups for their present convenience. Books classified in libraries, in other words, *structurally* organized, are to be thus grouped and re-grouped for the varying purposes and interests of students and readers, that is, *functionally* organized for the various special services.

4. Collocation of Related Classes for Convenience

For all types of library use classification is a convenience and an economy, but for the research types especially convenience requires that the closely related classes should be shelved in propinquity, or *collocation,* and that there should be *systematic reference to related classes* that are located elsewhere. The more general classes should consistently be followed by the relevant special classes and their respective sub-classes; and these should be arranged so that the most closely related specific groups should be in closest proximity, with regard to the dominant or the most important interest, so far as that can be determined, if the classification is to be relatively permanent. Thus the student may conveniently pass from the one group to the others that are likely to contain subject-matter of his research. He may turn from the general to the special for specific points and details or from the special to the general for basic statements and comprehensive views, or from the particular special to the relevant special for data bearing on his quest. He would be impatient, if conditions required him too often to pass to distant shelves or floors or rooms, or to the catalog. This convenience depends on two principles of utmost importance, which we term *Subordination* of special (or specific) to relevant general (or generic) classes, and *Collocation* of closely related classes, subordinate and coördinate.[5]

Having stated these principles, let us proceed to exemplify them. An applicant of type C comes asking for some book on cost-accounting. The subject-catalog

[5] These principles are numbered respectively VII and XIV in the list in the preceding volume, and Subordination is described in the second section of this chapter.

under that heading names only five books, let us suppose, and two of them are in use and the others are too old; so the reference librarian shows the way to the shelf labeled Accounting. The convenience of the collocation becomes evident when it is found that there are chapters on cost-accounting in several books on methods and also in the group for Special accounting.

To exemplify type D, suppose a school-teacher presents a list of books on Education. In the subject-catalog she is confronted by such an array of cards under this heading and its subdivisions that she turns in dismay to the reference librarian and together tney go to the shelves. There are too many references for the teacher's limited time, so a selection is made from the books examined. Both the teacher and the reference librarian save considerable time and trouble because of the collocation of such subjects as Philosophy of Education, Educational Psychology, Pedagogics, Methods of Teaching, The Psychology of Children, and Educational Tests. If many of the available books were to be brought to a table, the propinquity of the classes would save time in gathering them, and there would be less waiting. Then in both the foregoing instances applicants of types C and D advance in the presence of good classification to the status of type E, gaining a more comprehensive view of their subjects and selecting from a broader range of relevant classes. On the educational value of access to a well classified collection of books we need not expatiate here. It is for research of types E and F that collocation is especially desiderated and access to the shelves is permitted even where the collections are regarded as precious.

Collocation is a principle applicable not only to specific but to generic classes. It is important that the sciences of Biology, Physiology, Anthropology, and Sociology should be classified in this order, with their respective sub-sciences and divisions in relative collocation. The relation of Education to Psychology on the one hand and to Sociology on the other hand is evident; and the relations of educational tests and measurements to psychological and anthropological. These exemplify larger subjects for collocation in a good classification. The problem of schedulizing such relations in practical classification will be dealt with more definitely in Chapter IV. Thru consistent collocation under classes properly subordinated a systematic, synthetic classification attains to *maximal efficiency*.

5. Maximal Efficiency Thru Subordination and Collocation

By *maximal efficiency* is meant the most efficient, economical, and convenient serviceability to the largest number of relevant and valid interests. This principle may be effectual only in the probable uses of the books; and this *potential efficiency* is attainable largely thru consistent subordination of the more special subjects to the more comprehensive classes and thru collocation of closely related coördinate classes. The principle again applies the fourteenth of our list in the preceding volume.

The study of education may extend to the fields of the three major sciences, Anthropology, Psychology, and Sociology; in other words, these sciences may be centered about the interests of research and synthesis in the study of Education. From Anthropology may be drawn many subjects, such as, Human Nature, Growth, Craniology, Neurology, Endocrinology, Mongolism, Eugenics, Hygiene, Physical Training, Recreation, etc.;

and under these there would be many subdivisions, such as Child-study, Play, School Hygiene, Fatigue, etc. From Psychology there would be larger branches like Social Psychology and Psychology of Childhood, and minor subjects like Mental Development, Learning, Mental Abilities, Mental Hygiene. From Sociology we might draw such subjects as Ethnic Sociology, Folk Psychology, the Family, Tradition, etc. We should of course be dealing not with thirty odd subjects thus roughly grouped, but with some three hundred or more. Now, if these subjects be classified with consistent subordination of the more special to the more comprehensive, the finding of relevant subjects, and consequently of selected or listed books, will be much facilitated. This convenience will be more fully served, if the subjects that are most closely related to the interests most often centered in these studies are subordinated and arranged with circumspect regard to their predominant natural, logical, and scientific relations.

If another interest, say hygienic research, extend into these same fields, the scene would shift accordingly in the anthropological or biological direction, more especially to the physiological, the pathological, the psychological, and the ethnographical; but the order would remain for the most part the same. This would be true again, should the scene be shifted in the opposite direction toward the sociological field. In all four of these fields of study, to all these view-points, the order of nature and of natural and logical classification is on the whole the same. But each synthesis would select the subjects important to its interest and would minimize or disregard those less relevant. We shall deal with this problem again in the chapter on Classification for Special Libraries.

In considering the "Point of View" [6] we found that there are three distinct views, which, tho divergent, are consistent surveys of the whole of knowledge. This is on the whole true of the entire gamut of the sciences, from Physics to Philology. Without breaks in the gradation from the most general to the more and more special, the order of the sciences grounded in the order of nature applies to all syntheses, to all natural classifications, and to all those of scientific and educational purpose. Moreover, because of the inherent relations, practical library classifications, constructed on those scientific foundations, with logical subordinations and consistent collocations, would prove most efficient in service. The principles of Subordination and Collocation would avail. Such structural classification provides for functional groupings and re-groupings in selecting or in using the books and effectuates a maximal efficiency.

This is not a hundred-per-cent efficiency. Too much must not be expected. However well a classification may be systemized, some relations will inevitably be distorted, some interests disserved; there will result some inconsistencies and inconveniences. The principle of Relativity obtains. Yet despite these limitations, a classification so constructed and systemized will provide for the maximal number of interests, will serve the maximal number of needs, and be most readily adaptable to the maximal number of purposes.

The foregoing arguments are corroborated by Dr. Kelley's partly statistical study of the efficiency of the Library of Congress Classification and the Decimal Classification, as unsatisfactorily applied in four major libraries, and in comparison with the efficiency of the dictionary catalogs in those same libraries. The effi-

[6] The preceding volume, Chapter XIII, section 2.

ciencies were very low — much lower than the writer had ever indicated in his own criticisms. The reasons for this inadequacy are not only the dispersion of related subjects in those systems but the lack of subordination of specific to generic in classificatory subjects. The hardly less important lack of places, or terms, for recently developed subjects was considered only indirectly in that investigation,[7] tho this must be regarded as none the less detrimental in those systems.

6. Library Classification in Relation to the Organization of Knowledge

A classification of books is a structural organization of knowledge. If it is well constructed, it will serve with maximal efficiency for functional organizations of knowledge in grouping and re-grouping the books with regard to the various uses and the probable requirements. A classification is best qualified to serve thus, if it conforms fundamentally to the organizations of knowledge established in the scientific and educational consensus.[8] If it does not, it will lack adequacy, efficiency, and educational value.

The distinction so often drawn between the classification of knowledge and the classification of books should not lead us to negative conclusions, such as those of the logician Jevons, the bibliographer Schneider,[9] and the classificationer, Melvil Dewey. There are indeed two kinds of classification, on the one hand the logical, natural, and scientific, on the other hand the practical, the arbitrary, the purposive; but for library classification

[7] Grace O. Kelley, *The Classification of Books,* cited on p. 10.

[8] What we mean by this is stated in the preceding volume, p. 16, 222, 300, and 301.

[9] Schneider, Georg, *Handbuch der Bibliographie,* Leipzig, 1923, p. 126-30.

we should join these two hands; the two purposes should be combined. To make the classification conform to the scientific and educational organization of knowledge is to make it the more practical. A logical and scientific organization of knowledge should be adapted to the practical requirements, the various bibliographic services, and the necessary economies. It were well too that we should bear in mind that a library is, in a higher view, a temple of knowledge, and its classification should be, not a haphazard, ramshackle structure, but an internal edifice worthy of its environment and itself of intellectual and educational value.

The more definite the concepts, the relations, and the principles of science, philosophy, and education become, the clearer and more stable the order of the sciences and studies in relation to learning and to life; and so the scientific and educational consensus becomes more dominant and more permanent.[10]

In these brief paragraphs we merely touch upon this subject of large importance. But we shall return to it and will amplify certain aspects of it in subsequent chapters. The main argument was more broadly outlined in our preceding volume;[11] and the system of the sciences and studies of life and art surveyed there furnish a basis for adaptation to a classification of books for libraries.

7. Summary of Principles of Classification for Libraries

In discussing the several aspects of bibliographic classification we have brought out certain principles derived partly from the fourteen general principles that appeared

[10] This is more adequately stated in the preceding volume, p. 209-11 and 219-22.

[11] Especially in Chapter V, sections 3-6 and Chapter XXI, sections 2-4.

in Part II of our preceding book, and partly from previous studies of the problems involved. We have not merely invented them, as is sometimes done to the discredit of theorizing. They are generally applicable to the problems and the practice of classifying subjects.

To complete this summary and enumeration several definitions that have been amplified in preceding pages will be included here. Others added here will be stated and discussed in the following chapters on Notation and on Schedulizing. After each item the citations in parenthesis refer to the more general statements in our preceding volume and also to passages in other books touching upon these principles;[12] but, to be frank, it has not been easy to discover passages, explicit or implicit, that approach to clear or adequate statement of these principles, and for some of them none has been found.

I. *Relativity of Knowledge and of Classes*: objects and realities exist in relations to one another and to minds, or subjects, which by likeness relate them in classes and correlative concepts. These relations are basic to knowledge, to its relativity, and to the classification of subject-matters.

(P.I-IV; I, 120,123; II, 22-4; BS.C., 29; BS.M., 72).

II. *Classes* are *Correlative* to *Class-concepts* and to *Class-names,* or *Terms*; and they are *definite*; they are definable by their like characters, or characteristics, and

[12] The principles listed in the preceding volume are here indicated by P, followed by the respective Roman numeral; other citations to that volume are preceded by I; and this volume is indicated by II. Citations to Richardson's *Classification*, 3rd ed., 1930, will be preceded by the initials R. C., those to Berwick Sayers' *Manual of Classification* (1926) by BS. M., and those to his *Canons of Classification*, London, 1915, by BS. C.

For another purpose—a comprehensive statement of "Theoretic Principles of Bibliographic Classification," from which a concise *theory* could be derived and summarized—these principles were embodied in a paper contributed to the XIVth Conference of the International Federation for Documentation, held at Oxford in September, 1938. This was published in the *Transactions*. Some of those modifications are adapted now to the simpler restatement of this edition, but citation in detail seems unnecessary.

by their properties, relations, and forms, conceptual or real, natural or physical, any of which, or any combination of which, common to the class, may consistently be regarded as characteristic; and the class may be defined by the respective terms.

(P.III; I, 119-24, 132-3,134-8; II, 22-5,27; R.C., 2; BS.C., 29-32; BS.M., 48-51).

III. *Plural Characteristics,* or relations, and composite contents or forms may combine in a bibliographic subject-matter or class of books or documents. Any of these, or any combination of them, may be selected and thus may successively be formed different classes, that is, *plural* classes, defined accordingly.

(P.IV; I, 123,130; II, 23,26; R.C., 4-5; BS.M., 24,43,47).

IV. *Terms distinctive*: the terms defining distinct classes should be *distinctive* and be used *consistently*; for a class, tho wholly *comprehensive* of its own sub-classes, is not always *exclusive* of the sub-classes of other coördinate classes, or their terms. A sub-class may be common or alternative to two or more coördinate classes.

(I, 124,141; II, 24; BS.C., 31; BS.M., 34, 66, 111,canons 3 and 8).

V. *Inclusiveness and Totality of Classes*: a bibliographic class comprises all the items and all copies of them that may be classed under its definition and named by its term, or terms.

(P.V; I, 120,132-3; II, 25-6).

VI. *Development and Adaptiveness of Classes*: new or additional specifications, relations, or aspects, not so important as to be regarded as characteristic, but merely varietal or developmental, may be admitted into classes or their definitions, without giving rise to new classes, or sub-classes, or names.

(P.IV; I, 119-23,136; II, 24; BS.M., 49-50,59-60).

VII. *Comprehensive Classes* may comprise books, etc. of many specific differences, or specifications, which may be disregarded in classifying them. Conversely, books may be assigned to, or subsumed under more general, or comprehensive, classes, which would not fit them individually but the definition of which comprises them in general, or in the *aggregate*.

(I, 119,121,123,136; II, 23,26).

VIII. *Relative Permanence* of comprehensive, developmental, and adaptive classes: the more general and adaptive they are, the more likely to remain relatively *stable and permanent.* Minor changes disturb their whole characters less than in more special classes.

(P.XIII; I, 219-22; II, 24,28,30,78; BS.C., 59).

IX. *Natural Classes are more available*: classes defined by *natural, essential,* or *intrinsic* characters or relations are more *extensively available* in classing books, etc. than are classes of *arbitrary* or *extrinsic* specifications and purposes.

(I, 219,244; II, 35; R.C., 28-9,41; BS.C., 28; BS.M., 51,67-8).

X. *Groups are composite,* are of concrete books, etc., *selective* from one or more classes, *enumerative, accidental, local,* and *temporary.* Their components may be *re-grouped.* They are *not* inclusive and comprehensive totalities, as classes are.

(P.VI; I, 131-2; II, 28-30).

XI. *Subordination*: a class may be *divided* into *subclasses,* and these into their *subordinate* sub-classes, in each case by more specific *differences* in characteristics, relations, etc. The specifications and terms are *intensive* (in the logical sense), and the divisions are *analytic,* whereas comprehension of the relevant specific is *synthetic.* Generic and specific are relative terms. Besides sub-classes having distinctive terms, other sub-classes may be deemed unimportant and may be subsumed under the term *remaining,* or *residual,* sub-classes. This may be regarded as a *residual class of sub-classes.*

(P.VII; I, 121,136,140-1,152-3; II, 25-7; R.C., 36; BS.C., 29, canon 6; BS.M., 37-41,68-9,canon 5).

XII. *Coördination*: classes, or sub-classes, of the same order of division are coördinate, whether of one or of several coördinate classes. They should be arranged and collocated with regard to their characteristics and relations and the interests and purposes in view.

(P.VIII; I, 152-3; II, 26; BS.C., 29; BS.M., 60,69,canon 6).

XIII. *Subordination and Coördination are relative and complementary.* Classes subordinate with respect to one character or relation may be coördinate in another aspect or mode of classifying.

(P.VIII; I, 152-5; II, 26,75; BS.M., 68-9).

XIV. *Serial Classification*: a class together with its sub-classes may be arranged as a columnar series; and so may several series of coördinate classes successively, so as to form a series of series, or serial classification, or columnar schedule; and under sub-classes there may be secondary and tertiary series of subdivisions, shown by indentions.

(P.VII; I, 152-5; II, 25,75; R.C., 14; BS.M., 40,59-60).

XV. *Branched and Scalar Classifications*: sub-classes may be regarded as branches, and their subdivisions as ramifications. If bifurcate in positive and negative terms, the negative terms may be excised, so that the positive terms form a series graded by successive specifications, or subordinations—a *scalar* series.

(I, 151-3, 245-9).

XVI. *Tabular Classifications and Schedules and Cross-classification*: coördinate classes may be arranged in horizontal series, and under each its sub-classes vertically. This forms a *tabular* classification or schedule, as distinct from *serial, columnar,* "linear," *indented,* and *scalar* forms. Horizontally across the columns terms may recur—consistently in cross-classification, which is limited to two dimensions, whereas serial forms may have three or more dimensions. But tabular and serial forms may be combined; and tabular forms may be converted into serial, or serial into tabular.

(P.VIII; I, 152-5,358-9; II, 89).

XVII. *Synthetic and Systematic Classifications* bring subject-matters into inherent and consistent relations, as contrasted with *analytic* subdivision and specific subject-indexing, which are dispersive of related subject-matters. Structurally subordination proceeds from the general to the more and more special, analytically; but functionally a systematic classification is *synthetic* too; it may be traversed from the special to the general as well as from the general to the special.

(P.IX,X; I, 148,155,164-9,237-9; II, 26,72,74,81; R.C., 14; BS.M., 59-60).

XVIII. *Collocation of Related Subjects*: in *synthetic* and *systematic* classification for libraries the subjects, special or general, that are most *closely related,* inherently, logically, or scientifically, should be *collocated,* for convenience to the interests to be served.

(P.XIV; I, 238,301,408; II, 31-3,34,103-4; R.C., 26-7; BS.C., 29,canon 7; BS.M., 28,60,111,canon 6).

XIX. *Organization of Knowledge in Libraries*: in classification, in subject-catalogs and in other bibliothecal services, knowledge should be *organized in consistency* with *the scientific and educational consensus,* which is *relatively stable* and tends to become more so as theory and system become more definitely and permanently established in general and increasingly in detail.

(P.XII and XIII; I, 16,101-3,112,186,231,244,301; II, 36-7, 73; R.C., 24,32-3; BS.C., 34; BS.M., 51,66,67,72).

XX. *Natural, Logical, and Scientific Classification* may be *adapted* to library services and economies, and to bibliography and documentation; it renders more *efficient service,* is more *extensively available,* and more *permanent* than arbitrary classifications.

(P.XII; I, 186,209-11,244,410; II, 35-7; R.C., 24,28,29,34; BS.C., 34,60,68; BS.M., 51,68,72,75).

XXI. *Relativity and Consistency of Classifications*: classes may be classified *variously* with regard to different principles, characteristics, relations, orders, views, or purposes; but, while the classification should be *consistent* with its chosen *principle* or purpose, it should also be consistent with the basic principles of classification and as consistent as possible with the order of nature and with relevant organizations of knowledge. Consistency should thus be threefold.

(P.XI; I, 147-51,239-44; II, 23-4, 74,97; BS.M., 42,66).

XXII. *Composite and Complex Classification*: a single class should logically be divided into sub-classes by only one *principle* or *characteristic*; but further subdivision may proceed from other characteristics or principles; and several coördinate classes, or series, divided by *several principles,* or characteristics, may be *combined* in a complex system of *composite* classification.

(P.VIII and IX; I, 151,155,166,168; II, 26,35,82-3; R.C., 34, 40; BS.M., 56-7,76,80).

XXIII. *Standardized Classification*: a classification of threefold consistency (as stated in XXI) may be approved and standardized tentatively, then permanently, by a community, association, or other body. There may be standards for special fields, national standards, a general standard, and an international, and all these in a system of standardization. A standard classification should provide explicitly, so far as is feasible, for alternative and divergent views and purposes, regarding special subjects as well as general subjects.

(P.XI and XII; I, 244; II, 15,20,74,104-5; BS.C., 59-60; BS.M., 66,218).

XXIV. *Special Library Classification*: for libraries of special scope and purpose classifications should be *consistent with the general standard classification,* tho they would be *less inclusive* of classes regarded as *irrelevant* and would subdivide them less, while *developing* and *expanding* the *relevant* classes more especially. For the several types of special libraries, etc. adaptable classifications consistent with the respective organizations of knowledge and purpose should be standardized.

(P.XI; I, 243; II, 35,74,102-3,104-5; BS.M., 33, 276).

XXV. *Maximal Efficiency in Library Classification*: this *desideratum* depends upon the principles of proper *subordination, collocation* of closely related subjects, *synthesis,* and logical and scientific *organization*; it depends also on *adaptation* to library conditions and services and uses of books.

(P.XIV; I, 238,244,301,401,408,410; II, 33,35,103-4; R.C., 27, 28-9; BS.M., 28,51).

XXVI. *Alternative Locations* and *Methods* of *classifying* for subjects general and special, with regard to the several views, interests, or purposes to be served, should be provided in a systematic bibliographic classification and should be indicated in its schedules; and the *decisions* regarding these for any library should be recorded in its *code.*

(II, 79-81,147-8).

XXVII. *Notation Correlative*: a classification for libraries should have a *correlative notation* thruout the schedules, on the books and on the shelves, and the notation should be adaptive, adjustable, and economical.

(II, 18,47-9,64-5,70-1;
R.C., 38; BS.M., 86,112,canon 11).

XXVIII. *Systematic Auxiliary Schedules* of subdivisions and specifications that are *recurrent*, or *common*, and *composite* in a system of bibliographic classification should *economize* its compilation, printing, revision, and use, providing for *composite* sub-classification for recurrent *forms*, methods, relations, aspects, languages, historical periods, countries, cities, etc. Where two or more of such specifications are combined in *complex* classification, any of them may precede, others being secondary and tertiary. These alternatives should be presented in the schedules, and the decisions regarding them for any library should be recorded in its *code*.

(II, 75,81-3,93; BS.C., 43, canon 11; BS.M., 112, canon 10; D.C., "Introduction,Mnemonics"; Brown's *S. C.*, "Categorical Table," p.15).

XXIX. *Index to the Classification*: an *alphabetic* index for all the subjects and terms should by means of the *notation* locate them in the schedules.

(II, 17,76,94; R.C., 41; BS.M., 84,106,110,319).

XXX. *Library Buildings* and book-stacks should be *planned* and *arranged* with regard to the classification of the books, which conversely should be adapted to the plan of the library and its services.

(I, 115,414; II, 14,19,152; R.C., 35-6; BS.M., 238-41).

XXXI. *Expansive and Adaptive* classification and notation are requisite for new and additional subjects and relations.

(P.X; I, 107; II, 19,73-4, 85; R.C., 23-4,32-4; BS.M. 61,70-2).

XXXII. *Reclassification* of a library may become *requisite,* whether entire or only for certain portions or for recent accessions. Notation should therefore be applied and economized with regard to probable future alteration.

PP. X, XIII; II, 310-312.

If the foregoing principles, definitions, and statements may be summarized and generalized as a theory, it may be stated as follows. As a systematic structural organization for available bibliographic services a classification of books, etc. by their *subjects, forms,* and *relations,* with regard to interests and to practical requirements and economies, attains to *maximal consistency* and *efficiency* by *subordination* of relevant special subjects to the comprehensive general subjects, by grading the fundamental sciences and the major derivative studies in order of their *speciality,* by dividing and subdividing these in consistency with the organizations of knowledge established in the *scientific and educational consensus,* by *collocation* and *synthesis* of related special subjects, *alternative locations,* provision for new subjects and adaptation to changing requirements. Such a classification serves with *maximal convenience and efficiency*; it is more extensively *available* and relatively more *permanent,* and it tends to *standardization.* Its *terminology* should be consistent, it should have a *correlative notation,* expansible, adjustable, adaptable, and economical; and by means of this a complete alphabetic *index* should serve to locate all its subjects by their terms. By *systematic auxiliary* schedules it should economize *recurrent* and *composite* specifications and relations.

CHAPTER III

NOTATION FOR CLASSIFICATION

1. Notation Is Correlative and Subsidiary

A notation is a system of marks or symbols in some order, denoting terms or members of a series or system of things. For a classification a notation serves to denote the classes and their order, without naming or defining them; but it is *not,* as has erroneously been said, a "short-hand" writing of names. If a classification be complemented by an alphabetic index to its terms, a notation may serve as the best means of connecting the *alphabetic* order with the *systematic* order.

For a library's classification a notation is not only convenient to denote the classes briefly but is *requisite* to maintain their systematic order in schedules and on shelves, and to locate them in this order by means of the complementary alphabetic index. The notation thus is a system of symbols in an order *correlative* to the order of the classification; it is complementary to it, as the alphabetic index is; and it is *subsidiary*; without the classification the notation and the index are meaningless.

The notation may also serve as a means for referring, or translating, the various terms, or classes, of one classification to those of another classification or of one in another language; but it can do this surely and with facility only where it is comparatively simple and the order of its symbols is readily discernible, or familiar.

Librarians have been so accustomed to seeing the notation come first in the schedules and on catalog-cards that they are prone to think of notation as the thing of first importance; but the truth is that the classification is the main thing, and that the notation, however real its service, does not make the classification, tho it may mar it. The utilities of these correlates have been too much confused.

As regards principles, notation for classification has some of its own; and several of the principles of classification apply to it also, so close is the correlation. Repetition of these would be needless here. The first principle has just been stated: Notation is correlative and complementary to classification.

2. Expansibility With Adjustable Correlation

The principle of *expansiveness* was numbered XXXI in the preceding enumeration. A notation for libraries should be inherently *expansive* from its inception, and should be further *expansible.* Both terms should apply; both have been current in the literature: Cutter's classification was "expansive," and Dewey's notation is still expansible. A classification and its notation are expansive in their divisions and subdivisions, which in the aggregate we may term the first and the second *expansions.* It would be illogical to term the unexpanded main classes the first expansion. For further subdivision the notation should be no less expansible than the classification. As this expands thru subdivision and by insertion of new classes or sub-classes, so the notation must expand by adding subordinate factors for multiplication of subsections and by employing the resulting coördinate class-marks that are unused. We shall return to this in the following chapter on Schedulizing.

Implied in this structural expansion is the intensive functional expansion, or development, of the subject-matters or contents of the classes. Development is the better term, as used in the study of Logic, and this term was distinctive in the sixth principle of our preceding enumeration.

More concretely the selected groups of books on the shelves increase by addition of new books. This kind of expansion necessitates adjustment of groups to shelves and to *stacks,* relative to classification and notation. *Relative location* was the term brought forth with Dewey's *Decimal Classification,* with meaning antithetic to *fixed,* as of labels fixed to shelves. *Adjustable,* the term used by certain English librarians, is more fitting; for all locations are relative, as the doctrine of "relativity" avers. So *adjustable correlation* of notation to classification and of both to shelves and book-stacks is the principle that we shall link with that of expansibility. It is implied that expansion should not distort the collocation of related subjects.

Theoretically there is no limit to such expansibility, but practically there is a limit of feasibility and convenience, when further subdivision would be too elaborate and the notation with the additional factors would be too lengthy and complicated. Classification and notation, however expansible, should be actually expansive only within the limits of convenience and economy. We shall have to estimate what this *economic limit* usually is, tho of course it varies with conditions.

3. Capacity of Notation

As a classification subdivides and its subdivisions multiply, its notation adds factors to multiply its permutations. The capacity of the notation to do this depends on the number of symbols employed and the number of these combined in the individual marks. It is not *combinations* in the mathematical sense that we are dealing with, but *permutations.* The expansion of a notation depends on the *permutative capacity* of the symbols employed. *Capacity of notation* will be a convenient term.

Combinations are irrespective of the order in which the things appear. Of the letters, A, B, C, D, and E, combined in threes, there are only six combinations: ABC, ABD, ABE, ACD, ACE, ADE. But each of these combinations may have six permutations; thus, ABC, ACB, BAC, BCA, CAB, CBA. This is without repeating any of the letters, and is what is usually meant by permutations of different things. If all possible repetitions be allowed (thus: AAA, AAB, AAC, ABA, ABB, ABC, ACA, ACB, ACC, etc.), three letters may have 27 permutations, the cube of 3. So the permutative capacity is much greater. If the five letters were taken thus, the number of permutations would be 125, the cube of 5. Notation for library classification may well employ this larger capacity.

The series of symbols employed may be termed the *base*; and the number of *factors,* or *components,* put into the permutations equals the exponent of the *power,* in the mathematical sense of the term. Thus the base 1–5, expanded to the third power, produces 125 permutations, each of three factors. The larger the base the more rapidly the capacity expands. The cube of 10 is 1,000; the third power of 25 is 15,625. Generalized, we have the simple formula $P=n^r$, that is, the number of permutations is equal to the number of the base raised to the power indicated by the exponent. This is much simpler than the ordinary mathematical formula for the number of permutations of n *different* things taken r at a time: ${}_nP_r=n(n-1)\ (n-2)\ \ldots\ (n-r+1)$. "Different" here means that there are to be no repetitions. In AAA and ABA the A is the same.

The number of symbols employed we will term the *length of base.* The second factor may analogously be termed the *breadth of base.* The product of the two factors, or second power, or square, we will term the *area of the base.* This is correlative to the first *expansion* of the classification into *sections.* The second expansion of the classification into sub-sections utilizes the third factor of the notation, analogous to the *depth.* The expansible *capacity* of the notation provides for the expansive *contents* of the classification.

Expansion should not, we repeat, exceed the limits of economy; subdivision should not surpass probable needs; the notation should not be too lengthy nor too complicated for economical marking and reading of marks on books and on cards.

It is customary to denote not only the class but the relative order of the individual author and book within the class; that is, the notation, or *mark,* for the book is complex, composed of the class-mark, then usually the initial and number for the author's name, and also some mark for the denoting and placing of the individual book; so three or four symbols besides the class-mark may be requisite. Most librarians will agree with the writer that marks of more than eight factors are too long for rapid reading and writing and ready remembering, and therefore exceed the economic limit. We must conclude that for the class-notation the economic limit is three or four factors. The writer thinks it is four rather than three; yet, to be on the safe side, he terms the capacity of the fourth power the *super-capacity.* This may be requisite, and it should be available, but, where used, its length should be compensated by a shorter author-number or book-notation.

The longer the base, the larger the capacity, increasing in geometrical progression; for equal capacity shorter notation. But there is another important advantage in length of base. It provides for a larger content of coördinate main classes. Why it is so advantageous to have an adequate number of main classes will be shown more especially in the next chapter. Each fundamental science, each major composite, and each important sub-science should have its main class and its own distinctive symbol, as a basis for subdivision and expansion. The requisite number is about twenty. Ten are certainly too few and a hundred too many. This content of the base is one of the most important considerations in practical classification and notation for libraries.

Important too is the *area,* or square, of the base; for many sciences and studies have a dozen or more branches, besides the recurrent *forms*; history, periodicals, miscellanies, etc. Twenty to thirty sections have in the writer's experience usually sufficed for the content, and twenty-five proves to be a convenient average. But of course classes differ; and so will opinions on this matter. It is evident, however, that for the sections as for the classes, ten are too often too few. For the present contents it seems fair to estimate that 400 to 500 sections are requisite, and for this the area of over 600 would amply provide, with provision for probable future requirements.

Some kinds of notation, using letters for the main classes and sections, differ in apportioning their subordinate contents to a consecutive series of numerals, so that certain numbers are assigned and others unassigned. The notation of the Library of Congress and that of the English system of Brown exemplify this method. Such notation is expansible either by insertion of subdivisions coördinate with those already assigned or by subordination under a subsidiary decimal notation.

Standing on its own method, its simplest marks are too long. In places where the assigned numbers are close, or dense (in the mathematical sense of the term), the limit may soon be reached. Its super-capacity, utilizing the decimal principle, tends to become still more uneconomical.

In the Library of Congress QC 455 is for Solar Spectrum, 457 for Infra-red spectrum, and 459 for Ultra-violet. It is not unlikely that more than one sub-section between those cited here will be requisite. The mark for Geology is QE, Mineralogy and Petrology having 351-499. In Mineralogy 58 of the 149 numbers are assigned, and one of these, 389, has fifteen decimal subdivisions, the Oxygen salts being .6 and their Carbonates attaining to the mark QE 389.61, which may be cited as a specimen of such *hyper-notation.* More detailed comment on this notation and on Brown's and on Ranganathan's will be deferred.

In the notation of automobile licenses such combinations as 2N-48-37-N.Y. exceed the economic limit and the speed-limit for instantaneous vision. Letters have been introduced, but not enough of them. If letters were used more consistently, the permutations of five could mark over a million vehicles. Such notation would be more quickly read in the flash of an eye or of a street light, when the speeders or robbers are flying fast; it would be more distinctly impressed on the sense and more accurately remembered.

4. Are Letters Less Legible Than Figures?

The question whether letters or figures are best for the notation of classification for libraries has long been a controversial one, and some of the obvious facts stated in the foregoing pages have been clouded with unreason. The prevalent prejudice in favor of the figures seems to persist for the supposed reason that they are simpler, more legible, and afford more homogeneous marks. Let us examine this reason a little more reasonably.

The notation on books and on cards should of course be as simple, as short, as legible, and as homogeneous as is compatible with the purposes to be served. It should be composed of not more than three or four kinds of familiar symbols and their combinations should not be too complicated. The letters of the English alphabet and the Arabic numerals are for English speaking peoples the most familiar symbols that are well adapted to the purpose. Other alphabets or other systems of symbols might be used, if they were not less familiar and less convenient.

Are the figures indeed so much more legible than the letters as to offset the economies of using these; in other words, are marks of *five* figures simpler or more legible than marks of *three* letters, even in unmeaning combinations? They are *not*. There is psychology as well as common sense back of this negative.

A generation ago, when this controversy among librarians was a live one, Wilhelm Wundt, the great leader in experimental psychology, had written that: "When the impressions are somewhat more complex but of a peculiar character, such as single lines, figures, and letters, three of four of them are generally apperceived simultaneously, or, under favorable conditions, even five." [1]

The American psychologist, Ladd, who with James, brought the experimental psychology to America, stated that "the discernment-time," or "apperception-time" depends upon the complexity of the operations required. "To recognize three letters at once required about half the time necessary to recognize five or six." But the time was so brief, .02 of a second for three letters, .04 for five letters, that the difference is immaterial. "In apperceiving figures, however, it requires little longer to master three than one, but considerably longer to master four than three. The

[1] *Outlines of Psychology*, tr. by Judd, Leipzig, 1897, p. 212.

obvious reason for this is our habit of grasping numbers in periods of three each." [2]

So experimental psychology had a generation ago given its answer to the question controversial among librarians then and since. In the following decade another eminent American experimentalist translated the work of another leading German authority, and from his summary of results in this investigation the following passage is quoted:

"The difference between simple and complex stimuli has received special attention in the domain of vision (letters, words, numbers, pictures). Within certain limits, increased complexity of the initiatory impression makes no difference to the length of the reaction: indeed, short words are cognized even more quickly than single letters, and numbers of two or three places hardly less quickly than simple numbers. A further increase in the number of constituents is required to produce a distinct increase of reaction time. This shows that the conditions of the sensory apprehension of complex impressions remain the same with those of the apprehension of simple stimuli up to a certain point of complexity, ..." [3]

The matter has been investigated since especially in the interest of the psychology of reading. It has been found that in reading the eyes move along the line in a succession of steps, or jumps, between which they pause for very brief instants to take in the words or letters or figures that are clearly enough perceived. Ingenious experiments allowing readers peeps only of from .1 to .01 of a second have shown that the average reader can instantaneously take in about ten letters, or three or four familiar words with meanings. But for combinations of unmeaning letters ("nonsense syllables," . . . . or unpronounceable, or all consonants) the limit of instantaneous apprehension is "four or five letters, in the majority of cases, although as many as six or seven letters may, in exceptional instances, be read." . . . . "Accordingly we find that readers recognize,

[2] Ladd, George T., *Outlines of Physiological Psychology*, 7th ed., 1898, p. 368 and 371.

[3] Külpe, Oswald, *Outlines of Psychology*, tr. by E. B. Titchener, London, 1909, p. 417-18.

apparently in one pulse of attention, four or five unrelated marks of different shapes, four or five letters in which such marks are unitarily combined, or four or five unrelated words which are still higher unitary complexes of these letters." [4]

More recent experimental findings may differ in details, but their outstanding reply to our question is that combinations of four or five letters and figures are taken in so nearly instantaneously that differences are not appreciable, but, when groups of five figures are measured against combinations of three letters, the shorter marks are recognized and read more quickly, easily, and accurately, as they may also be written. If the letters spell familiar words, they are recognized the more readily. MARK is read more quickly than 4723; CAT is manifest, while 853 may not be free from error. If we can put two and two together instantaneously, we may conclude that 2 and A and B in such combinations as 2AB, BA2, and even B2A may be read almost instantaneously. They present no real obstacle in notation. If four figures can be read more quickly, the difference is inappreciable.

So we are justified in our statement that a notation of letters or of letters and figures combined is virtually as legible as a notation of figures alone, and it is shorter to write and is more readily remembered or carried in the mind, especially in transferring records.

Some short words or combinations of letters may have objectionable meanings or may appear ludicrous. Such may be omitted from the notation. It need not LEER; it should not CUSS; and ROT may be held to be unfit for a shelf in a library. But there are very few really objectionable words of three letters. Moreover, as we become accustomed to marks of this kind on the backs

[4] Huey, E. B., *The Psychology and Pedagogy of Reading*, 1908, Chapters II and III, particularly p. 48, 56, 63, 64, and 69. This author rested his statements on the investigations of Erdman and Dodge in Germany and of Dearborn and of Cattell in this country.

of the books, we cease to regard them as words and do not notice their linguistic meanings. So this objection too should not be thought to outweigh the manifest economies of a notation of letters. Indeed it is more than offset by the mnemonic values of words and even of letters. Short marks that may be more easily read and remembered are a real economy; and long marks scrawled on the backs of books are obtrusively objectionable.

5. Homogeneity Is Not Requisite

Several kinds of symbols may be used distinctively for different *orders* or *forms,* but such combinations, if overdone, tend to lengthen and complicate the notation. Moreover objection to combinations of letters and figures has been urged on the ground that they are confusing to the eye or to the mind. There is something in this. And, where there is a prejudice, there may be a kind of mental resistance. But the disadvantage is not enough to offset the advantages of feasible economy.

If homogeneity were the prime requisite, either the letters or the figures could be used alone. The figures may be used as decimals in successive expansions, and they might be applied to mark not only the class but the order of the books within the class; and the notation would again be expansive. But such homogeneity is *not* the prime requisite. In *book-notation* (as distinguished from *class-notation*) it has been found convenient and economical to combine the initial of the author's surname with one or two figures relative to alphabetic order. Such marks are by a professional metonymy called *Cutter numbers,* or *author-numbers,* tho only the suffix is a number and the main thing is the initial; so they are certainly not homogeneous; yet librarians have adopted the device as simple and unobjectionable. They have even added a third kind of symbol in the lower-case letters that indicate the titles of the books. Such marks as B46d are *not* homogeneous, not "pure," but they have long been established in American library economy, and they are economical — and familiar. Such marks as B46, 4BC, and CB6 are *not* disconcerting; they are familiar to librarians in book-notation, to clerks who classify and mark goods, to stenographers who file business correspondence, to theater-goers, to high-school students of algebra and to everybody on automobiles. If C94 is simple and economical to designate Cutter's name, is it not just as simple and economical to designate Antiquated textbooks in Chemistry? It is briefer than 541.8, and simpler too. If R, prefixed to a number and standing for Reading-room, is convenient, why not 3, prefixed to a class-mark of two or three letters, such as 3LB, standing for Biographical dictionaries in the Reading-room? We must conclude that homogeneity is not requisite.

6. The Value of Mnemonics

Notation, as a kind of symbolical language, depends extensively on memory of meanings. In learning to read and write a new language we gradually learn the words and their meanings and remember more and more of them. In like manner librarians and the users of libraries gradually learn the order of the classes and remember the class-marks, tho they continue to make use of the catalogs, shelf-lists, and index to the schedules. The more systematic the system is, the more readily they will learn and the more efficiently they will remember. This is the natural and rational ground for a system of *mnemonics,* or symbols that may be readily and systematically remembered.

Any kind of symbol, or combination of such, may thru usage come to signify a meaning, an idea, or in language a word. It does not need to look like, or sound like, the thing signified by it. *Giraffe* does not look like the animal with the long neck. *Bee* does, however, sound somewhat like the bee's breezy wings. Language thus has its onomatopœic elements and tendencies. They add to the significance of words and they may facilitate the memory of terms. *Whirr* and *purr, snarl* and *howl, drowsy* and *curt* are intrinsically expressive and *intensively mnemonic.* Most words are commonly, or extensively, mnemonic.

But numbers are *not* mnemonic, for the figures that compose them are not; and, if they are or must be remembered, it is despite this lack. Of course neither are letters alone mnemonic; but combinations of letters tend more readily than numbers to become mnemonic, for the very reason that we are all accustomed to the common mnemonic values of such combinations in words. Figures and numbers are arithmetical not linguistical; they have other uses than to express meanings; they are just numbers. Yet librarians remember numbers of the notation of the Decimal Classification; but in this they are working against nature and against linguistic tendencies. A literal notation is more readily remembered, because it is more linguistic and the letters are more distinctive; they "stick better" to the captions. Again a literal notation is more easily remembered because it affords shorter marks for a larger number of the important subjects. For instance, CB for Physical Chemistry is easier to remember than 541.3, because shorter; but, if C is mnemonic for Chemistry, and the main class Physics is marked B, the mark CB for Physical Chemistry is doubly mnemonic, and intensively mnemonic. It is very convenient to have such mnemonics to carry in the mind in many processes of library work.

But intensive mnemonics should be casual; they should just fall into the system, fit there, and belong there; they should not be forced into place. We should not use A for Astronomy and B for Biology, nor A for Art and B for Bibliography, nor any other arbitrary choice and combination. Mnemonics in library notation should not displace apt collocations nor subordinations and coördinations; if arbitrary, they may distort classification and cost more than they are worth. It is because of such misuse that mnemonics were in the controversial past condemned without proper hearing.

The most important kind of mnemonics are what we shall call *systematic mnemonics*. They are recurrent thruout the system more or less constantly. Those that always denote one caption, or kind of class, one form or kind of book, we shall term *constant*, or invariable; those that are used sometimes for one caption, sometimes for another, we shall term *variable mnemonics*. Systematic mnemonics may be quite extensive in scope and application, while many are quite intensive. They should make for economy in the system without overburdening the memory or confusing the mind of the classifier.

In a notation combining letters and figures the figures may be used distinctively for recurrent specifications of certain subjects antecedent to the specific subdivisions and relative to the *form* or kind of book or to some special collection, e.g., Periodicals, Miscellanies, History and scope of the subject, Bibliography, Dictionaries, Manuals, etc. The value of such mnemonics is recognized by some such provision in the leading systems. In the Library of Congress, however, they are minimized. Mnemonics that indicate locations, rooms, or special collections may be termed *locative,* or *indicative,* while those that specify *format,* or forms, or kinds of books, may be termed *form-mnemonics.* In library parlance the meaning of *form* has been extended. "Common subdivisions" is a term of too general applicability. We shall return to this matter in the next chapter.[5]

7. How Requisite Capacity With Requisite Economy Is Attainable

The shorter and simpler the notation is, the more readily it is remembered and recorded. To attain the requisite capacity without exceeding the economic limit we must utilize a base as long as is feasible. The figures alone are inadequate. A notation based on the 26 letters of the English alphabet would have an *area* of 676 sections, and the maximum capacity of its second expansion would be 17,576 sub-sections, plus 676 sections and 26 main classes, or 18,278. A notation of three letters has a capacity about eighteen times that of three figures. To attain as much capacity a notation of figures would have to be expanded to five factors, and this exceeds the economic limit.

A notation combining 24 or 25 letters with the nine figures is advocated here, and such a notation has been tried out in the system proposed by the writer years ago and now published. The figures would be used as systematic mnemonics for preliminary or antecedent captions, *forms,* departmental and special collections, etc. The cipher should not be used, because similar to the letter O. The letters Z and S, when hastily written,

[5] See the writer's article "Form in Classification" in *The Librarian,* v.26, p. 128-130, Jan., 1937.

may be confused with 2 and 5, but if the handwriting in libraries be careful enough, these may be retained.

The base of 25 letters provides adequately for the major sciences and studies. Together with nine numeral main classes, the *area* of the 34 main classes is 1156 sections; the maximum capacity would be 39,304 sub-sections, plus 1156 sections, plus 34 main classes, a total of 40,494. But deductions must be made. The *feasible,* or practical, capacity is considerably less than the *maximum* capacity, but it should be greater than the *requisite* capacity. We do not carry a pail brimful of water — indeed not when its feasible capacity is more than is requisite. Again we should distinguish between the present *contents* and the *requirement,* in which some provision should be made for the future, tho of course only by estimate. The feasible capacity should always be ample for this requirement.

The chief deductions are for the sake of system and mnemonics; then there should be deductions for objectionable spellings and combinations of letters and figures. The systematic mnemonics are not always applicable. Even the *constant* mnemonics may not be required in some sections and sub-sections. Thus, under Biography of Chemists there would be no need for Periodicals. Some of the numeral classes might have very meager contents. The class for Bibliography, including Library Economy, etc., might have contents for a quarter of its capacity. The same may be found for the class for Miscellanies. But the numeral classes for Special Collections and Departmental Libraries might require all of their feasible capacity.

For the literal main classes some of the constant mnemonics will be useless; some of the variable mnemonics will be irrelevant. For the numeral sections few literal sub-divisions would be required. This would minimize the occurrence of such marks as B8K, which may be objectionable. In the numeral classes such marks would not be extensively used, except in the special collections; but here the mnemonic prefix would be advantageous. These items cannot be estimated closely, but the opinion is offered here that the several deductions would amount to about 5,000. The total deductions considered here would amount to something like 11,000. The feasible capacity of the entire notation would be considerably over 29,500, say in round numbers about 30,000. The requirement would of course depend on the scope, size, and specialization of the collection. Specifications by country, language, or historical period might indeed utilize super-capacity. For more complex specifications and relations, for pamphlets, documents, periodicals, clippings, etc. further "expansions," partly by means of mnemonic schedules, may be requisite, tho for libraries and for bibliographies they may not be economical. But for books and pamphlets on specific subjects the feasible capacity of the second expansion would usually suffice even for very large libraries. It would seem that the limit of expansion would be reached in the classification sooner than in the notation. Of course, wherever requisite, the *super-capacity* might be utilized by adding a fourth factor. Another means occasionally available would be intercalation of lower-case letters for certain subsidiary sub-sections.

Some classes and sections have more expansive contents than others and tend to exceed their capacity sooner. Such inequalities are inevitable in any system. Those whom we have helped so far to see into this complicated problem will perceive that herein lies a strong argument for length of base and breadth of *area* — to provide for enough main classes and sections.

Those who associate their preference for a notation of figures with fealty to the father of the Decimal Classification should know that Dr. Dewey was also the uncle of the heterogeneous notations which Mr. Cutter so earnestly reared as his well-favored offspring. In those days of argumentative tilting, when the foundations of library economy were being laid, those two brothers in arms were not always on the same side of the controversy; but in this question of notation they agreed in so far as the two following passages from Dr. Dewey's writings would show:

"Of the comparative advantages of figures and letters Mr. Cutter has given a summary which agrees perfectly with my experience. . . . .

"Probably most librarians would vote for the simpler figures even though they were not so compact; but my strong leaning to the shortest of all methods leads me to find all possible advantages in the letter method. At Amherst, after careful consideration, the balance of advantages rested with the numbers, and we adopted the simplest numerical scheme. I should like to see some one else test the letters thoroughly."

"As often stated, my claims for the Amherst plan were based not on the way it is filled out, but upon the central idea of a complete index, ... Its merits and some additional would all be in a classification and index adapted to this scheme. [Notation of letters and figures combined]. If a competent committee would prepare it, I have faith to believe it might be the best yet offered."[6]

From the foregoing considerations we must conclude that a notation of letters combined with figures for anterior systematic mnemonics would have ample capacity within the economic limit of three or four factors, would be as simple as an adequate notation of figures, and for any objectionable features or details would more than compensate by the economies of its systematic mnemonics and by the shortness of its marks. Such notation is homogeneous thruout the body of its main classes and sections, such class-marks as BA, BGA, and BAG being the rule, and such marks as B3T being exceptional. The figures would regularly appear either as mnemonic pre-

[6] *Library Journal*, v. 3, p. 248, and v. 4, p. 10 and 78.

fixes for anterior classes, such as 1 for Reference collection, 7 for Miscellanies, and 8 for Special collection; or as mnemonic suffixes relevant to a systematic schedule, e.g. BA7 for Miscellanies in Theoretical Physics. The figures would rarely be used except as mnemonics. The letters too would often be mnemonic, casually and advantageously. In such notation for library classification we should most conveniently attain the requisite capacity with the requisite economy.

8. Internal Notation

It is the notation of classification and of systematic mnemonic schedules that we have so far been considering. But notation for libraries usually provides also for designating the individuals of the class, whether authors, books, or other things, and for maintaining the order of their *arrangement within* the class. It is more consistent, simpler, and more economical to regard the book as the individual to be so designated, rather than the author; for thus we avoid intermediate designation of the author and complication of the notation by the customary addition of a mnemonic lower-case letter (or sometimes two letters) to indicate the title, and sometimes further addition to indicate duplicate copies, as cop. 2, etc. Such complications are heterogeneous, cumbersome, and objectionable. Advocates of such notation should cast out the *beams* in their own notation before they carp at the *motes* in class-marks of other systems.

To exemplify the simpler notation, the mark $\substack{\text{JTR}\\ \text{H8}}$ for Huey's *Psychology and Pedagogy of Reading* indicates the subject Teaching Reading and that the relative place of that book within that sub-section of Education is marked by H8. The entire mark designates and locates the individual book. A second copy may have the internal notation H8.2.

The *Alfabetic-order Table,* devised by Charles A. Cutter some fifty years ago, assigns numbers to follow initials of surnames correlative to a conceptual alphabetic order of all authors' surnames; for example, D55 corresponds to any surname beginning with Dick; it may be Dickens, while D56 may stand for Dickinson; but other names may be assigned to the numbers, or conversely, other proximate numbers to these names. It is a matter of adjustment. The numbers are regarded as decimals, and thus the notation is indefinitely expansible. In the printed Table two-figure numbers are arranged in columnar sequence between two columns of letters representing truncated surnames the initials of which are consonants, except Q, S, X, Y, and Z, which are arranged, together with the vowel-initials, in a supplementary portion of the table, as requiring a second letter (and Sch a third letter), tho with but one figure. After some years this Table was "altered and fitted with three figures" by Miss Kate E. Sanborn, the vowels and S still being separated in a supplementary portion of the table. This, and indeed the simpler original table, seem needlessly cumbersome and inconvenient. They seem to rest on a misconception of their use, which is not to designate names, but to indicate relative order of names. For classes having very many authors such tables may have their reason, but for most classes they are too elaborate and require too much time.

In an article on "Simplified Book-notation" in *The Library Journal* for December, 1910, the writer maintained that the number should indicate not the author but the individual book; that the table should be simplified by reduction to one placard of numbers of one figure (except for B, C, D, and M, each of which may well include the two-figure numbers ending with 5, e.g. 25); that the vowels and S should not be separated and treated differently; that the table should be used as a starter, or finder, to indicate the approximate alphabetical place, not as a designator or assigner of the numbers; that the lower-case letters should not be used to mark titles, except where they prove more economical than decimal numbers; and finally that the volume-numbers may well be added to complete the marks of the books. The simplified table then referred to was printed in *The Library Journal* for February, 1912, with examples of simplified marks. Before then some librarians had been omitting the numbers and arranging books merely by the author's initial. Such economies have since been widely adopted.

A few specimen marks will show how economical this notation combining letters and figures really is. To facilitate printing here, the entire marks are placed in single lines with a comma between their parts. These are transcribed directly from the backs of a group of books on a shelf at the writer's elbow, which were selected not for this but for another purpose.

AFA,	F6	Flint, *Philosophy as Scientia Scientiarum.*
AL,	J9	Joseph, *Introduction to Logic.*
AKA,	P32	Pearson, *Grammar of Science,* 2nd ed.
AKA,	P3/1	Pearson, *Grammar of Science,* 3rd ed., v. 1.
AKA,	P77	Poincaré, *Science et l'hypothèse.*
AKA,	P78	Poincaré, *Science et Méthode.*
A7,	W9/1	Wundt, *Philosophische Studien,* Band 1.
AK,	08	Ostwald, *Natural Philosophy.*
IAE,	H6.2	Hobhouse, *Mind in Evolution,* copy 2.
ALA,	S4B/2	Sigwart's *Logic,* Bosanquet tr., v. 2.
IA,	J3.2/2	James, *Psychology,* copy 2, v. 2.
E,	C4	Chamberlin and Salisbury, *Introduction to Geology.*

In connection with *systematic* schedules there are special economies and conveniences which sometimes require an extra letter or figure, or even both, to be suffixed to the class-mark. But in the proposed system these expansions into super-capacity are compensated by mnemonic values and other systematic economies.

From time to time in the development of library economy special devices or methods in order-notation have been proposed. Mr. H. S. Biscoe in 1885 advocated[7] arrangement of books within a class by date of publication, or of acces-

[7] *Library Journal,* v. 10, p. 246-7.

sion, with internal notation composed of a capital letter and a figure, so that the year 1472 may be marked C472, and 1743 more briefly F43; and 1829 reduces to I9. But the precise date is less requisite than subdivision by time-periods might be, and this would be a matter for classification rather than for order-notation,[8] and for that a single letter would suffice. A somewhat similar method of representing dates, but by numbers alone was proposed[9] by Mr. W. S. Merrill in 1912. This was shown in two sister tables: I, for representing alphabetized surnames by decimal numbers without initial letters, and II, for likewise representing the titles of periodical publications. Tho this notation is in so far homogeneous, it has less capacity and might soon exceed its economic limit of two or three figures. These and similar devices may serve special purposes. Some librarians, however, regard internal notation unnecessary. On the contrary it appears that the lack of it in one of the great American libraries makes designation and location of the books very difficult, slow, and uncertain.

9. The Problem of Changing Marks

While classification, being relative and adaptable, should be altered without much difficulty by inserting new captions or re-writing the schedules, the notation, marked on books and on cards, is not readily alterable. In course of time some sections, or classes, not yet stabilized in their development, may need to be reclassified, while in other sections only a few additions or alterations may be required. But changing the marks is a more serious consideration; it costs much time, and too often it mars the books. Notation, fixed to books, therefore lacks freedom in correlation to classification; it is an

[8] A proposal to subordinate subject-classification to historical or bibliographical periods was made by John J. Lund and Mortimer Taube jointly in *The Library Quarterly*, v. 7, p. 373-394 (July, 1937). This was criticised adversely by the writer and by Mr. W. S. Merrill in the issue of the following January (p. 120-6).

[9] *Public Libraries*, v. 17, p. 127.

obstacle to re-classification. Hence the conservative side of the economy, and of the argument.

Yet classification must be relatively free; it must permit of at least some alteration and adaptation. If books must be marked, then marks must be changed, some sooner, some later. In some cases the books will survive the marks; in some cases the marks will survive the books, or at least the covers of the books. Sometimes the class-mark will have to be changed, sometimes only the internal notation. But for changes notation must provide. Librarians must face this problem.

On cards the marks may be carefully erased, and the shorter the marks the more easily. Or new cards may be filed. Within the books the marks should be in pencil, rather than in ink; but, if in ink, a small gummed label may cover the supplanted mark, and the new mark may be written thereon. This may be done on the cards too, but, if many consecutive cards are so to be altered, it becomes necessary to paste small "stickers" on other corners to equalize the thickness. An electrically driven eraser may serve for efficiency and neatness.

But to change marks on the backs of books is a matter less easily disposed of, especially if they have been impressed in gilt, for gilt marks are neatest and most durable. Where marks must be gilded three alternatives are presented: the books may be sent to a bookbinder, or a bookbinder may come to the library for the purpose, or one of the library's staff may use bookbinders' methods. A label of leather or cloth may have to be pasted over the old mark and then the notation gilded on that. An electrical stylus gilds from a thin ribbon of gold, and, if used skillfully, marks neatly enough. Gummed paper labels, protected with a coat of shellac or other varnish, may last somewhat longer. If they stick too well to come off readily for alterations, they may usually be removed neatly enough with a knife — and a little skill and care. If the backs of the books be marred, slightly larger labels may be applied to cover the places. Another method is to paint a band across the back with some dark paint, preferably of *tempora* vehicle, because such dries more rapidly; this, when quite dry, can be marked with white ink, and later a coat of shellac should be applied to protect the marks.

If these simple methods are unsatisfactory, the problem of changing notation should be investigated for the application of a little scientific technology. This would be a valuable project in a course of "library science," where science would indeed be available. Classification should be adaptable and is subject to alteration. Notation is correlative and should likewise be alterable. Notation fixed to books is a hindrance to growth and adaptation hardly less than notation "fixed" to shelves. False economy should not be allowed to stand in the way of higher considerations of service and purpose. Good economy accepts some adaptation and expense.

10. Principles of Notation Summarized

I. For library classification notation is *correlative* and *complementary*. It should not predominate.

II. The notation should be *expansive*, with *adjustable correlation*.

III. The notation should be as *simple* as is feasible with regard to its uses and economies. It should be composed of familiar symbols.

IV. The notation of *classes* (class-marks) should be separated and distinguished from the *internal notation* of the books within the classes.

V. Requisite *capacity* with requisite *economy* should be provided for both in the notation of the classification and in the internal notation.

VI. The notation should be as *short* as is feasible. For the class-notation the *economic limit* is three or four factors, and for the internal notation four factors.

VII. The *base* should provide for at least twenty main classes, besides marks for *forms* and for special and reference collections.

VIII. A *complementary* notation for certain *auxiliary systematic schedules* should so far as is feasible be composite and *intensively mnemonic*.

IX. The *mnemonics* should be *casual* and *systematic*, not forced, and should not distort classification, nor conflict with its principles.

X. Notation for library classification should for length of base, for requisite capacity, for shortness of marks, and for mnemonic values, *combine letters and figures* as simply as is compatible with the requisites.

XI. Complicated and confusing combinations should be avoided or minimized, and objectionable spellings should be omitted. The cipher and the letter l should be discarded.

XII. The notation should be so marked on the books and the cards that, where alteration or reclassifying becomes requisite, the marks may be removed or erased with the minimum of trouble and expense and with comparative neatness.

CHAPTER IV

SYSTEMIZING AND SCHEDULIZING

1. General and Standard Schemes and Synopses

Organization, classification, and system are inherently correlated, but in system the relations, which in classification are merely implied and structural, become effectual and functional.[1] In a system of bibliographic classification we have to deal not only with the order of sciences and studies, the coördination of classes and the subordination of divisions, but also with the multifarious interweaving relations, in a thousand ramifying interests in the ever varying aspects of knowledge and thought. System becomes the more requisite for subject-classifications that are elaborated more expansively than for books to provide for the multiplicity of subject-matter in documents, pamphlets, periodicals, abstracts, clippings, and other resources of information, research, and the recently extended scope of "documentation." [2]

The distinction between the classification of knowledge and the classification of things we have considered elsewhere. Here we will merely remark that classifications of books and of all bibliographical resources are at once classifications for knowledge and classifications of things.

Preliminary to systematic bibliographic classification is the structural *scheme*, or plan, which may be regarded

[1] *Cf. The Organization of Knowledge*, p. 148 and 168.

[2] This term has superseded Bibliography in the name of L'Institut International de Documentation. The reasons for this were stated in several articles of the transactions of the conferences in the years 1931 and 1932.

as the conceptual, pre-existent state to be developed in the expansive system of functional schedules. This is virtually an organization for knowledge, of subjects, terms, and symbols, of classes, divisions, and notations. The *scheme* should be explicit in a *synopsis* and an "outline" of the main classes, also of the notation and of the *systematic schedules.* A bibliographic classification of general scope and purpose would have a *general scheme* with its *general synopsis.* This should be relatively stable, because based on relatively permanent principles and persistent purposes; and it should be consistent with the organization of knowledge inherent in the scientific and educational consensus. But, if the scope and purpose be *special,* there would be a *special scheme,* adapted and developed for the special field; yet this should not be inconsistent with the general synopsis. If the scope should change in the future, the synopsis would then more nearly conform to the organization of knowledge, in which special subjects are subordinated to general subjects and related to the system of knowledge as parts of a comprehensive whole. The main classes that are especially within this scope may be subdivided more minutely while other classes may have less subdivision and some may even be unused. Furthermore, a larger portion of the base may, if requisite, be assigned to the specialty, so that the larger content need not exceed the capacity, and the notation may thus be kept within the economic limit. This would of course require special schedules and a special index. This interesting subject will be treated more adequately in the next chapter.

The developed, or expanded, schedules should in their details be adaptable, but even so they are likely to be comparatively temporary, portions of them being merely tentative. Alternatives should, where desired, be provided for. New subjects may develop, new classes be defined, and these may require adjustment. Revision of the schedules and reclassification of books and cards should therefore be regarded as an occasional service of real value. All this is consistent with the principle of Relativity and Adaptability of Classifications.

Libraries have individuality; they belong to different communities; they have different groups of readers and serve different interests. They may have special collections that require differences in classification and notation. But libraries *per se* may be classified, and the individual libraries of a class will probably be similar enough to adapt a scheme and schedules constructed for a *typical* library of that class in conformity with a general scheme. In brief, a system of classification may be *standardized* for a type of library, and other libraries of that class may adapt it to their particular needs and purposes.

In systemizing a general bibliographic classification the first stage comprises five steps: (1) the *general synopsis,* showing its relations to the general organization of knowledge, and its main divisions and coördinations; (2) the schedule of *main classes,* correlative to the general synopsis; (3) the *notation* and its *mnemonics,* briefly stated; (4) the *systematic schedules* outlined; (5) the most important *alternatives* stated.

A synopsis of classification is a systemic organization of knowledge, on which is to be constructed a classification which deals with subject-matter of knowledge as classificatory and which is analytic in subdivision while also synthetic in coördination and collocation. In other words, a synopsis surveys a system of concepts, of branches of knowledge, and of the studies that develop coherently from them, whereas the expansive structural classification *systemizes* and *schedulizes* the multiplicity of subjects and relations with regard to interests and uses and in this sense is functional. The synopsis should appear as an introductory table of captions, without notation. Or two such tables, a Condensed Synopsis followed by an Expanded Synopsis, may provide a more comprehensive approach to the study of the system. Besides the general synopsis, there may be synopses of the several main divisions or sciences or groups of sciences (e.g. of Biology). These *class-synopses* would be introductory to the respective main classes or sub-classes.

The second step is to make a table of the main classes. This series would be *graded in speciality,* and its classes, while coördinate structurally, would be successively subordinate logically and functionally, that is, each would not only precede but would generalize subject-matter of the subordinate classes and thus would in a sense comprehend them. The series would, however, be adapted to certain purposive and practical considerations, and perhaps in places to the exigencies of notation. Schematically the main classes would comprise fundamental sciences or groups of sciences or studies.

The schedule of main classes should be prepared before the notation and the systematic schedules are devised, because it is better to adjust the notation to the classification than it is to force the classification to fit the notation.

The third step is to determine what notation to apply to the system, what symbols to employ, what the *length* and the *area* of the *base* shall be, and which mnemonics to make *systematic,* which *constant,* and which *variable.* The principles underlying this problem were stated and discussed in the preceding chapter; and it was found that a notation combining letters and figures is most economical and may comprise systematic mnemonics and avail of casual literal intensive mnemonics. In such a system the schedule of main classes may be preceded by a schedule of certain anterior classes, preferably marked by mnemonic numerals. These may be termed the *anterior numeral classes*. But a notation of figures may be preferred, with perhaps a few complementary letters as mnemonics. Whichever be chosen, the classification may afterwards be adjusted to another notation. Moreover we may translate, in a sense, a standard, or older, classification into an adapted classification, or the reverse, by means of the notation and the index. On principle, notation is complementary and subsidiary, and it should be adapted to the classification.

2. Apportionment of Notation to Classification

Determining the notation, we have said, is the third step of the first stage of systemizing the classification. Apportionment, adjustment, and correlation of the notation to the classes of the main classification may be regarded as the second stage of systemizing; it is very important in schedulizing a classification for libraries. If the structure be out of proportion, some of the classes, or sections, will the sooner become overcrowded. Apportionment implies both partition and proportion. What portion of the *area* shall be assigned to the systematic mnemonics, what portion to the languages and literatures, what to the natural sciences, to the social sciences, to history, to the arts? In the second stage the notation is *tentatively* apportioned to the main divisions of the classification with regard to the purposes of the library and the probable requirements of the respective classes. Some sciences and studies may require more, others less than an entire main class. But each *fundamental* science and each *major* study should have a main class as its particular domain, marked by its distinctive symbol. This primary apportionment may, however, be modified in view of the unequal contents of certain studies which may or may not be regarded as major, depending on the point of view and the purposes to be served. Thus Logic and Mathematics may be regarded as major, or they may be regarded as sub-classes of General Science and Philosophy; but they would require an entire main class only in a library specialized in these studies. Astronomy, tho not a fundamental science, may be regarded as a major subject. Geology is so closely related to Physical Geography that it seems best to treat the two as members of the group of Geological Sciences, or Earth Sciences. Sub-sciences, such as Ethnology and Hygiene, may usually be subordinated as sub-classes, but some have so much content that they require entire main classes, as do Botany, Zoölogy, Political Science, and Law. The immense detail of History and of Philology exceeds the capacity of single main classes, and to each of these great subjects three main classes should be assigned, if the base be literal. The arts too should have two main classes, one for the Fine Arts and one for the Useful, or Industrial, Arts (excluding the more scientific technologies that should be classified under the respective sciences). More adequate treatment of the classification and apportionment of the several sciences will be given in a third volume.

Not only the present requirement should be considered, but we should peer into the future and estimate, as well as we can, how much to allow for *future* contents. The contents of a class or section, at present only partly filled, may in the future overflow its capacity. Certain systems now exhibit this over-crowded condition.

History and the literatures of course need room for future development, as also do the arts. We should distinguish here between the probable future requirements for unassigned sub-sections and the less probable need of assigning sections to new sciences. The need for new main classes is much less likely.[3] New subjects would most probably be subordinated. Some main classes may, however, after a half-century or so, need to be reclassified on a reconstructed plan. These considerations apply also to the future contents of many sections. The sciences, imperfect tho their development be, may be regarded as relatively coherent in their fundamental relations and relatively permanent as regards their chief branches. In minor details they may change in a decade, but in their main structures they seem likely to change little in a century.

The *basic,* or *major,* classes having been assigned, the residual main classes may be distributed for the larger contents of History and Philology, and for alternative locations for certain major subjects. The apportionment of the notation is thus completed.

The third stage is that of *first expansion.* The first step of this is again a plan, or synopsis, for each basic class, and a correlative tentative schedule of sections. The class-synopsis should of course be consistent with the general synopsis. On the bases of these tentative schedules the *areas* may be apportioned to the contents. The main branches of the studies would each have its section and distinctive mark. The subordinate branches are to be treated as structurally coördinate. The present content of some sections will be less than the capacity; but sub-sciences or larger branches may require more

[3] With regard to the stability of the fundamental sciences see Principle VIII at the end of Chapter II, and the references there on the relative permanence of general classes.

than one section for their contents or a group of sections, or a sub-class. For some of these, e.g., Medical Sciences, a synopsis may be of value. On the other hand for some sciences or sub-sciences of minor importance or small content one section suffices. Certain sections may be assigned to the subdivision of the subject by the *systematic schedules,* especially by the *Geographic schedule.* Again certain *alternatives* should be provided for. Moreover one or more sections may be reserved for probable future developments. Thus the entire area may be apportioned and the first expansion may be schedulized.

The *second expansion* (into sub-sections) — the fourth stage of systemizing — is a stage of schedulizing rather than of apportionment, and as such will be considered farther on. Beyond the first expansion apportionment is less requisite and less precise. Some sections for some types of libraries may not for the present need any second expansion. Other sections may require but few sub-sections for present content, and the relations between these may not be very important. Still other sections may have present contents for many sub-sections which should be collocated for certain types of research. When the subdivisions of the subject have been tentatively schedulized, its present *requirement,* and also its probable future requirement, may be estimated. Generally in the second expansion there should be a much larger proportion of unassigned sub-sections. But, if not, most new subjects may be adjusted to the older captions, some of which may need to be changed.

3. Alternative Locations

Classifications are relative and should be adaptive, and systems should, so far as is feasible, serve various tho not incompatible interests. Alternative locations should therefore be provided in the schedules for certain studies or sciences regarded from different points of view or preferred in other allocations.

A few of these *alternatives* will be mentioned here. Psychology may either in the naturalistic view be coördinated with other natural sciences or subordinated to Anthropology, or in the epistemological view this science may be collocated with Epistemology and Logic. Social Psychology may be regarded either as a branch of Psychology or as a branch of Sociology, and alternative sections should be provided accordingly. Theology may either as the Philosophy of Religion be subordinated to Religion and Ethics or it may be subordinated under General Philosophy and Metaphysics.[4] Philosophy may be regarded as a system of generalized and comprehensive thought grounded on knowledge but criticising intuitive beliefs and the rational foundations of science. As such it should be in the same class with General Science, Logic, Mathematics, and abstract Theology. But Philosophy may otherwise be regarded as reflective thought transfusing human experience, transcending positive knowledge, and extending into all the interests of life. As such it is but more rational literature. Engineering, civil and mechanical, may be included in the residual class of Useful Arts or subordinated under Physics as a sub-class to be collocated with Mechanics. Mineralogy may be subordinated to Geology or preferably to Chemistry. Biochemistry may be subordinated either to Biology or to Chemistry. Paleontology may be regarded as ancillary to Geology, but properly it is a branch of Biology to be collocated with Phylogeny. The Physiology of Plants and of Animals may be subsumed under Biology and General Physiology or subordinated respectively under Botany and Zoölogy. Biography may be unitary under History, as an auxiliary interest, or it may be distributed according to the more special interests involved in the portrayal of personali-

[4] *Cf.* Stumpf, Carl, *Zur Einteilung der Wissenschaften*, in *K. Preuss. Akademie d. Wissenschaften, Abhandlungen, Philosophisch-Historische Classe*, V, p. 90-1. (1906).

ties in their peculiar environments and activities, for instance, the biography of artists may be classified under Fine Arts, and that of scientists under the several sciences.

Of course the schedules of a classification are not required nor expected to provide for all divergent views but only for those that are consistent with the assumed point of view and the various purposes to be served. In the proposed system the point of view is dominantly that of natural science and is consistent with the humanistic; and the purpose is mainly the structural organization of knowledge as functioning in libraries. The naturalistic view we have found not inconsistent with the psychological and the humanistic. In a scientific age it is the predominant view. The proposed system, however, provides, so far as is feasible, for other tho somewhat divergent views, not only for such major studies as Philosophy, Theology, Psychology, and Engineering, but also for such subordinate studies as Biochemistry, Crystallography, Paleontology, Social Psychology, Economic History, Constitutional Law, and Photography. The arbitrary systems in vogue neither provide well for alternative locations nor comprise other relevant points of view.

4. Systematic Schedules

One of the most important economies of the scheme of a system of classification we have termed its *systematic schedules*. These are systematic not only in the ordinary sense but in that they are applicable more or less extensively thruout the system. Some may be applicable, wholly or partly, under any class, others only under certain classes or sections. On the whole they tend with familiarity in use to become *extensively* mnemonic, and they may have several *constant* and *intensive* mnemonics.

In a notation combining the figures with the letters the figures may be always thus mnemonic. A table of these auxiliary and mnemonic schedules should appear in the front part of the schedulized system.

Systematic schedules are a means of economizing the writing, printing, and use of the system. Their convenience and economy become a matter of conviction. For lack of such economies certain systems have become too cumbersome for economical use. They are encumbered with hundreds of pages of repetitious details in history, in geography, in the social sciences, and in the languages and literatures.

Let us consider some of these economies more closely. To nearly all studies certain modes of approach and of treatment are applicable; nearly every study has its history, its bibliography, and its method; then its material may be presented historically, or methodically in treatises, or theoretically or philosophically; it may be treated in an elementary or popular way, or analytically, or mathematically; the treatment may be comprehensive; the material may be systematized in manuals, handbooks, or epitomes, or alphabetically arranged in dictionaries; or it may be fragmentary and miscellaneous in essays, lectures, notes, or pamphlets; sometimes it may be statistical, or merely illustrative; sometimes its scope may be geographical, or it may be presented with regard to nationality, and sometimes with respect to educational or professional interests. All these aspects may be reduced to systematic schedules. This is done more or less in the leading systems, but not so economically and systematically as should be.

Dictionaries, encyclopedias, compendiums, manuals, and bibliographies are distinct *kinds* of books embodying materials for convenient reference in condensed rather than in descriptive *form*. Periodicals, miscellanies, essays, lectures, addresses, studies, contributions, notes, readings, selections, collections, etc. are composite and fragmentary as regards both authorship and subject-matter. Somewhat similar in these regards are the reports, proceedings, transactions, etc. of congresses, conferences, and committees. Still more miscellaneous and crude are the illustrative materials in exhibitions, catalogs, illustrations, atlases, and charts. These and also biographical and statistical materials may be termed *ancillary* to the descriptive, the historical, and the geographical treatment of certain subjects.

All these *forms* and kinds (in the sense of *format*, make-up, composition, or condition of content, but not of its scope, definition, or relations) may for convenience be subsumed under the terms *anterior* and *ancillary*, not to the study but to its classification systematically regarded. If the notation employs figures, these may conveniently as *mnemonic numerals* be assigned to appropriate captions, to which the anterior and ancillary may be reduced or subsumed. Those captions that are most generally or commonly applicable or recurrent thruout the classes, sections, and subsections would correspond to the mnemonics that we have termed *constant*, while those captions that are only occasionally or contingently required would be distinguished and grouped as *variable* mnemonics.[5]

5. Schedulizing the Contents of Sections

The principles of the Relativity of Classification, of Coördination, and of Subordination of the specific to the generic are everywhere involved in the schedules of the sections, to which apply also other generalizations adduced for the classification of the main classes. Apportionment is less feasible under sections and is much freer and less complete. There should be a much larger proportion of reserved sub-sections. Moreover there should be provision for alternatives where desirable.

Adequate knowledge of the contents is prerequisite to proper classification. The systemizer should have

[5] *Cf. ante,* p. 60. For some discussion see the writer's article, "Form in Classification," in *The Librarian*, Jan., 1937, v. 26, p. 128-130.

enough acquaintance with the sciences or studies and their branches to enable him to outline the chief coördinations and subordinations and to collocate the closely related specialties. On this knowledge and discriminating ability will depend the "efficiency" of the system. If the classifier does not know enough of the subject, he should inform himself or should seek assistance or coöperation. One mind can hardly do justice, even in a decade, to the whole classification. For the general synopsis and the apportionment of the main classes scientific and philosophic comprehension are essential, and this grasp of the synthetic mind should extend to the whole area of the sections, that is, the first expansion. For the second expansion, however, and for further subdivision of some subjects special knowledge as well as expert mastery may be requisite, but for other subjects a knowledge of the outlines may prove adequate. The classifier should be well grounded by well organized education and reading and especially by a survey of the relations of the branches of knowledge.

To make a classification of Chemistry or of Biology it is hardly necessary to pursue post-graduate courses in those subjects. On the other hand it will not suffice to copy or to cull from the contents-pages of treatises. There is an important difference between the contents of a book and the contents of a classification for books. Some of the captions of a book are matters for chapters or paragraphs rather than for volumes, and some never will be more than that. In the Library of Congress schedule for General Biology, QH 301, there appear, for instance, the following subjects: 343, Comparative study of living and non-living matter; 347, Differences and resemblances between plants and animals; 650, Influence of physical and chemical energies. If there be books or pamphlets on these subjects, they should be classed under more distinctive captions, to which other books of similar contents could be assimilated.

To classify a subject certain steps, learned in long experience, are advisable. First read an outline text, then scan two or three comprehensive treatises, listing main branches and important subdivisions—the crude contents of a *section* in distinct terms; then draft a synopsis and on this basis make a tentative schedule. If a bibliography be available, compare its divisions, if it be classified—or else its titles—with the tentative details; then compare this schedule with other classifications, with relevant groups of books on library shelves, and with shelf-lists. After this, typewrite the schedule, prove it in use for a time, and, later, if alterations have complicated it, clarify it by again rewriting it.

In the gradual process of schedulizing an expansive classification the established or accepted classifications of scientists and bibliographers as well as other organizations of knowledge should be utilized. The product, however, should be regarded as tentative. It should be tested by applying it to a collection of books to which it is adaptable structurally, and then for a considerable time it should serve functionally, while new materials would be classified and assimilated to its classes, thus testing its adaptability. In the meantime new captions would be added or inserted, diverse relations would be discovered, collocations and coördinations would be altered, and definitions or terms would be changed. After a period of growth and adaptation, the schedule may be rewritten or "revised." Some well directed reading on recent developments in the field may be of especial value in a re-survey of the classification. But again and again a classification for books should be tested, adapted, and altered to keep it efficient as a functional organization of knowledge.

The writer kept the second expansion of his classification for over ten years in this growing condition on cards in two trays; then for ten years more, only partly on typewritten sheets, with many alterations and annotations, it was plastic to every positive requirement.

Directional Calculus was to me an unfamiliar term, when years ago it came before me on the title-page of a book by E. W. Hyde, published in 1890, and entitled *The*

Directional Calculus based upon the methods of Hermann Grassmann. The term, conjoined with Grassmann's name, at once suggested that great mathematician's theory usually designated by the German term *Ausdehnungslehre.* But the term *directional* also suggested Vector Analysis, a closely related subject, which may be regarded as a calculus of *directed extension.* Hyde's Preface moreover proposed the *Theory of Extension* as the English equivalent of *Ausdehnungslehre.* So one might hesitate whether to class this book under this last term or under Vector Analysis. The preface opened with an unusually clear indication for the Theory of Extension. But neither that term nor Directional Calculus appeared in my schedules, nor in those of the Library of Congress, nor in the Decimal Classification, tho the index of the former refers from Directional Calculus to *Ausdehnungslehre* and the index of the latter from Calculus of Direction to Quaternions, a closely related subject, but not the same. In all three classifications there is occasion here for emendation. In my schedule I accordingly added both terms, Directional Calculus, as more generally comprising *Ausdehnungslehre,* and Theory of Extension, as the equivalent English term.

6. Terminology, Captions and Typography

The captions of classification schedules should be distinct and as simple as befits the requisite precision. Common names and *catchwords* are better than descriptive phrases and inverted complex terms. But scientific, technical, and philosophic terms should be used where they are briefer or more distinctive than phrases in familiar terms. The schedules are for classifiers, and classifiers should be masters of terminology.

The term *Epistemology* is not only briefer but more distinctive than the phrases, Theory of knowledge, Philosophy of knowledge, and Ground, scope, and limits of knowledge; and it makes the best caption; the phrases should be subsumed under it in smaller type. *Metrology* is simpler, more distinctive, and more comprehensive than the phrase, Measures and Weights. *Kinematics* is more distinctive than the Science of Motion. There is an applicable distinction between the name of the *subject* of study and the name of the science, or *study* of the subject. Thus *Botany* and *Zoölogy* are preferable to Plants and Animals. But *Stars* as a caption is more comprehensive than *Astrophysics*. On the other hand *Ethics* is more comprehensive, while more abstract, than the Science of Morals, for it comprises not only the descriptive science but the theoretic or philosophic study. So in general, when there are several nearly synonymous specific terms, the more comprehensive and the more distinctive terms should precede or be preferred.

Sometimes two distinctive terms are nearly synonymous but one is less familiar, tho it may be either simpler or more precise. *Physiography* is briefer than Physical Geography, *Geophysics* than Physical Geology, and *Geochemistry* than Chemical Geology. Yet in these cases the more familiar terms should be assigned to the captions, because they are somewhat more comprehensive, and the more precise scientific terms should be subsumed. But some synonyms seem to have little difference in scientific usage. *Petrology*, the science of Rocks, is also called *Lithology*, while its descriptive counterpart is termed *Petrography*.

Generally, terms ending in *ology*, *ic*, or *ics*, and *ogeny* are the more abstract and theoretical, while those ending in *ography*, *ometry*, and *y* are more concrete and descriptive.[6] Compare Biology, Cosmology, and Ethnology with Biography, Cosmography, and Ethnography; then compare Ethnogeny, Ontogeny, and Phylogeny with Microscopy and Stereotomy; then Logic, Physics, Graphics, Optics, Ethics, Economics, and Pedagogics with Economy, Pedagogy, Philately, and Psychiatry; then Anthropology and Anthropogeny with Anthropometry and Trigonometry. There are, however, notable exceptions, especially to the derivatives in *ics*: Numismatics, Sphragistics, Dramatics, Polytechnics,

[6] *Cf.* our preceding volume, Chapter XIII, section 4.

and Civics remain for the greater part descriptive. Geometry and Geodesy, originally metric, have become abstract and theoretic. It is evident that generalization about scientific terminology in the English language must be qualified. Sometimes the theoretic term is to be subsumed under the more comprehensive heading, and sometimes *au contraire* the caption of the main class should be the theoretic term, e.g. Economics.

Some captions are not simple, but indeed composite. Economy in apportionment will sometimes necessitate grouping two or more subjects which, tho closely related, have no name to comprise them. In our system Astronomy and Geology are brought together as Class D, Sociology and Ethnology as Class K, and Religion and Ethics as Class P.

Sometimes the schedules should provide for such composites of lesser sciences, studies, or pairs of arts as Logic and Algebra, Ethics and Æsthetics, Sculpture and Keramics, Birds and Reptiles. There should also be provision for special treatment of sciences, such as Mathematical Physics, and Medical Physics.

Definition is an important correlate of classification. Concise definitions of main classes and sub-classes may well be placed at the heads of their synopses; and elsewhere thruout the schedules unfamiliar terms or those of various denotation should be briefly defined in notes. Comments and suggestions are often appropriate, especially respecting the applicability of the systematic schedules; and instructions are requisite in many places, with occasional examples. All notes should be in smaller type and deeply indented. Alternative locations should be plainly indicated by notations, and should be in a distinctly different type at the right-hand margin.

On the style and distinctness with which the schedules have been printed will largely depend their clearness and economy in use. The principal headings should stand out in more prominent type, tho not in display; and the subordinate headings should be in two or three sizes of type, the smallest being for terms subsumed under the captions of sub-sections; and this should be distinct from that of notes, definitions, instructions, etc., and again distinct from that of alternatives and heading-references, or cross-references. Sufficient distinctness with economy of space, clear and concise captions and notations, notes and annotations, details and directions, these should render the schedules compact and convenient to handle.

The notation should be in a regular column on the left-hand side of the pages, without indentions. If, however, its *super-capacity* is in places expressed, it should be indented well beyond the column, or even subsumed. Any subordinate captions may be indented where this seems conducive to clearness.

The captions of the schedules are mostly printed as coördinate, but of course they cover many implicit subordinations. The proper place to show the chief subordinations is the Synopsis; and the several synopses of the main classes and sub-classes should suffice to show the secondary and tertiary subordinations; and further subordination may be shown as we have advised above.

Classification has repeatedly been compared to a trellis, to which the tree of knowledge is trained for certain purposes. Schedules of classification, like the successive slats of the trellis, impose the restriction that they are successive in one direction, at least in so far as notation is successive in the one expansion. The two-dimensional trellis here seems reduced to a one-dimensional series. By its first and its second expansions it becomes, as we have seen before, first virtually two-dimensional, then three-dimensional. It is an important problem in schedulizing so to treat these serial coördinations and subordinations that they will conduce to efficiency in collocations, while maintaining coherent and consistent order of the interrelated branches.

As the contents and captions of the sections are less permanent than those of the main classes, it seems advisable to print the schedules only on the *verso* side of the leaves, so that additions and emendations may be written on the *recto* side (the right-hand page when the book is open) opposite the printed schedules; and it would be better to bind the leaves in the loose-leaf mode, so that they may from time to time be replaced, when schedules are reclassified or the leaves are soiled or torn or worn. It has proved convenient to have the schedules on large cards in trays, with guide-cards, showing the synopses.

Classification and cataloging for the subject-approach have been made too dependent on terms in alphabetic order. Terms indeed are correlative to their classes, and so to the correlative concepts. But there are many synonyms and usage is various. A subject may require a dozen terms. Simple terms may not suffice to denote some classes; multiplex and complex terms may be requisite in definitions. Adjectives in English regularly precede the substantives. Sometimes they are more general and sometimes more specific. Complications and confusions too often result. Is *Chemical Analysis* the same concept as Analytical Chemistry? In the former *Analysis* is the generic term, and Chemical the specific. In the latter, Analytical (or Analytic) is the specific term. In the inverted form is Chemistry, Analytical, the same class as Analysis, Chemical? Is not the one the name of a branch of Chemistry, while the other is the term for a kind of analysis, a general method, which may be applied in many sciences and technologies? A similar case is the customary term *Agricultural Chemistry*. And there are many others. In an alphabetic *subject-index* of terms referring to classes the synonyms and references should resolve this complication of terminology; but in an alphabetic order of *subjects* the *subject-matters* remain dispersed.

7. Specific Distinguished from Subject-Classification

Most library catalogers are disposed to regard a book on a certain broad *subject,* e.g. Education, as just a book on education, no matter what its particular contents may be or its point of view. They have neither time nor interest to look for differences, so they put the subject-card for the book under the subject, Education, in the card-catalog, and they do not bother to sub-classify that subject, which indeed is a rather difficult undertaking. If there are a thousand books on education, there are perhaps a hundred different kinds, for which the classification should provide.[7] Of a hundred readers ten may want only one of these kinds, another ten another kind, and so on continually. Yet neither Dewey nor Cutter provided for such differences under their general captions. The International Institute of Documentation (Bibliography) in its *Classification décimale* has, however, undertaken to provide for manifold relations, aspects, and differences, but with detail too elaborate and notation too complicated.

General treatises, "principles," and "systems" should be distinct from elementary and introductory books, text-books and manuals, hand-books and compends. Then other books less systematic, tho not less general, may also be distinguished — discourses, lectures, addresses, essays, studies, aspects, etc. How close such

[7] Dr. Kelley's argument implies that very specific classification is usually futile because dispersive and vaguely apprehended.—Kelley, Grace O. *The Classification of Books*, New York, Wilson, 1937, p. 20,59,69,73, *et passim.* This argument we do not admit for reasons indicated above and on other pages.

distinctions may feasibly and serviceably be drawn depends on the nature of the subject and upon the requirements of the users of the books. For most sections it seems worth while to distinguish at least four such classes of books general in scope; these may be subsumed under the captions: Elements, Treatises, Discourses, Miscellanies. The discourses, essays, studies, and aspects may cover the entire field, or they may touch upon certain portions only in certain aspects, yet they may be so wide in range as to be deemed general in scope.

It is important to distinguish between special *branches* of a study or science and special *aspects* of it. There may be special aspects of the general *field*; it may be surveyed from different points of view, or with diverse special purposes. Conversely, general treatises may be addressed to special interests, special professions, or special classes of readers. Then the general books on a subject may be classified with regard to their dates of publication; or they may be selected with respect to their reputation. On the other hand, there may be *general aspects of a special field,* that is, a special subject may be treated generally or comparatively, or it may be regarded in its relations in a comprehensive aspect. But *special topics* are special in both those senses, while they are general in neither of these senses; and they are to be distinguished from special subjects or branches, aspects, results, and methods. *Special* in these contexts means either more specific in definition or in some relation or aspect.[8]

[8] The term *Special general,* which has figured in the schedule of the Library of Congress, confuses the two terms in a rather meaningless way. They are indeed relative terms but they do not mix well in one spoonful. Does this combination mean that the general in scope is treated in a special aspect, or mode; or does it mean that the special subject is treated in general; or does it mean something else, or sometimes the one thing and elsewhere the other thing?

The classification of knowledge proceeds analytically from the general to the special thru grades of subordination and specification. The classification of books involves similarly successive subordination and gradation, not only for the main classes but also for the sections and even for sub-sections. The following table shows graded specifications that are applicable to the systematic subdivision of most subjects, general or special.

General in Scope:

- Bibliographical.
- Historical and Critical:
  - Historical;
  - Method, scope, and relations of the subject to others;
  - Critical;
  - Biographical;
  - Ancillary: Statistics, Illustrations, etc.; Documents, Reports, etc.
- Miscellaneous:
  - Periodicals and Serials of Societies, etc.;
  - Collections, selections, readings, miscellanies, essays.

General in Scope and in Treatment:

- Elementary, Introductory;
- Manuals, Compends;
- Treatises, Principles, Comprehensive studies;
- Discourses.

General in Scope and Special in Treatment:

- Theoretical treatises;
- Aspects of the general subject;
- Treatment for special interests, purposes, professions, etc.;
- Geographical and National relations and aspects;
- Technical;
- Experimental and Laboratory.

Special in Scope and in Treatment:

- Special subjects;
- Special Theories;
- Aspects in special interests;
- Special Topics;
- Special Methods, Experiments, etc.
- Statistical Treatment;
- Pamphlets of special content, and other special materials.

The distinction between *specific* classification, analytic and synthetic, and "subject" classification, or rather subject-indexing, of the "practical," pigeon-holing kind, should be emphasized and understood. Such schemes depend too much on the approach thru the alphabetic index. In this they are not much superior to alphabetic orders. They lean too heavily on the erroneous notions that specific subjects are not merely distinct but separate and no less stable than generic subjects. Valid subject-classification is based on the fundamental principle that specific subjects are essentially and logically subordinate to more generic subjects, or classes; and these are more stable. Subject-classification properly implies the "subject-approach" to subjects in relation to other subjects. This is plainly antithetic to the alphabetic approach and the author-approach, on which catalogers have expended immense efforts and extensive funds. The alphabetic-subject-approach is intermediary but it is not equivalent to the logical and systematic subject-approach for which subject-classification should stand, and for which library services should more efficiently provide.

But for logical and systematic subject-classifications also the alphabetic index is a requisite complement, and it should be complete, with synonyms and alternatives.

In short, subject-classification is classification by subjects, the general logically comprehending the relevant special, relatively more special, and very special, or *specific,* which thus, if logical, are not separated and dispersed, as Dr. Kelley's book says they are, but are comprised and *synthesized*. It is *illogical* subject-classification that separates, and alphabetic order that disperses, related subject-matters, and it is to these that the objection truly applies.

CHAPTER V

CLASSIFICATION FOR "SPECIAL" LIBRARIES

> "This above all: to thine own self be true,
> And it must follow, as the night the day,
> Thou canst not then be false to any man."
>
> *Hamlet*, Act I, sc. iii.

1. Four Fundamentals of the Special In General

The writer must at the outset in candor confess that he does not know much about "special" libraries. He would not advise their librarians as to the conditions affecting them and the problems that have emerged. It may be that they have not yet completely "found themselves," as we sometimes say of the young people. They should not take umbrage at this remark, but just take the proffered hand; for about classification there be matters "of great pith and moment" that we may consider together to mutual advantage.

There are many species of special libraries, and some are more special than others. Their plurality is no less bewildering than their specialization is disconcerting to cut and dried conservative standardization. Statements may apply to certain kinds but not to others, and views may likewise be partial. But some librarians of special libraries say that their conditions, services, and problems differ less in fundamentals than in details.[1] This opinion

[1] See, for instance, Julia A. Elliott's clear and forceful article in *The Library Journal*, February 1, 1926 (p. 125). In *Special Libraries*, February, 1926, an extended article by several contributors considered the distinctive recurrent problems of several types of special libraries.

More recent attempts, particularly in *Special Libraries* for 1937-38, to frame a definition generally applicable have been more interesting perhaps than positively successful.

is in certain aspects probably true, and herein lies the applicability of the quotation placed at the head of this chapter. There is another classical quotation that applies well from another aspect:

"Homo sum; humani nihil a me alienum puto."[1]

There should be many contacts between the spheres of special librarians and the fundamentals laid down in the preceding chapters. The very term *special* invokes our fundamental principle of the *Subordination* of the *Special* to the *General.* And one of the fundamental principles on which the system of the sciences stands is termed *Gradation by Speciality.* How do these principles apply? Why, special subjects or specialties are of relative degrees of speciality, and to be mastered effectually they should be related, at least in surveys, to the relevant general subjects to which they are subordinate in the system of the sciences and studies.

Some special libraries, more special than others, serve very special interests intensively, without regard to neighbors or even to relatives. They follow their *lines* — exclusively. Others sooner or later become more or less *inclusive* of side lines, of related interests. Such broadening out may be too much like the departmental drugstore, but even such conglomerations can usually be brought into an orderly system. Most live interests *look about* even while following their lines, and they find that their paths pass thru *fields,* neighbor fields that have some interests in common; and that paths branch and cross. The specialist, whether in science or in business, may be centered on his point, or confined to his line, but he must confess that this is not the hub of the world, nor

[1] This well known line from a play of Terence with a long Greek name, being interpreted, means: I am a librarian, and I feel free from none of the problems of librarians.

the only spoke of the wheel. Each specialty has its place in the system of knowledge and of human affairs; and it has its relations to other interests. The question is which relations are to be considered relevant, and what is the point of view. To scientists and educators these truths have long been established in their doctrines of *the unity and relativity of knowledge*, and *the relativity of classes and of classifications.*

In some concerns the specialty may from the beginning have been developed *comprehensively*. But aside from all modes of specialization here considered, we should distinguish the treatment of a *general* subject with regard to a *special aspect* or interest. For instance, Human Geography may be studied in the special interest of a commercial tariff. Conversely a transportation corporation may conduct investigations of human-geographic relations.

If these distinctions seem of little import, you have not got down to the roots of your problem of classification; and you have not read profitably certain preceding chapters. Now the four fundamental principles that are applicable to special libraries may briefly be recapitulated:

I. The Relativity of Classes and of Classifications.
II. The Subordination of the Special to the General.
III. Gradation of specialties by their relative speciality.
IV. Special aspects of general subjects are distinct from general aspects of special subjects.

2. Is the Specialty a "Line," an "Interest," or a "Field"?

In planning a classification for a special library the first thing to consider is whether it is purposed to follow its specialty exclusively, or to include related subjects, or to develop its field of interest comprehensively and in relation to other fields of interest. To exemplify these three stages of development the following items are selected from the Special Libraries Directory.

(1) General Electric Company, Pittsfield, Mass., library of electrical subjects exclusively, founded in 1912 and organized to serve electrical engineers.
(2) General Electric Company, New York City; organized to serve sales organization; comprises "electrical engineering with its many ramifications."
(3) General Electric Company, Main Library, Schenectady, N. Y., organized to serve the entire company, including factories and sales offices; comprises "electrical engineering, mechanical engineering, commercial research, employee relations, business conditions, industrial organization, physico-chemical research, advertising and selling," and of course many other subjects. This looks conglomerate, but it is probably more systematic than it looks.
(4) General Electric Company, National Lamp Works, Cleveland; organized to serve the research laboratories; comprises "general physics, radiation, optics, color, electrophysics, chemistry, physical chemistry, mathematics, electrical engineering, illuminating engineering, physiology, physiological optics, psychology. This covers a broad field; it looks systematic, and it doubtless is systematic.

The three following examples are drawn from other pages of the *Directory*.
(5) American Institute of Accountants, New York City. This is their "line": accountancy, auditing, bookkeeping, costs and cost accounting, depreciation, statistics, valuation.
(6) United Drug Company, Boston; organized to serve executives, members of the company, and stockholders; the most important subjects comprised are: "advertising, buying, candy, chain-stores, credits, collections, drugs, druggists' sundries, foreign trade, formulas, legislation, management, medicines, pharmacy, retailing, rubber goods, salesmanship; selling plans, soda fountains, special sales, stationery, toilet goods, window displays." There is the "drug-store" conglomeration.

(7) Chamber of Commerce of the United States of America, Washington; organized to serve the departments of this organization; comprises: finance, industrial relations, foreign trade, tariff, taxation, transportation, insurance, coal, trade associations, agricultural statistics, municipal affairs, foreign relations, banks and banking." This might be made systematic by good classification.

It appears that few special libraries follow their lines exclusively, because they really extend into *fields*. This is to be expected, and it makes the librarian's problem more interesting. Tho the special library may be still following a line, the question is likely soon to arise how can its classification be brought to cover its field? It would be wiser and more economical to have planned more adequately for expansive development. The problem involves the relation of classification to notation; so let us consider what that relation is.

3. Notation Is Subsidiary

Of all librarians the special librarian should be most chary of notation. We have emphasized that notation is the subsidiary correlate of classification. Yes, they are brothers, but they have been worst enemies. The decimal notation has been a fetish, we said long ago. Mnemonics — as misapplied — have been a delusion and a snare. Lengthy numerals, whether complicated by letters or not, constitute an elaborate waste of print. These unnecessary burdens and nuisances have been devised by notation fiends for the undoing of classification friends.

But the worst is that they make the occasionally desirable *undoing* of classification the more difficult and expensive. Reclassification becomes a nightmare, because notation has to be changed on books and cards and what not. If, however, the notation of the improved classification can also at the same time be improved by making it shorter and more readily alterable, the resulting economy in continually classifying, grouping, and recording books, cards, etc. would soon compensate for the cost of the improvement. This argument is especially relevant to special libraries.

The functional organization of knowledge should be adaptive and its structural classification therefore should be adaptable. This is a restatement of a principle adduced before. Special libraries are functional organizations of knowledge. They are judged by their fruits, and these are desired fresh. The corollary of the principle just stated is that either the notation should be brief and readily changeable, or else it should not be affixed to the books and cards so as to make its erasure or alteration uneconomical or unsightly. That notation for libraries has not been concise, that librarians have become conservative as to reclassification, these are two reasons for saying that notation has been classification's worst enemy. This opposition is very discreditable to librarianship. Classification has deserved better consideration. It is one of the most important means toward organizing knowledge. In special libraries it is likely to be more important even than cataloging. It behooves the special librarian therefore to make notation, if possible, his pliant tool, and to free his, or her, youthful spirit from the fetish and the incubus.

4. Apportionment of Notation

Apportionment is the backbone of economy and efficiency in notation. There should be due regard to the probable requirements, and the *base* of the notation should be utilized as fully as is feasible, so as to have short distinctive marks for the most important subjects, and so as to provide for sufficient expansion without exceeding the *economic limit.* The results of disproportion in certain established library classifications are likely to be aggravated in special libraries, the more so, if the specialty is a subordinate subject, for instance, forestry, or bacteriology. One reason why special librarians are so much concerned with the problem of classification is that in applying a portion of an inadaptable classification they become entangled in its lengthy notation. Plainly it is to the interest of special librarians to get rid of this incubus.

Apportionment means assigning a place and a portion to each special subject with regard to the relations of subjects to one another, whether special or general, whether subordinate or coördinate. It implies system and order. It is no informational breadline waiting to be served under a "subject-index illusion."

Not only present requirements should be provided for but probable future requirements — so far as these may be foreseen and estimated. Foreseeing the future requirements of a classification for a special library does not depend upon looking straight ahead in a line; it depends not less on looking *about* in providing for the relations to neighbor subjects that are very likely to develop. For some specialties these may be readily anticipated; the tendencies are already apparent. For other specialties the future — even the near future — is very uncertain. In general there is enough uncertainty as regards specialties to justify reducing the expectation to a general scientific basis rather than to an inspired prediction. That is to say that for special libraries as for general libraries it is in the long run most practical and economical to plan classification with due regard to the system of the sciences and studies as maintained in the scientific and educational consensus of the period.

But how can we adopt such a general scientific system and at the same time specialize our classification and still economize its notation? By apportionment, and by reapportionment. While remaining consistent with the standard classification, or the fundamental classification of knowledge, the apportionment of the special classification would minimize subdivision of subjects irrelevant or less important to its interests, leaving larger capacity for expansion of subjects germane to its interests. It is consistency with the scientific system that is prerequisite — not conformity. Enhanced adaptability and efficiency inhere in such consistency, but not in the "procrustean bed" of a standardized schedule. In consistency with the scientific system, and, so far as seems justified, in conformity with a standard system for a similar class, or *type,* of libraries, the classification of a special library should be planned and an economical notation should be apportioned. If conformity to a standard system be close enough, its schedules may be utilized with the notation of the special classification affixed parallel to its own. In adapting a special classification to a general or a standard system, and in apportioning, or reapportioning, the notation, the special librarian should consider the tendency from the first to the third stage of those distinguished in the second section of this chapter. Our answer to the question raised there is in this section.

The interests of life, of studies, and of business, however complicated, are organized in such coherence that, whatever subject is specialized, its relevant interests involved with it, are subordinate to some general subject.

The ramifications of neighbor branches are for the most part more closely interwoven than those of the other parts of the tree of knowledge. There may be different points of view; so alternative relationships should be provided for. For special libraries a whole chapter might be written on this topic alone. Yet despite all complications, the principle obtains that for special libraries as for general the adaptable and efficient classification is that which is consistent with the organization of knowledge as maintained in the educational and scientific consensus.[8] This is stated here as a general principle; tho not applicable invariably and in all particulars, it is the kind of truth that scientists, educators, and business men admit into their theories, programs, and estimates.

5. The Principle of Maximal Efficiency Again

The principle of Maximal Efficiency proceeds from the fundamental principles of Subordination of the Specific to the Generic and of Collocation of closely related classes, or subjects. These principles have been stated and discussed in preceding chapters, and very little need be added here; but one thing may well be emphasized: as special libraries tend to develop systemized organization, their feasible efficiency increases toward the maximal. The principle of collocation is opposed to unsystematic and haphazard division and arrangement. Analytic division tends to dispersion. But synthesis, either collocative or systematic, places subjects in effectual relation and efficient organization. A collocative synthesis does not, however, forego analysis, which in-

[8] The writer has considered these questions more fully in an article on "Consistent Classification for Special Libraries" in the March, 1938, issue of *Special Libraries*.

evitably issues from subdivision; but it collocates the results of analytic subdivision. This is the very nature of systematic classification. It opposes the false theory that disorder and dispersion can be obviated or compensated by an alphabetic key or subject-index. The key can unlock the thousand doors indeed, but it is more convenient to have rooms and alcoves connecting without so many doors and locks and devious passageways. The alphabetic subject-index is an essential complement to a systematic classification, but it is not a satisfactory substitute for it. It serves some uses, but it fails to serve others that are more important in the organization of knowledge. The false supposition that it compensates for dispersion we have given the sobriquet of "the subject-index illusion."

6. Standardized Special Classifications

A thousand special libraries must permit of considerable classifying of the libraries themselves by whatever features, extrinsic or intrinsic, foundation, purposes, or services. The *Special Libraries Directory,* as a "classified list," shows some forty such classes, besides many sub-classes, or sub-groups. For instance, Horticultural libraries are properly subordinated to Agricultural libraries. The question concerns us, are the libraries of these classes, or groups, enough alike to make standard classifications feasible? Where the specialty is definite, it indeed seems feasible. But for standardization conformity is requisite — conformity to a classification, more or less adaptable, planned and developed for the special class or type of library.[4]

[4] *Cf.* the writer's article on "Standardization in Classification" in *Special Libraries,* March, 1929. See also his article on "Consistent Classification," cited on the preceding page.

Librarians and specialists may think and work along their lines, but such individual views are transient and become de-personalized. A community of interests develops. The relevant interests of botany, biology, geology, chemistry, agriculture, arboriculture, landscape gardening, even something of poetry and painting, enter into the more intelligent, cultured, broad-minded interest in horticulture, — also the economic, the vivid, the beautiful, and the healthful — and this is no longer a narrow specialty following its line. It develops synthetically; it probably is reorganized; it enters the systematic stage. The more it tends this way, the more requisite and the more feasible is a systematic classification in consistency with the established organizations of knowledge.

Differentiation is another matter, pointing rather in the opposite direction. There should indeed be room for differentiation, as for specialization. Where special libraries are located rather near to each other, and while their interests and services are rather different, they may indeed differentiate in their originally separate or subsequently divergent lines. Yet, even so, even if they differentiated years after adopting a standard classification, they might be the better off for retaining it as a broad-minded basis for their different developments. They might, however, reapportion their notations to economize a specialized expansion of their classifications.

7. Coöperative Services

It would follow that coöperation between like special libraries is a means to efficiency and economy. This would apply not only to the classifying but also to the cataloging and even to the lending and exchange of the material, as well as to certain bibliographic services. But, where the individual libraries or groups are consciously competitive, coöperation may indeed be beyond business-nature. Even in the business world, however, this stricture would probably affect few groups, or classes, of libraries.

Special libraries are, more than general libraries, maintained as functional organizations of knowledge. They are not mere collections of books and pamphlets. Indeed in many of them bound books form but a smaller portion of their enumerable contents — considering number rather than bulk. Some of them collect and systemize a mass of ephemeral print, typewritten material, clippings, illustrations, memoranda, etc. Such material does not fall into the ordinary methods of library cataloging; but it may well be classified and indexed. On the adequacy of the classification and the completeness of the index depend the efficiency of such functional organization of knowledge.

But interests ramify and extend from lines into fields; systems and syntheses overlap, involve, even comprise other systems and organizations. Special libraries may, indeed often should, become coördinated with and coöperative with other special libraries, whether of the same class or of some related class. Moreover they may, and indeed should, become in some respects coöperative with general libraries, and with library organizations and other organizations. So long as distinctive individual development is not too much constrained, there should be no limit to so good a thing in general as coöperation and organization.[5]

[5] In a paper read before the Catalog Section of the A. L. A. in June, 1927, and printed in the *Proceedings*, p. 352-4, the writer outlined a definite plan for "More adequate coöperative cataloging and classifying."

8. From Information Service to Special Research

Where does information end, and where does research begin — in any library? These questions provoke the reply that there are no definite demarkations to the various modes of seeking knowledge. Information may be asked in a single question: What is the population of Pawtucket, R. I.? That may be answered from a reference book. But supposing you have reason to question that answer? To ascertain the precise number for that population on a given date and according to certain definitions, that indeed is a problem and a task for its census bureau. Again, to learn the minute of sunset today is a simple matter of looking into an almanac; but to learn how to determine the local time requires a study of astronomical geography. If, moreover, one should become interested in the question whether the sun-spots affect the terrestrial climate, that would be an astronomical research of the second or third magnitude, and the researcher would have recourse to an observatory and a library. These things are generally understood by educated people, and it is needless to expatiate on the theme that there is no boundary between information and research.

Yet it would appear that special libraries tend to differentiate in the one or the other direction. Most business libraries are regarded as organized mainly for information service to the company or office or staff. Their librarian is — or should be — expert in furnishing information in the special lines on the press of a button, or very soon afterwards. Regarding on the other hand the relation of research libraries to industrial research we will quote an opinion of Dr. Arthur D. Little, the eminent chemist:

> "These laboratories should each be developed around a special library, the business of which should be to collect, compile, and classify in a way to make instantly available every scrap of information bearing upon the materials, products and requirements of the industry concerned. Modern progress can no longer depend upon accidental discoveries. Each advance in industrial science must be studied, organized and fought like a military campaign. . . . . I regard the special library as not merely the heart, but the arterial system as well, of any adequately organized research laboratory."[6]

Special libraries organized for research, scientific, technical, industrial, economic, geographic, sociological, or historical, generally have more books and pamphlets in a wider range of subjects. Such libraries are of course much used for mere information on points, on facts, on questions; they may have an information service, which may do somewhat toward functionally organizing knowledge in certain lines. On the whole, however, there is evident differentiation between information service and organization for research. This difference becomes more pronounced as the research library becomes larger and more comprehensive. But there are libraries that may be regarded either as special reference or research libraries or as *general* reference or research libraries; and there are intermediate kinds.[7]

Some libraries usually regarded as "special" have well over a hundred thousand volumes. A few may be instanced: The U. S. Department of Agriculture Library, the Library of the U. S. Surgeon-General's Office, The New York Academy of Medicine, Harvard University Law Library,

[6] *Special Libraries*, May, 1919.

[7] Dr. Tse-Chien Tai, in his *Professional Education for Librarianship*, distinguishes between the "static" and the "dynamic" types of special libraries, instancing as of the static type, among others, the Library of The Metropolitan Museum of Art in New York. The distinction seems unclear, but "dynamic" seems to apply rather to the information service type of business library.

The New York Bar Assn. More strictly special in field yet nearly as large are the Library of The Hispanic Society of New York and that of the Bureau of Railway Economics, in Washington. From a quarter to a half of this size are the libraries of The Interstate Commerce Commission, of The Metropolitan Life Insurance Co., and of The National City Bank of New York.

Any of these libraries is likely to have demands for service beyond what it is organized and equipped to render. The information service may have occasional demands for real research. If it is not organized for it, then the service will by so much be discredited. It is then that poor classification costs, or poor book selection. On the other hand a research library, having books enough and classification good enough and cataloging nearly complete, may yet lack the finer analysis, more specific indexing, and functional organization of the efficient information service.

This trend of thought leads to the conclusion that libraries, both general and special, should be organized to function both ways and administered to serve both requirements. The departmental development of the large reference public libraries, e. g. Cleveland, Detroit, and Los Angeles, would serve special research as definitely as the departmental collections and facilities in universities. The regular and urgent services that the library purposes to serve should of course come first. Economies may require that no more be attempted. If more be desired, the librarian may refer to libraries purposed to serve such needs. The value of coöperation may therein be realized; and there may be great possibilities in this. Quest, however, for knowledge as for results, is likely to be impatient. Most inquirers desire the immediate service of the library called upon. This human fact affords reason for the maintenance of information services in offices and laboratories, and in libraries, whether special or general. It has long been recognized as the pedagogic root of the professor's collection of books in his room, tho the college library is but a minute away; and from this has developed the problem of departmental libraries in colleges and universities. Yes, the professor, the lawyer, the doctor, the engineer, the banker, or the manufacturer will go to the library uptown, or will wait for a book from Washington, if he *must*, but he greatly prefers to have it in the next room, or the answer in the next minute.

The *raison d'être* and the course of development of special libraries of the information service type in commercial and industrial corporations were well described by the late Mr. John Cotton Dana in *Encyclopedia Americana*, v. 17, p. 379. A background for this rapid development existed in the prevalent growth first of trade journals then later of technical and business literature, bringing forth and disseminating "fresh ideas, new devices and broader views."

"Then came industrial and commercial libraries. Great organizations found that they needed, for their proper growth, all the knowledge, wisdom, technique, science and suggestion anywhere to be found; that they needed to know every day all that inquirers, in the special field of each organization, had learned the previous day; that they needed to know of all experimentation by others that they might avoid costly experiments for themselves; that they needed, in fact, as complete a collection as could be made of the recent, and of some of the older, books, journals and pamphlets on their activities; that they needed . . . . to have them so arranged, filed and indexed as to bring out all they contained of value to them; and that they needed to have that part of their contents which particularly fitted their work digested, arranged by topics and presented daily, weekly or monthly to all the directors of special activities in their whole army of workers.

"A commercial or industrial library, then, is the resultant of two things, — the great modern growth of organizations and the great modern flood of business, technical and scientific literature; and it is, briefly, a carefully controlled collection of such printed material, relating to the work of the organization which it serves, as a librarian, expert in print, and his assistants can gather, index, digest and present to all its personnel."

9. Consistent Classifications and Competent Classifiers

Special libraries serve specialized interests and even individualized needs. They are individual, but they are also grouped — classified by kinds or types: Commercial, Banking, Insurance, Law, Medicine, Scientific, Technological, etc. These various classes can not be served adequately by standard general classifications constructed for other purposes — nor even by parts of them. But for each class an adaptable classification may be coöperatively constructed and standardized; and these special classifications may be consistent with a general standard classification, may be adapted to it, without conforming to it in detail.[8]

The special interests depend on librarians of special competence, who should be educated and trained for this competence. They depend on special classification and indexing probably more than on ordinary library cataloging. They should have ability to coöperate in compiling special classifications adaptable to the various individual libraries and standardized after being proved. These special standards should be consistent with the general organizations of knowledge, in which they are interrelated specialties. They should be revised from time to

[8] *Cf.* "Special, related to General, Bibliographic Classification," the writer's paper, read and discussed at the Conference of the Library Association at Scarborough, England, June, 1937.

time and readjusted. Here are projects for groups and committees.

It is needless to elaborate the argument; we must hasten to affirm our conclusion. Those who have read the preceding chapters with the attention that arises from interest will probably be prepared to accept the principles as previously stated and to admit the conclusions on the strength of arguments already confirmed. In this chapter we have found that those conclusions apply not only to general libraries but at least in some measure to special libraries also, depending somewhat on whether the library is following a line, or extending over a field of interests, or developing systematically. Few libraries continue to follow a line. For a time a single mind or group of minds of narrowed interests may keep in a groove; but those minds will pass, other interests will supervene. Business reaches out; research ramifies; so does information, as every detective knows from experience. In planning a classification for a special library it is advisable — if not requisite — to provide for both information service and research. But research cannot be adequately provided for without a systematic classification. The subject-index method is only half a method, and that half is only half efficient. For information services too a *functional* organization is inadequate without a coherent *structural* classification. For *maximal efficiency* there should be *collocation* of related *special* subjects, and this depends on logical *subordination* and consistent *coördination* to the relevant general subjects. There must be subordination of the specific to the generic; there should be *gradation by speciality*; and the special details must be arranged under these principles. To be efficient a functional organization of knowledge must be systematic.

PART II

CLASSIFYING, SUBJECT-CATALOGING, AND BIBLIOGRAPHY

"Such a schedule functions only after the classifier has determined the *subject* of the book. Therefore the classifier must work from the book to the classification system and not from the classification schedule to the book. The schedule will aid the classifier, but it cannot classify the book."

Margaret Mann.

"Adequate classification of books depends upon modern systems of classification and on the competent use made of such systems. . . . .

"But how is the prospective cataloger to acquire real interest and competent judgment so as to qualify for the subject approach to books? . . . . "

* * *

"A systematic arrangement of books according to their subject-matter seems to be the most helpful kind of order that can be devised for the greater number of fields which constitute our growing collections of books; but the application of any such system calls for a clear understanding of all that happens before, and even after, the books finally rest upon the shelves."

Grace Osgood Kelley.

CHAPTER VI

THE ART OF CLASSIFYING BOOKS

1. Classing Books Distinguished From Classifying

When librarians speak of classifying books, they usually mean assigning them severally to appropriate classes in an adopted system of classification. According to the distinctions drawn in our chapter on "Classification," [1] this would more properly be termed *classing* the books. This interesting and difficult service involves two closely related processes: first, finding out the main *subjects* of the books, their most important contents and predominant interests, that is, the characters by which they are to be classed, then locating these subjects in the adopted classification, or assimilating them to the most nearly similar subjects in that system, or adjusting new classes there for such books by inserting in the schedules appropriate terms, with or without definition, and class-marks consistent with the notation of the system. The second process may involve reference to the *shelf-list* for comparison with books previously assigned to the several related classes. It may further involve shifting or rearranging several classes and making references from other parts of the classification. It may sometimes involve re-classing and re-marking certain books and their cards in the catalogs, etc. In brief, it may involve *classifying* books and their classes, and it may occasionally involve reclassifying them to some extent. Some-

[1] In the preceding volume, Chapter VIII, section 1.

times classing and classifying are done at the same time; but usually the classing is done subsequently. Most new books are assimilated to pre-existent classes; and only a few new subjects are adjusted to the adopted classification. It is only occasionally that classifying is involved or that reclassifying is undertaken.

In order to classify books the subjects or the characters by which they are to be classed relative to the classification must first be determined. In this the books are usually treated individually. But, when a book is assigned to a class, it becomes a member of a system or organization of classes. The interests and relationships of the individual book should be considered with regard to the others of the group or class; for it is no longer an individual book but a *social* book. All this is implied in *classing* and *classifying* books. Classifying implies a plurality, a society, of books and a system of classification that has been, or is being, prepared or adopted. If we are dealing with live subjects in a live way, we are aware that the classification is, or should be, always in process of adaptation. Rigid, undiscriminating methods in rigid conservative systems that have not been adapted to changing requirements because they are inadaptable have resulted in much unsatisfactory classification for libraries.

The classification of knowledge is dominantly scientific and indeed progressive. Classifying books for libraries, however, is in a sense a plastic art. Every art has its method — and so has every artist. Ergo the art of classifying books for a library has its methods, and each individual classifier may have his own peculiar methods. With what warrant then should one classifier tell another how to classify books? Why, just as one artist tells another how he works. It is implied that classifiers are ever students of their art. Artists say that they are always art-students — always learning, not from nature alone, but from every voice that speaks to them of art sincerely from genuine experience or from true spiritual insights.

Three questions arise: what especially is the subject of the book and its main purpose or interest? Have other similar books been placed in the library, and, if so, in what class, that is, how is the class termed and how marked? To what class shall this book be assigned, to what term and specification may it most appropriately be assimilated, and what class-mark shall be given to it?

This triad of questions implies a simple syllogistic judgment. For instance, take the statement: this book is on Scotland, is more descriptive than historical or sociological or ethnographical, and it is for the general reader. This statement may be regarded as a minor premise. The major premise follows: there is a class of books descriptive of Scotland, including geographical and historical matter, with descriptions of the country and its cities, the social life of the people, etc., and in this library this class of books is marked MW3. The conclusion is: this particular book should be classed in that class and should have the class-mark MW3. This is a very simple judgment. It is instanced here to enforce the statement that to class a book involves judgment. And the judgment usually takes this simple deductive form. The particular book is likened and assimilated to a class and is marked with that class-mark.

But often the judgment is not so simple; neither the contents-pages nor the preface, nor the first chapter nor the last, may reveal the dominant purpose or interest of the author or the book's probable values and uses in the library. The individuality and the social relations of a book may be very elusive. More careful examination may be requisite, and more adequate knowledge of the subjects involved and their relations in the system of knowledge. All this calls for classifiers of knowledge and judgment.

If the book on Scotland is not mainly geographic and historical, but consists of descriptive and narrative chapters together with a mélange of literary and scientific observations and reflections on the national traits and institutions, also considerable social philosophy in the last chapters, the judgment is indeed complex and the decision may be uncertain.

Centralized and standardized classifying together with cataloging may indeed prove to be an economy and an adequate service, showing what the subjects of books are and where they should be placed in standardized classifications; but entire dependence on such services is a confession of ignorance and incompetence. Librarians should usually know the subjects of books before purchasing them, and classifiers before arranging them with their companions in their local classifications, by whatever system, whether standard or not. But we shall consider this question in the last section of this chapter.

2. Some Examples and Comments and Some Advice

The first book that comes to hand to exemplify the classifier's need of knowledge and judgment is entitled *The Epoch of Reform,* by Justin McCarthy, M.P. The epoch of English history in which the great Reform Bill was debated and passed by Parliament in 1832 is here extended to 1850 in order to trace how the principles then established were gradually worked into the political and economic life of the people. This author wrote for the most part political history. This is not a book of social reform in the broad sense; it is not sociological; and closer examination shows that it is not a social history of the period. Nor is this a history of the Reform Bill in Parliament merely. The author's first sentence makes this clear:

"The Epoch of Reform in England is the period of transition during which the representative system in Parliament and the constitutional system in Monarchy became settled institutions." Then on the fourth page he says: "The two most significant reforms accomplished and established in England during the period which this history describes are the reforms in representation and the changes gradually made in the relation of the sovereign towards the people. These principles were formally established in England between the years 1830 and 1850."

The judgment is confirmed; the title of the book is not misleading; the book is about the Reform Bill *and* its effects in that epoch of the *political* history of England. But the political and the social are interwoven; the general term *social-political* history implies this; and a system of classification should provide for the social-political history under the several nations, as well as for the *social* history as distinct from the political, or social-political. This book should accordingly be assigned to the Social-political history of England during the period 1830-50.

Within that period the Chartist agitation, called Chartism, in which the workingmen strove for the rights of suffrage, may be regarded as sufficiently distinct and important to become the caption of a class of books. But this would *not* involve the question whether the Chartist movement was political or social or both. The caption would comprise the whole subject.

A third book is entitled *Star Chamber Cases*, London, 1630. The unhistorical classifier would soon see that this rare old book is neither an astronomical diversion nor scandalous theatrical biography; but he might not know what the Star Chamber was; and, after he found out, he might be at a loss as to what to do with the book — whether to class it under the History of English Law or in the History of England in the time of Charles I. It looks like legal literature; its purpose was mainly to show "what cases belong to the cognizance of that court." The cases were "collected for the most part out of Mr. Crompton his Booke, entitled the *Iurisdiction of divers Courts.*" Yet the contents would now probably be of interest mainly as illustrative of the conduct of the government of Charles I.

Here is a little book on *The Bayeux Tapestry,* "an historical tale of the eleventh century, from the French of Madame L. . . . , with a fac-simile of the tapestry," Brighton, 1858. A scarce book this, of an uncommon kind. The intent is plainly to popularize the history of the famous tapestry and the important history it illustrates of the Norman conquest of England. It is in the form of a romance, however, and doubtless introduces matter more or less fictitious. Its "fac-simile" is only six plates of drawings reproduced lithographically. It is not worth classing with books on Tapestries, in the Fine Arts. Few modern readers would accept it as a romance. The only fitting place is the Bayeux Tapestry, as a special historical subject in the period of the Norman Conquest. This case exemplifies classing by the negative method of *elimination.*

A more typical example of *multiple aspects,* not merely for a particular book but for the whole class, is presented in *Shakespearean Playhouses,* by J. Q. Adams, Boston, 1917. The caption Elizabethan Theater, as subordinate to Elizabethan Drama, would appear under History of English Literature of the Elizabethan Period. But there would be an alternative in the History of the English Drama; and there would be a third alternative in the section for Drama and Theater subordinate to Comparative Literature. Still a fourth would arise, if all the topics about Shakespeare were classified under that great name. There are four generic captions under which this special subject may be specified — four ways of classing it: (1) English Literature, History, Elizabethan, Drama, Theater, Shakespearean; (2) Engl. Lit., Hist., Drama, Elizab'n, Shaks'n, Theater;

(3) Drama, Engl., Elizab'n, Shaks'n, Theater; (4) Engl. Lit., Hist., Shaks., Theater. Of course there are several other variant ways of specifying or classing this subject; but they involve questions in schedulizing rather than in classifying books. This type exemplifies one form of complex judgment, requiring consultation of a *code for classifying* such as will be outlined in the next chapter, or even of the library's *shelf-list,* or both, to ascertain how other similar books, if there be any, have been classified.

In the science of Physics two or more subjects may be correlated, or treated as relevant, in a treatise, study, or investigation; and the book may therefore be difficult to classify, requiring some knowledge of the subject and judgment as to its relations and interests. For instance, McClung's *Conduction of Electricity through Gases and Radioactivity* might be classed either under Electricity, Conduction thru Gases; or it might be classed in Physics of Gases, under the caption Ionization.

Another example is the book entitled *X-Rays and Crystal Structure,* by Professor William Henry Bragg and his lamented, war-stricken son, William Lawrence. This penetrating investigation has been more important as an application of X-rays to the study of the structure and classification of crystals than to the study of the constitution and properties of matter. A book with a similar purpose, but without special regard to the X-rays, is Tutton's *Crystalline Structure and Chemical Constitution.* These two books may be classed in Physical Chemistry under the caption Chemical Constitution or both be placed under the term Crystal Structure in the sub-science Crystallography. It would depend on the interest and the point of view.

A more difficult book is Larmor's *Æther and Matter,* "a development of the dynamical relations of Æther to material systems on the basis of the Atomic Constitution of Matter, including a discussion of the influence of the Earth's motion on optical phenomena." To ascertain what this well-known book is about and what the chief interest in it is likely to be in the classifier's library calls for considerable knowledge of physical science; and to determine which of several classes to place it in requires discriminating judgment. The title-page immediately suggests certain captions in the schedules, Æther, Matter, Ætherial Radiation in relation to the Earth's motion. This last involves the question of the *entraînement* of the Æther, which has led to the discussions of the relativity of motion and to the doctrines of Einstein. The book involves matter of prime importance to physical science. It is, however, thirty years old, and therefore, considering its subject-matter, is mainly of historic interest. More careful examination is called for in this case. The Preface of eleven pages is not very clear and is somewhat involved in style. It tells us that the original purpose was to develop an atomic theory of electricity. Furthermore: "It is incumbent on us to recognize an ætherial substratum to matter. . . . " Then the theory of the "elastic ætherial medium" is found adaptable to the electrodynamic theory. The discussion thus extends to the very fundamentals of physics, involving a wide range of physical theories, of the nature of the æther, of the constitution of matter, of the relations of matter to æther, and of the relations of electrical phenomena to both matter and æther. Let us pass to the Introductory Chapter of five pages, more clearly written. "The scheme of this essay" is there fortunately summarized as having five sections. The first treats historically "of the influence of the motion of matter through the æther on phenomena directly connected with that medium." That clearly relates to the ground of Einstein's theory of Relativity. "The second section develops the general theory of the relations between matter and æther. . . . . In the treatment here given, the essential distinction between molecular theory and mechanical theory, and the principles involved in effecting the transition from the former to the latter, are carefully traced." Well, that is going deeply and very generally into the fundamentals of physics. The third section considers more speculatively the consequences of the electron theory of matter or of radiation thru the æther. The fourth section considers these theoretical results with regard to the negative inferences from "the optical rotary power of quartz" being independent of the direction of the light as referred to the Earth's motion. "The fifth section treats of the subject of the radiation of material systems." These three sections also relate especially to the Relativity question. Having spent an hour in the quest, we must think hard for five minutes in order to decide which of these several subjects it should be assigned to. Viewed broadly as a special discussion, the matter is mainly of historic interest; but to relegate this important work to the historic would be going too fast into the future of physical science. Regarded in its special interest to the theory of Relativity, it deals less with the theory itself than with the problems out of which the theory has arisen. It does not belong with the books on Relativity, or on Relativity of Motion, which is subordinate to Kinematics. Nor is it to be classed with the books on the Æther, nor with those on the Constitution of Matter, nor with those on the nature of Electricity, nor with those on Radiation. It should not be confined to any of these special classes. Neither should it be extended to the broader scope of General Physics. But, considering its contents and interests, it should be brought under the caption, Matter, Æther, and Radiation, in a sub-section for Special Discussions. If the schedule for Physics has not that caption or one similar to it, it is deficient and should be amended.

Scientific terms are more confusingly combined in the title *Substance and Function and Einstein's Theory of Relativity*, by Ernst Cassirer, Chicago, 1923, which is indeed a work on the philosophy of science. To the classifier with library-school equipment the term *substance* might suggest chemistry and *function* might recall physiology, and the rest of the subject might be lost in the mazes of inscrutable physics. Nor would the book itself be crystal clear. The more specially trained librarian might mistake this for a book on the "substance philosophy," as specially branded by philosophers; and he might suppose that *function* in the mathematical sense was here invoked to expound substance; and Einstein's theory is often defended as being incomprehensible to the unmathematical mind. But this book does not deal with the theory of Einstein enough to justify that part of its title. Its professed purposes are to discuss the philosophy of science and the critique of knowledge. One wonders why the title — why substance.

In view of misleading titles, catalogers, dealing with the subjects of books, should be educated and trained as classifiers too. This need is exemplified in the following three instances of unfit classifying by the catalogers of a library well known to the writer of these reflections, — who hastens to admit the advantage that he has read these three books. The sincere little book on *The Art of Thinking,* by Ernest Dimnet, was classed as Psychology of Thinking; but it is not psychological in the scientific sense. Applying our broadest rule, this garland of engaging chapters on mental traits and intellectual activities, and of course many other things, is not science, nor philosophy, nor history; it is literature. Similarly applying this rule to Walter Lippmann's *Preface to Morals,* which one of these classifiers had put under Ethics, but which deals with religion and social life more broadly than with morals and ethics, we find that this most interesting and influential book too is literature; while prefatory to any — or all — of these studies, it is neither theology, nor philosophy, nor sociology, nor ethics; it is at once something less than these and something more — very good literature. Thirdly, *The Universe Around Us,* by Sir James Jeans, one might be inclined to treat as literature too, tho the author is an eminent physicist. This is not because the book is so well written, nor because so well advertised, but because it is really not scientific in matter or treatment; it is far too speculative and imaginative for that — even for "popular" or literary science. Yet, out of respect for the author and for the interest of many of its thoughtful readers, this classifier would ascribe it to the subject Cosmology, under Astronomy. He would not, however, term this *Cosmogony,* as certain critics and scientific writers have done in the confused terminology. Nor would he accept this matter as scientific *astrophysics* Still less would he admit this book to be descriptive astronomy, as at least one fallible classifier has done.

Another difficult case now comes to hand, Whittaker's *Course of Modern Analysis*: "an introduction to the general theory of infinite series and of analytic functions." Cambridge University Press, 1902. A noted mathematical work is this, and very mathematical, with all the difficulty to the classifier which that implies. Apparently this is not an ordinary treatise on the higher mathematical analysis. Indeed the brief preface conveniently tells us that: "The first half of this book contains an account of those methods and processes of higher mathematical analysis, which seem to be of greatest importance at the present time. . . . . In the second half of the book the methods of the earlier part are applied in order to furnish the theory of the principal functions of analysis, ... " Here is a book that is neither comprehensive in scope nor special either as to content, to method, to aspect, or to subject-matter. It is a broad eclectic study of infinite series, of Higher Analysis and of Theory of Functions too. Referring from the class-mark of this book, we find that our schedule for Higher Analysis has an appropriate caption, with the following definition: "Higher Analysis, general in scope but special in treatment; not comprehensive, nor Functions only, nor Applications only." While this case is hardly typical, the difficulty involved is likely to recur in other cases.

To distinguish between new special aspects of a subject and new subdivisions of it is a duty continually before the classifier; who will have to decide in each case whether to make a new caption or to subordinate under an old caption, or merely to subsume under some proximate caption that may be elastic enough to include the new matter.

3. The Complexities of Sociologico-Philosophical Literature

Not only philosophy but, as we have seen in the first chapter, history is comprehensive of the whole range of studies from Logic to Linguistics. Scientific data and theories have historical antecedents and are subject to historical treatment. And all these studies, when embodied in writings, may be said to be literature.

Nearly every philosophical study that is sound rests upon scientific data, and nearly every philosophical book has something scientific in it. On the other hand, nearly every scientific treatise has in it something philosophical. Again nearly every serious literary writing has something of the historical and philosophical. All such writings are in the broadest sense literature; and much literature is in this sense quadruplex in its content. Often the four components are so mingled that it is difficult to judge whether the writing is principally scientific, philosophic, historical, or literary. This is especially true of the literature of the social studies.

A good example of this kind of complexity is *The Mind in the Making: the relation of intelligence to social reform,* by James Harvey Robinson. As literature this book is excellent reading. Its author has a high reputation as a historian, especially of cultural and intellectual history. The book, however, combines much scientific matter with well reasoned social philosophy. From its contents, tho hardly from its title, it may without much question be brought under Social Psychology. Its title alone suggests Mental development (psychological), but its sub-title, while indicative of interest to *apply* sociology to ameliorating social conditions, is suggestive of the broader social science and philosophy that inform the larger part of the book. So we have classed it with such sociological companions as Baldwin's *Social and Ethical Interpretations in Mental Development,* and Lester Ward's *Psychic Factors in Civilization.*

In some cases the title is more misleading. *Progress and Poverty* by Henry George was not on progress generally nor on poverty especially, but mainly on the nationalization of land, or more especially on the re-distribution of wealth thru a single tax on land. *The Great Society, a psychological analysis,* is the title that Graham Wallas gave to a book that, purporting in the first half to be mainly social psychology, devotes the latter half, under the captions of The Organization of Thought, of Will, and of Happiness, to rather concrete discussions of political and social conditions and remedies. The title, *The Great Society,* however, suggests not social psychology but either a socialistic utopia or a study of some great social organization. Wallas had previously designated as *The Great Industry* the dominant industrial development of modern society. By the analogous term, *Great Society,* he would imply that there is a developing tendency to reorganize society more thoroly as a social and political system.

More expressly socialistic is *The New Society* by Walther Rathenau; yet we have not classed this book under Socialism, but in the section for Descriptive Sociology have assigned it to a sub-section provided for Social Conditions and Tendencies. This differs from the preceding instance in that it has little to do with social psychology, is not indeed a sociological study but rather is literary and hortatory in manner; nevertheless, because of its content and purpose, it should be classed under Sociology rather than as literature.

On the contrary, Walter Lippmann's *Public Opinion* must be regarded as literary rather than scientific or philosophic. It is not, however, a mere collection of essays, but has a general trend, like most of this brilliant writer's books, to the liberation of thought from its trammels and prejudices. Yet its general purpose is neither sociological nor psychological nor historical; nor is it philosophy in the proper sense. It must be regarded as literature, and it should be placed under a caption provided for such purposive discussions in Recent English Literature.

Several of the books of H. G. Wells are at once literary and philosophic. Some that are in the form of novels have the purport of sociological or ethical discourses. This applies of course to many purposive, or "problem," novels. In most cases, however, the purpose is not so explicit that a classifier would perceive it in cursorily classing the book. If it is a matter of advertisement and of knowledge to readers, the book may be classed under the subject. Bellamy's *Looking Backward* may well be classed under Socialism, in a sub-section provided for such romances or novels;

and there may conveniently be a sub-section of English Literature for such speculative or prophetic books as Wells' *Anticipations*.

As regards misleading or baffling titles, what shall we say to the following: *Boon, the Mind of the Race, the Wild Asses of the Devil, and the Last Trump; being a first selection from the literary remains of George Boon, appropriate to the times, prepared for publication by Reginald Bliss; with an ambiguous introduction by H. G. Wells.* All this title belongs to a single book, and it is enough to arouse the curiosity of almost any reader. How shall we find out in five minutes what it is all about? There are ten continuous chapters, which are probably as facetious as the interspersed whimsical drawings in juvenile style that increase our curiosity. Cursory perusal of a few pages shows that, while fiction in form, the matter is mainly satirical and ironical, humorous and facetious, and quite imaginative. It is no mere series of essays or sketches. In which of the sub-sections of Miscellaneous English Literature that are available for such books we should class this one will depend on what kinds of books have already been classified in those sub-sections. Perhaps other classifiers would not agree with us, and perhaps the reviewers might be found to hold different views, if it seemed worth while for us to look up what they said about the book on its publication.

4. Advice On Classifying Philosophy and Literature

Philosophy, we have seen, merges on the one side into science and on the other side into literature. The philosophy of science may be regarded either as philosophy or as science, and such books as Spencer's *First Principles* and Pearson's *Grammar of Science* have much in common. The two interests differ, however, in that the one is for the scientific point of view and the other for the philosophic. This difference the classifier should at least be able to distinguish, and, if so, he will be able to distinguish most other philosophic studies from the related scientific studies. He will recognize Hodgson's *Time and Space*, for instance, as philosophic, and Mach's *Space and Geometry* as scientific.

Another point, books termed Metaphysics may be confined to ontology or they may comprise epistemology, as do, for example, Hamilton's, Lotze's, and Taylor's. This is just a matter of scope and definition. The scope of a treatise may be unclear from the confusion that infects the term *reality,* implying sometimes existence independent of knowledge and sometimes existence dependent on knowledge.

A kindred vagueness affects the scope of Logic, which is often held to comprise most of epistemology, or even of metaphysics, and which may involve much psychology, but which on the other hand is often confined to *formal* logic, or the forms of valid thinking.

In providing an alternative for Psychology under Philosophy, we had in mind the older study called Mental Philosophy. Modern psychology has, we have shown, its place among the sciences of human nature. But the older books, under whatever title, and those most closely akin to epistemology, might be classified in contiguity with this caption, or even subordinate to it.[2]

The term *human nature* has similar duplicity. Hume's *Treatise of Human Nature* was philosophic. So was Hartley's *Observations on Man.* Büchner's *Stellung des Menschen in der Natur* was philosophic rather than anthropologic in the scientific sense. Charron's *De la Sagesse* belongs to the olden literature of philosophic anthropology, but *wisdom* in this title does not imply *knowledge,* and the book should not be classed in Epistemology. Of recent books Eucken's *Problem of Human Life* (1912), Hocking's

[2] Three typical examples will be cited here: Hickok's *Rational Psychology,* 1849, Dugald Stewart's *Philosophy of the Human Mind,* 3 v., 1792-1827, and Taine's important work, *Théorie de l'Intelligence,* 1870.

Human Nature and its Remaking (1918), Paton's *Human Behavior* (1921), and Edman's *Human Traits in their Social significance* (1920) all treat of the philosophy of human nature and life rather than of scientific psychology or anthropology.

An Introduction to Reflective Thinking by Columbia Associates in Philosophy presents a special problem to the classifier. Thinking is a subject that has its psychological literature as well as its scientific psychology; but this book is neither literary nor psychological in interest and treatment. Then there is a logic of thinking, the analysis of thinking and logical processes, and the "laws of thought," and the tests of the validity of thoughts or judgments. In this book, however, these logical matters are merely ancillary. A broader philosophic and scientific purpose is here professed — to serve in introductory courses in philosophy and science. Yet this book is quite different from those ordinarily termed *Introductions* to philosophy. Tho it deals with logical methods, it differs from methodology too. Where then shall we place it? Well, since it belongs neither under Psychology nor under Logic, since it is not strictly scientific but is ancillary rather to philosophy and to methodology, the subject may properly be designated as Thinking, reflective, philosophic and scientific, and this definition should be subordinated under the section for Books about Philosophy.

Creative Intelligence, essays in the pragmatic attitude, by John Dewey and others, might be classed with certain books on the psychology of intelligence. An undiscriminating use of the Index to the classification might lead to this, as it might mislead also in the preceding instance. *Intelligence* stands first in the title and *pragmatism* might be overlooked, tho it is the leading subject in this book, as, I think, most classifiers would find. Having indicated caution here, no further comment need be made on this type of error.

Again such books as *The Tragic Sense of Life,* by the Spanish author, Unamuno, challenge careful judgment as to whether they should be regarded as literature or as philosophy of life. The decision may well depend on the point of view.

Some classifiers may regard most philosophical books as just "philosophy," even as they may regard most educational books as "just education," without bothering about specifications; but a little more knowledge and discrimination would bring these unphilosophic classifiers to recognize that most philosophic writings assimilate in general to four main captions: historical, critical, speculative, and systematic. In modern works the systematic may be so closely combined with the critical that it is not easy to judge which predominates; but in most cases the systematic should be chosen as the more important. Certain works of James, Ormond, Royce, Croce, and others may be distinguished thus, without distinctive names being assigned to their systems. Sometimes, when the systematic purpose is professed, it is difficult to define or characterize it, that is, to classify it. Some philosophers who profess the systematic purpose deprecate being ascribed to any systematic name, or *ism*. If, however, distinctive names have become well established, captions for them may appear in the schedules, e.g., Pragmatism, Voluntarism, etc. But a philosopher may have adopted a subsequent name for his developed or improved system. James in his later essays preferred to call his thought *radical empiricism*, not, as before, pragmatism. When there is a distinct caption, books that are especially critical may be classed with those that are mainly systematic in intent, and so may works that combine the historical and the critical. Thus the caption may stand for the broader scope, e.g. Pragmatism and Humanism (in the philosophic sense), and the class may include such titles as the following: *Principles of Pragmatism* (critical) by Bawden, *Philosophy of Humanism* (systematic and critical) by Haldane, James' *Pragmatism* (systematic and critical), Moore's *Pragmatism and its critics* (critical), Schiller's *Humanism* (systematic and critical).

Philosophy, we have said, approaches literature. Some philosophers have literary talent; they have poetry in their souls, and in their pages; they are delightfully vague; and they are vaguely read by those who delight in them. It seems unfair to relegate Plato and Kant, Schopenhauer and Nietzsche, James and Bergson, Croce and Santayana, to unalluring philosophy, while Lucretius and Goethe, Coleridge and Tennyson, who were also of fealty to philosophy, are crowned as poets and honored as *élite* in literature. Literary thought may indeed be philosophic, yet it is not very difficult to distinguish this thoughtful literature from literary philosophy. The history of thought is moreover to be distinguished from the history of philosophy. Much æsthetic and religious thinking, much political and moralistic discussion should be comprised in the history of thought and opinion. Lecky's *History of European Morals* belongs to History rather than to Ethics, and Merz's *History of European Thought* may be treated as the history of intellectual progress and culture rather than, more strictly, of its science and philosophy.

5. Classing With Regard to the Index, the Code, and the Shelf-List

Some classifiers, many librarians, and, perhaps we should say, most readers do not approve of such close distinctions. The difficulties, however, of classifying books and the uncertainties in locating them, whether on the part of librarians or of readers, are not much increased by definite and specific classification, but the special services and conveniences so often requisite are thereby greatly enhanced. The uncertainties may usually be removed by ready reference to the Index of the classification or to the catalog under author or subject. On the other hand the difficulties of finding special kinds of books in unclassified collections are much greater and more vexatious. So we would classify even literature and philosophy as definitely as is feasible, tho not too elaborately for the real requirements.

On referring to the index, however, the classifier may find two or three locations, sometimes for alternatives, sometimes for different treatment of the subject, which may belong to the fields of two related sciences. Thus the subject, Family, is referred to Sociology and to Ethnology, for there are the two distinct tho related studies, the one descriptive, statistical, and sociological, the other comparative, historical, and ethnographical under the caption Social Ethnology.

Consulting for instance the shelf-list of our college library, the writer found classified there in the sociological subject the following books, among others: Helen Bosanquet's *The Family,* James Q. Dealey's study of *The Family in its sociological aspects,* Willystine Goodsell's *History of the Family as a social and educational institution,* Grove's *Social Problems of the Family,* Messer's *The Family in the Making,* Mowrer's *Family Disorganization,* and Spencer's *The Family and its Members.* In the ethnological subject are two books, Starke's *The Primitive Family, in its origin and development,* and Westermarck's *History of Human Marriage.* Elsie Clews Parson's book on *The Family, an ethnographical and historical study,* covers both fields, but the interest is sociological rather than ethnological, and the book belongs in Sociology, Descriptive, as the broader field. But the actual placing of such books, in all overlapping subjects, should have due regard to the tendencies shown in the shelf-list; they should not indiscriminately follow the terms of the schedules as located by the index. That short cut may fall far short of adequate classifying. As Mr. Berwick Sayers has remarked, it may not be classifying at all.[8] It proceeds from what we have called "the subject-index illusion," and it may lead to many errors and much confusion.

The tendencies shown in the shelf-list should be reconsidered from time to time; and occasionally it may be necessary to transfer a book or two from the one place to the other. The schedule may, however, present the alternative of placing the entire subject in the one science or in the other. If so, the judgment is reduced to considering a note in the schedule or to a decision or definition in a

[8] *Manual of Classification,* sections 82 and 115.

code. Not only decisions but tendencies may be recorded or anticipated. The terms or notes in the schedules and the definitions expressed or implied in these may be further specified or amplified. This may be done so as to apply to cases likely to occur in the individual library or the statements may be more generally applicable to many libraries of the same type.[4] For Literature and Philosophy a code is indeed requisite. We shall outline the principles and limitations of such codes in the next chapter.

The index would refer the subject Learning both to Psychology of Learning and to Learning Process, in Educational Psychology. Those who separate Education under Sociology from Psychology here run against the crux of the problem. Educational Psychology *is* psychology *and* education. In the subject of Learning, and in many other subjects, the two branches overlap; the two views converge. Yet for convenience of the two groups of students, those coming from the studies of psychology and those from the educational studies, the two classes of books should be distinguished, as in the following incomplete selection:

In Psychology of Learning:

Cameron. *Cerebral Destruction in its relation to Maze Learning.*
Kjerstad. *Form of the Learning Curves for Memory.*
Koch. *Influence of Mechanical Guidance upon Maze Learning.*
Myers. *The Learner and his Attitude.*
Snoddy. *Experimental analysis of a case of Trial and Error Learning in the Human Subject.*
Sullivan. *Attitude in relation to Learning.*
Thurstone. *The Learning Curve Equation.*

In Educational Psychology, Learning Process:

Colvin. *The Learning Process.*
Edwards. *Fundamental principles of Learning and Study.*
Freeman. *How Children Learn.*
Pyle. *Psychology of Learning.* (Because of interest rather than by title).

[4] Mr. Merrill's *Code for Classifiers* has entertained this broader purpose.

The index to the classification is also an index to any shelf-list that is correlative to it. We should bear in mind that in an alphabetical index, however convenient to locate subjects or books, the subjects are dispersed, lacking collocation; and the more specific the index is, the more dispersive it is. But, if it subordinates under many subjects their more specific subdivisions, aspects, and topics, and their more intrinsic relations to other subjects (in cross-references), the dispersion will in so far be diminished. This, however, requires many duplicate entries. Few indexes can bear so much systematic burden. This is a reason why classifying from the index without due reference to the schedules and occasionally to the shelf-list, and to the *code,* may be so unsatisfactory. Hasty classifiers should avoid the habit, particularly where it is a kind of rough and tumble short-cut thru the complications of systematic classification and the labyrinthine tangles of scientific terminology.

6. Prefaces and Introductions As Aids to the Classifier

Often a preface tells the classifier in the author's own words what he deems the scope of his book and its point of view and purposes. This is especially welcome when the title, for literary or commercial or other reason, is peculiar or even misleading. But of course we should not always take the author's own estimate, nor his terms; and his point of view may not be that from which such books are classified in our library. However, it behooves the classifier, when in doubt and in problematic cases, to consult the preface and the introduction, if there be one. He may then pass to the summary or the conclusion, if there be one. In some books there is a summary at the end, or at the beginning, of each chapter, part, or section; and examining a few of these may suffice.

Perhaps Randolph Greenfield Adams had some of the difficulties of classifiers in mind, when he wrote at the beginning of the preface to his book, *Political Ideals of the American Revolution,* this declaration of its purport: "This work is intended in the first place as a contribution to International Law. In the second place, it is a chapter of Britannic Imperial History, and in the third place it may be regarded as a fragment of the History of the United States." The title implies the third of those subjects, while the sub-title, "Britannic-American contributions to the problem of imperial organization," implies the second. In this case we can hardly say that the author has solved the classifier's problem. More of the preface must be read and the contents-pages scanned, and certain chapters interrogated. This classifier did not class this book in the first place under International Law, nor in the second place under the history of the British Empire, or of Great Britain's imperial policy, nor in the third place under the history of the American Revolution. For the general purposes of his library he thought it best to take the author's second subject in connection with the term *imperial organization* stated in the subtitle, and to classify the book under Political Science in a sub-section for Imperialism (as a national policy or form of political organization). This caption is for the subject in general, for historical as well as theoretical treatment. Tho the book is historical rather than general or theoretical, it seems best not to confine it to the interest in the American Revolution, nor to the history of Great Britain's imperialism.

Introductions are not always so clear and positive at the outset as the first pages of Professor Cubberley's editor's introduction to Freeman's *Psychology of the Common Branches,* published by Houghton Mifflin Company. It is worth while to quote from it at some length as an example:

"The present volume is . . . . a very successful attempt to apply the knowledge which we have recently accumulated in the scientific applications of psychology to the concrete problems of instruction in the elementary school. It is neither a scientific treatise on psychology nor a book of special methods, though embracing something of the content of each. Instead, the present volume occupies a field lying between the two, being a presentation of the psychological principles underlying the most effective instruction in the commonly recognized subjects of the elementary-school curriculum. . . .

"In between these two extremes of psychology on the one hand and special or general methods on the other lie two new fields in applied psychology — genetic psychology, which attempts to organize psychological knowledge in terms of mental evolution, and the psychology of the process of learning to write, read, spell, calculate, etc. Genetic psychology lies nearer to the pure psychology end, and the psychology of learning lies nearer to the methods end.

"The present volume is a treatise on the second of these two intermediate fields, namely the psychology of the learning process, and as applied to the so-called fundamental subjects of the elementary-school course."

Relation to a series is generally indicative of the scope, trend or bias of the component books. Another of the *Riverside Textbooks* is Terman's *Measurement of Intelligence.* This title might indicate the broader subject under psychology, but in relation to that series it indicates that this book should be classed in a special sub-section of Educational Psychology that should be termed Intelligence, Tests and Measurements.

There is indeed a manifest tendency to state the purpose and scope of a book in its preface or elsewhere. This is shown in a large proportion of the books that have come to this classifier's hands during recent years. A particularly interesting instance, where there would seem some intent to assist librarians, as well as publishers and booksellers, is the preface to Pintner's *Intelligence Testing,* published by The Henry Holt Company, with whose permission we quote:

"This book is an attempt to give a simple account of intelligence testing and the results which have so far been achieved by the testing movement. It is designed for use as a text in a college course, and it is hoped that it will prove useful in serving as a guide to the thousands of teachers who are now becoming interested in the use of intelligence tests in their schools.

"The book is not a treatise on measurement in education or psychology. For this purpose, we have already the valuable works of Thorndike, Rugg, and others. Nor does it deal with the technique of test construction, which has been recently covered by McCall. Furthermore, it does not deal with educational tests, that is, with tests of achievement in school subjects, for in this field there are now many books. It is rather an attempt to tell the reader what is meant by intelligence testing, what means are employed to test general intelligence, and what results have been achieved."

But sometimes in literary books the author's preface is like a mask, thru which he teases the gentle, or the ungentle or irritable, reader with grimaces that conceal more than they reveal. It is unnecessary to exemplify this charming annoyance. Most readers have had experience in this literary pastime. Here, however, is a modish book sporting the title *Masks and Demons,* by Kenneth MacGowan and Herman Rosse, which whimsically employs the caption "Initiation," instead of *Preface,* and thus initiates the topic, or the reader (Harcourt, Brace & Co. permit us to quote):

"The mask is not to be carelessly assumed or lightly put off. Primitive man knows that there must be initiation and a certain ceremony. If he puts on a false face without the proper incantation, there will be no power in it. It may be the same with books — or at any rate with a book about the mask.

"There are certain things that one should know before looking at a mask. They have to do with the mind and the faith of primitive man. This book, with its pictures and its words, is intended to tell the man who looks at a mask drawn by Craig or a mask made by Dulac, Stern, or Benda various facts that he should know about their ancestors, the holy masks of simpler men. This foreword is intended to initiate him into those mysteries of medicine men and demons which he must know before he can put on knowledge of the mask."

7. Coöperative and Centralized Classifying

The system of knowledge, we have maintained, is unitary and is correlative to the persistent order of nature. *A valid classification of knowledge tends to become standardized with regard to a scientific and educational consensus.* A classification of the subjects of study, properly correlated to the system of knowledge and adapted to the uses and economies of libraries, should therefore be generally applicable and relatively stable.

In more or less close conformity with such standard classification various special classifications respective to types of libraries may be developed, each with its own notation, index, and *code*. Adaptation to different requirements or points of view should, so far as is feasible, be provided for by *alternatives* presented in the standard system, or systems.

Centralized cataloging is distinguished from coöperative[5] cataloging. A number of libraries may *coöperate* in selection, search, methods, rules, typewriting, microphotography, printing, and distributing catalog-cards that indicate subjects of books and class-marks for specific notations; and in this service authors, editors, publishers, and booksellers may also coöperate. This, broadly, is *coöperative* cataloging and classifying. Then, if these processes and services are concentrated in one library or agency, national, state, institutional, or central, this is *centralized* cataloging and classifying. To combine the centralized and coöperative plans is advantageous or requisite if the central library or agency has not all the resources, information, funds, and personnel. In the various services and undertakings in this country and in Germany, Great Britain, France, and other countries there are important tendencies toward such completeness.

Coöperative classifying together with cataloging for a group or system of libraries, general or special, and centralized printing, storage, and distribution of the cards have not yet passed thru the stages of experimentation and discussion, for the systems and services are still incomplete and unsatisfactory. This would not slight the estimable services of the Library of Congress and of the

[5] David J. Haykin, "Cooperative Cataloging in North America—Problems and Possibilities." *Catalogers' and Classifiers' Yearbook*. No. 6. 1937. p. 26-7.

Committees of the American Library Association, nor would it criticise them. Those and other agencies, national and international, comprehensive and special, are developing in the stage of *organization.* Various plans have been and are being proposed,[6] and some of these are being proved.

As there are many different kinds of libraries, their collections, purposes, services, and rules will differ, and so should their catalogs and classifications. Each individual library will have its *individual* classification and catalog. These may in certain respects be adaptively *consistent with standards*; and they may conform even in many details; but to plan that *all* libraries of all lands should be cataloged by one code of rules and classified in detail by one "universal" classification is impractical and uneconomical — is too much organization. The individual library should conform only in certain respects to the standards of its class and type. Special types and standards should be consistent with general, national, and international standards only in so far as such consistency seems serviceable and economical. A class or group of libraries may, however, be extensive — coextensive with a country — so a general or a national standard may be adopted, or adapted, generally, or nationally, or even internationally.

A coöperating group of special libraries, with their fields delimited, could at the same time coöperate in contributing "copy" for printing on cards to be supplied from the central service. In this way a large percentage of the new books selectively purchased by American libraries could be handled economically, efficiently, and promptly. How much could be accomplished with the less recent books or those of the past would of course

[6] At a Round-Table of the Catalog Section of the A. L. A. on the subject of "Extension of Coöperative Cataloging," June 23, 1927, the writer put forth a plan for "More Adequate Coöperative Classifying and Cataloging." See also his article in *Special Libraries,* March, 1929.

depend on how much would be subscribed by coöperating libraries and how much revenue would accrue from the sale of the cards. In any case the fact of and the need for judicious selection is manifest.

The most important economy of all would be the *coöperative selection* of books and designation of fields of specialization for selections and collections. This great problem indeed would require itself a volume of study. Libraries generally would select for most subjects and collect for a few.

But this coöperation could go a step farther: the cards for books coöperatively selected and therefore in considerable demand might be supplied wholesale to publishers and booksellers to be retailed to libraries with the respective books, when so ordered. A library might obtain some of its cards this way and some from the central service. The publishers and booksellers would be compensated not only by a small profit on the cards but by the increased purchasing power resulting from the economy of the library funds, and by the enhanced good will. Moreover, for books selected coöperatively the cards might be sent "on approval," as sometimes the books are at present, and they would tend to sell the books as well as to inform the librarians. Unsold cards should be returnable to the central stock.

The economy second in importance is *indication of the subject,* or subjects, general and specific, on the cards in terms of a standard alphabetic system, or "List" of subjects and references. This should be revised and reissued as often as economies allow. The scope of the subject could be defined by authors and publishers with regard to the related fields of knowledge; and with reference to a standard classification. This indication of subjects and classing in standard systems would of course be merely tentative and preliminary to classifying by librarians according to their own schedules, rules and codes, whether general or special. The subjects and the notations on the cards could be translated into the terms and notations of any other classification, often by means of its index. For two other standard classifications also the notations might be printed on the cards, so as to serve more directly than thru an index.

But for coöperative classifying and subject-cataloging it is altogether *needless and uneconomic* to adopt the individual classification of an individual library. However great, rich, and liberal this may be, it may *not be typical,* and, if not, its classification will be fit for few other libraries. The older and the more extensive it is, the more conservative and inadaptable its system will probably be. And, if its system is inherently faulty and objectionable, it becomes detrimental. There is no real need to adopt it and no real economy in employing it. What is actually needed is better coöperative standards and a better coöperative service.

By coöperation of librarians and publishers in some such way as is suggested here, subject-cataloging and classifying for libraries would be greatly facilitated and economized and also rendered more satisfactory. Successful coöperation in this country for these purposes would lead to similar coöperation in other countries. Coöperation in bibliography is tending to become international.

CHAPTER VII

OUTLINES OF A CODE FOR CLASSIFYING BOOKS

1. Preliminary Considerations

In preceding chapters there have been allusions to a "code for classifying." What is meant by this will now be outlined, what its uses may be and what its limitations, what it should contain, according to our principles, and what it should not undertake.

A classification for a growing library is an expansive, developing system; and it should be adaptive, the more so if purposed, as a standard, to serve many libraries, whether of one class or of many classes. New subjects will need to be inserted and adjusted, and old subjects will develop new aspects, requiring different definition. In adaptation too there may be choice of alternative locations for certain subjects, general or special, and of alternative methods of classifying certain major subjects: literature, philosophy, history, biography, travels, geography, etc. Many questions will arise involving study of the schedules of classification and of the definitions and directions that should complement them. Comparison with other systems of classification may be advisable. The choices and decisions for an individual library may well be recorded in the schedules, or in a supplement following, or paralleling, their order and notation. This may be done in annotations on the margins of the schedules; or on *recto* pages left blank for the purpose, the original schedules being printed or typewritten on the *verso* pages only; or it may be on interleaved pages, or in a separate loose-leaf book, or on large cards. This record would be essentially not a printed and finished thing, but open to much addition and alteration. If it be in book form and systematic, paralleling the schedules, it should be fully indexed alphabetically. If it be marginal to the schedules, the data should be intercalated in the Index to the schedules. But it may in itself be *arranged alphabetically* by distinctive terms and catch-word headings for the subjects, and with cross-references.

The closer the record of decisions to the choices and alternatives presented, and the closer the exceptions stand to the stated rules, the more convenient the record will be and the more efficient in the process of classifying books. This may lead to the complementary or parallel arrangement in the schedules. But the alphabetic arrangement may on the other hand prove simpler and more direct.

Some choices, alternatives, and rules may be generalized as to statement and applicability. Such may well be embodied in a book, compiled and published for use in many libraries. The *Code for Classifiers,* compiled by Mr. William Stetson Merrill, with collaboration of Miss Grace Osgood Kelley and Miss Julia Pettee, has undertaken to meet this need. We should remark that this code is for *classifiers* — in the plural.

In the classifications for libraries established in the past such definitions, directions, and alternatives have been lacking in the schedules or inadequate. In applying these systems it has become necessary to supplement them thus with material that should in part have been complementary. This seems to have been the main reason for the printed code just mentioned. There has also been a recognized need for more adequate statement of rules and instructions for classifying books than the meager literature on this subject has heretofore furnished. But, whether for classifiers or for students in the library-school courses, such rules and instructions are, educationally and practically, material for text-books and manuals rather than for codes such as we are here considering; and the study of much of this material might be extended to a volume of critical discussions. In short, some items should have place in text-books, some in manuals, some in codes, or records, and some in the schedules of classification.[1]

Aside from manuals, text-books, and lectures, let us consider more especially what such "codes" should embody. The schedules of classification should originally contain, besides their captions and terms for the classes or subjects, certain complementary data: specifications of classes, definitions of terms, alternatives of location and of method, cross-references, directions, and annotations of special import. For all of these the schedules are the proper place, within limits of economy. Not all subjects would be defined there, but only those where definition is most likely to be of positive assistance to the classifier while at work — *not* in study. The studies of definitions, of relations of subjects, and of the intricacies of terminology belong in informative and educative books. But the schedules would serve the

[1] It is significant that the Index to Mr. Berwick Sayers' *Manual of Classification* contains neither term *code* nor *alternative*; but much is implied in his own "Rules for Classifying" in his section 252, and particularly in his last rule, "Index all decisions." The importance of this rule he again emphasizes in his section 261. Dr. Richardson's book does not touch upon this question. The *Classified Catalogue Code* of Ranganathan is introduced as a code of rules generally applicable to classified catalogs, tho there is reference thruout to the author's *Colon Classification*, so this Code exemplifies a guide and elucidation that is purposed also as a manual for other libraries with other classifications and catalogs.

better for functional classifying, if they present definitions and directions to guide classifiers at cross-roads and places of perplexity and in the depths of the forests of science and philosophy.

2. What a "Code" May Well Contain

(1) *Definitions of subjects* that are not defined in the schedules and that may have various content and relations, e.g. Anthropology. Also Ethnology and Ethnography, cognate subjects confused in the terminology, may well be defined. But special subjects such as Philately and Sphragistics may be defined in the schedules, while such general subjects as Metaphysics, History, and Philology should be defined or discussed in manuals or in more comprehensive books.

(2) *Definition of terms* variously used or likely to be misused, such as Journals, Memoirs, Literary history. But such terms as Chrestomathies, Drama, Merchandising, and Monographs should be defined elsewhere, tho for the first two the choices in allocation should be recorded in the Code.

(3) *Distinctive synonyms* should be *specified* in the Code, whether this be of general or of individual application, and, where requisite, the allocations should be recorded. For instance Antiquities and Archæology, Dramatics and Theatricals, Collections and Selections, Economic and Human Geography, Colonies and Dependencies, and Introductions to Philosophy, which may be general or historical only.

(4) *Heading-references* and *Cross-references* should in the Code, if alphabetically arranged, supplement the Index to the Classification. If in any case there be two or more locations or specifications, these should also be

indicated: e. g. Textiles, refer to Industries, Textile, and to Arts, Textile; Diaries, refer to Autobiographies, and from Journals; Queens, refer to Kings and Queens, or to Rulers.

(5) *Alternative allocations of special subjects,* sometimes indicated in the schedules and their index, should be determined in the Code, and reasons for the decisions may be recorded there, tho less adequately than in a treatise or discussion: for example, Economic History, National traits, Teaching botany, and Art education. For major general subjects alternative locations should be shown in the schedules. Discussion of reasons would have place in an Introduction to the Classification or in a separate study or treatise.

(6) *Alternative methods of classifying subjects,* general or special, such as Biography, Philosophy, Travels, Literature, Criticism, Translations, Periods of history, Forms of Poetry, Bibliographies, Concordances, Correspondence, Inscriptions, Battles, Wars, Rivers, should be indicated in the schedules, and should in any case have the choice recorded in the Code. Some of the major alternatives would be discussed more fully in a treatise or study of classification for libraries.

(7) *Duplex,* or *complex, subdivision* of subjects, scientific, historical, or philological, by specification, by nationality, country, or locality, by historical periods, by literary forms, *format* of books, etc., involving alternatives and choice as to which should precede in the order of subdivision, all require that the choices and decisions should be recorded in the Code; e. g. Cross-fertilization of Orchids, Stratigraphy of the Devonian in England, History of Egyptian Art, Medieval French romances.

History of subjects, general or special, may be treated generally or comparatively, or with particular regard to one country or nation or group of nations. If treated generally, subordinate either under General History or else under the subject, utilizing the respective mnemonic. But, if the subject be treated nationally, there are again two alternatives: to classify by subject and sub-classify by nations, applying the systematic schedule; or to classify under the history of the nation, or country, where subdivisions for such subjects may be provided for.

The classifier should consider which interest predominates. But it is inconsistent to subdivide General History first for the subjects treated generally and then to subordinate the national there, thus separating the latter both from the history of the nation and also from the general and descriptive study of the subject; e.g. History of British Commerce should be subordinated either to History of Great Britain or to Commerce, History, but *not* to History, Economic, Commerce.

History of Elementary Education in France should class with other books on elementary education in France, or else it should be collocated with other History of Education, but it should not be subordinated to General History, nor should the History of Education. If there be exceptions to this tendency, the individual Code should note them.

(8) *Duplex, or complex, relation, or reference, to other subjects,* with regard to effects, influences, aspects, viewpoints, treatment, interest, etc., requiring choice as to which should be subordinated, may well have such decisions recorded in a code; e. g. French assistance to the American Revolution, Prohibition of liquor traffic viewed by a criminologist, Old Norse sagas' influence on English poetry, Byron's influence on Shelley, The Ethical import of Darwinism, Myth as the origin of religion.

The last two of these examples are taken from Merrill's *Code,* where they appear under the 11th and 14th "Directions applicable to any class of material." The particular directions there are to class the *myth* subject under Religion and the Darwinism subject under Ethics. Those decisions may be valid for some interests, but not for all interests, nor for all libraries; and the same may be said of the other sixteen directions in that category. The principle affirmed here is that, however generalized the *direction* may be, or the *rule* in a generalized code, the *individual ruling,* or *decision,* should be stated in a code for the individual library.

(9) Rules, precepts, and directions generally applicable but not comprised by the foregoing rules: see below for instance the items: Inscriptions and Islands.

(10) Rulings and decisions for individual libraries not comprised by the foregoing items: e. g. Mathematics for Chemists class under Chemistry.

There may be so many rulings of particular or individual reference that the Code may become unduly increased in bulk. This would indicate economy in including only those general rules and definitions that are not properly part of the schedules; it would also be a reason for excluding general principles of classifying and educational instructions.

With the size and complexity of the Code the uncertainty as to what terms the specific subjects would appear under would of course increase, and the index would need to be the more complete, or, if the arrangement be alphabetical, the heading-references would need to be adequate.

A code of rules and rulings cannot prescribe for all the individual peculiarities of books but only for recurrent similarities, more or less specific, with characters and particulars common to them. On the other hand a code can generalize usefully only within limits, because the generalizations would comprise too many cases, indeed most of the books classified for a library, and classifiers would have neither need nor time to refer most classings not only to the schedules but to the code. Of course many of those rules would be remembered, but so would the instructions of the text-book and the teacher; and classifiers should be trained in these beforehand. For particulars the shelf-list is in many cases the more satisfactory reference. But the Code may well record decisions in choices that are likely to recur, and those that recur often may be generalized in rules that are generally applicable. In a generalized code, however, such merely redundant rules as "Political History class in History" and such alternatives as depend on choices that should be recorded in an individual code of rulings, for example, History of economic conditions class in Economic history — and without direction as to whether to classify Economic history under History or under Economics — such rules are of little avail to economize the classifying of books for libraries.

Such a code as we have outlined would be supplementary rather than complementary to the schedules; it would be for ready reference in the actual work of classifying books, and therefore it would be alphabetical rather than systematic in arrangement; but, if complementary to a system of classification and parallel to that in its order, it should be furnished with a specific alphabetic index, with alternative and synonymous terms and all requisite heading-references. Such a code would not be for instruction as a text-book for library-school classes, tho as a class-manual it might serve in practice work in classifying. It should duplicate few of the definitions and directions that should more conveniently appear in the schedules of classification. Statement and discussion of principles, problems, and methods of classifying, and general instruction and advice in these matters should have no place in it, being material for other books.

3. Definitions in a Schedule

Economic Geography is to be distinguished from Commercial Geography, from Human Geography, and from Historical Geography.

Briefly, Economic Geography comprises more of the physical, mineral, and biological, while Commercial Geography is less physiographic than the Economic and less theoretical than the Anthropogeographic, which is more biologic, ecologic, and ethnologic.

Antiques class under the respective arts, sculpture, furniture, etc., rather than under History, Antiquities.

Antiquities: archæological antiquities are to be distinguished from ethnological antiquities and from historical antiquities.

The fields denoted by these three terms overlap. Archæological implies the more ancient historic and the prehistoric remains, while ethnologic implies the primitive stages of cultural development and comparative studies of the materials; but such historical antiquities as furniture, spinning-wheels, clocks, bells, and playing-cards are usually regarded neither as archæological, nor as ethnological, nor as artistic.

Archæology: see the distinctions under the item Antiquities.

See also in the schedules of classification the notes under Archæology, Ethnology, and Ethnic Archæology.

Inscriptions of general historical interest are to be classified with the accessory studies under History.

Those that relate particularly to the history of a nation, or to a period of its history, are provided for by the systematic schedule for the history of the nations. But inscriptions of palæographic interest might be preferred under Palæography, and those of linguistic interest chiefly should be provided for under the linguistics of the language.

4. Decisions for a Complementary Code

Author's influence on a foreign literature usually class under the latter; but an author's influence on another author usually class under the author influenced.

Byronism in Italy is classed under special topics in the History of Italian Literature. But Milton's relation to Vondel and to Dante would be classed under Milton in the History of English Literature.

Bookbindings artistic, or illustrative of the art, classify under the art of Bookbinding; those of special value place in the special collection segregated for safety.

Islands belong with the adjacent countries or coasts or with those of which they are dependencies.

Where scientific interests predominate over the descriptive and narrative, classify under Regional Geography and Natural History rather than under the geography and history of the countries.

Literature, Method of classifying adopted: English literature classify by Method IV, except for the early periods.[2] Classify the criticism with the history and biography. Chief European literatures classify according to Schedule 5. Other languages and literatures classify according to Schedule 4.

Mountains:

Classify the Pyrenees under Spain, as provided in the schedule. The Ural Mountains classify under Russia; the Alps under Switzerland, if description predominates. But scientific geographic books should be under Regional Physical Geography, where places for the great ranges or systems should be distinctly provided.

Rivers:

The Danube regard as continental, the Volga as European, the Rhine as German, the Nile as Egyptian. Compare this with the item Mountains.

[2] These references apply to "Systematic Schedules" in the author's *System of Bibliographic Classification*, published in 1935.

History of special subjects under Economics or other Social sciences should be subordinated to those subjects.

But in using the Systematic Schedules distinguish between branches where the interest is mainly economic or scientific and on the other hand those where it is mainly historical. The History of Money is economic, and so is the History of Coinage, but the History of Coins (concrete) is likely to be treated as numismatic.

Scientific treatises or texts in one science for workers in another field place under the science treated rather than in that to be served.

Literature, History of, Periods and subordinate topics:

Whether topics should be subordinated to periods, or periods to topics, does not admit of a general rule. Special subjects and topics usually may best be subordinated to the periods: e.g. Elizabethan Romances. But Elizabethan Drama might be treated either way, also the Elizabethan Sonnet might be subordinate to the Sonnet as a form of poetry. This problem extends to Comparative Literature and to Literary Forms in general.

Pro and Con Arguments usually consider both sides, tho it may be unfairly; and most readers do likewise; so it is better not to attempt to separate the pros from the cons. But some subjects may have separate headings in the schedules.

Rivers not within one country may be regarded as continental, but they may sometimes be regarded as belonging to the country to which they are most important.

Most of the books are to be classified under Geography, Physical, Regional, or Historical (under the several countries, or continents), or under Travels, or Explorations.

CHAPTER VIII

SOME RELATIONS TO SUBJECT-CATALOGING

1. Pointed Remarks On Cataloging

For the organization of knowledge in libraries a systematic subject-catalog is hardly less requisite than classification, and hardly less problematic. Less direct and satisfactory in some respects, it is in other respects more plastic and more complete. But each complements the other and both are essential to complete functional efficiency. Cataloging and classifying, tho distinct, are closely related steps in bibliothecal service; and they should be combined in the same office or coöperative in the same department of organization.

Finding out what the subject of a book is, looking up the class, or classes, that correspond to that subject in the individual classification, comparing the book in hand with other books in that class, and deciding which class to assign it to, perhaps with the aid of the Code of Rulings — these are the successive steps in *classing* the book; and the first and essential step is ascertaining the *subject*. This often takes more time and mental effort than all the other steps that follow it; it is the most difficult part of the process, requiring knowledge and judgment, and sometimes more of these mental commodities than cataloger or classifier has at his, or her, immediate command. To take the step twice, first with the classifier's foot and then with the cataloger's, may have the advantage of companionate work, of bringing two minds to bear on the problematic cases, if there be effective coöperation between cataloger and classifier; it may moreover lessen the likelihood of error or idiosyncrasy; but it surely does not seem necessary for the ordinary run of books, nor as a general practice does it seem consistent with library economy. Where there is coöperative cataloging or classifying, it is evident that the two branches of the service should, so far as is feasible, be combined.

Tho closely related, classifying and subject-cataloging should not, however, be mistaken for the same process with the same principles and rules. That notion has resulted in what we have termed "the subject-index illusion." Valid subject-classification rests on the fundamental principle that specific classes or subjects are essentially and logically subordinate to more general classes or subjects. This is very different from "subject-classification" (so called) that treats special subjects as separate and as stable as their relevant general subjects.[1]

But special subjects are not logically separate from the relevant general subjects, nor are they developmentally more stable or permanent. Can the reader think of a special subject that is not related to or dependent on or derivative from some more general subject? Anthracite is coal and coal is fuel and fuel becomes heat. More complexly oranges are fruits and fruits are foods; but oranges are *citrous* fruits and so are lemons and limes. Here in elementary subjects we are dealing with the fundamental principles of logical *subordination* and relevant *coördination,* on which depends *collocation* for convenience. These principles are as valid in subject-cataloging as they are in subject-classification.

As regards permanence, special subject-matters come and go and grow more transiently than the general subjects that comprehend them — house them, something

[1] *Cf. ante,* p. 93-4.

like roomers in a lodging-house. In a changing world — mental world — they come and go and grow and change from day to day, while their lodging-house remains year after year, tho with some alteration or development to accomodate them and their various requirements. There is truth in this analogy both for subject-cataloging and for subject-classification.[2]

But between these two systems there is this important distinction. While both deal with subjects in their relations, classification objectively arranges classes, or groups, of books, or cards, whereas cataloging arranges terms and titles, names, and mere bibliographical data *on* cards or *on* pages — less directly, less objectively.

Whether subordination of specific subjects should also obtain in subject-catalogs more extensively and systematically than at present in most libraries, that is a question we shall consider a little farther on in this chapter. But first we should take some account of the differences between catalogs and classifications.

Adequate treatment of the art and methods of cataloging would in itself require another volume. Many points might be reconsidered; some rules might be revised; matters of abbreviation, capitalization, and punctuation might be brought into closer consistency with educational and literary custom. Large catalogs should be developed not only as means of convenient reference and access to individual books, and to small groups of books, but also as aids to completer research into subjects in relation to other subjects.

In general, an author-catalog serves for access to individual books, whereas a classification serves for group-

[2] "Permanence through Change" was the title of a thoughtful paper by Mr. Currier, of the Harvard College Library, published in the Catalogers' and Classifiers' Yearbook for 1938, in which he compares: "with the slow but constant development of the forest the slow and constant growth, pruning and renewal of our huge card-catalogs."

ing books by subject or other definite likeness, and especially for the purposes of research. A subject-catalog may, or should, serve both these uses, and others besides; it may facilitate access to particular books, when the subjects are known but the authors are not, or are forgotten, or their forenames are, where the catalog presents a disconcerting array of cards under the surnames. On the other hand, a subject-catalog may serve as a preliminary to research in special subjects, and it may complement the classification by including under the subjects those books of the respective classes that are temporarily absent from the shelves and moreover those books that are classed in other related classes; furthermore it may include *analytical* items for books of composite nature.[3] Still another advantage the subject-catalog has over the classification: it may provide for subjects that relate to certain general ideas rather than to classes of books, for instance, Youth. At the other extreme, the subject-catalog may subdivide much more minutely than is feasible in the classification. At the same time it may be more plastic in showing the relations of subjects, and it may be no less adaptive within certain limits of economy, considering the cost of making extensive and complicated changes. In brief, the subject-catalog may be more complete, more inclusive, more analytic, more specific, and more plastic; but in becoming these it tends to become too complicated, cumbersome, and expensive. Moreover to most interests it is less satisfactory than access to the books themselves, even tho the groups in the classes are more or less incomplete. A

[3] Dr. G. O. Kelley's *Classification of Books*, p. 126-9, states conclusions regarding current classification and subject-cataloging that—from another aspect—confirm the present writer's arguments on these questions. The advantages of good subject-catalogs over inadequate classifications are evident. But one may on the other hand show the advantages of good classifications over inadequate subject-catalogs.

mass of cards is so uninviting, to follow their dry details in disconnected succession is so irksome, there is so much irrelevant material, so much "dead wood," so much bibliographic jargon, that the reader thrusts the tray from him and turns to consult the books, some of which at least are suffused with vivid interests. It is in consideration of this desire and need for more intimate and informative contact with the books that classification is maintained in modern libraries and access to the shelves is allowed.

Classification is of especial service to research; but it also facilitates access to particular books by placing them in smaller groups and consequently simplifying their arrangement and notation within the classes. In the same way it facilitates reference to a number of books in the class, or in the more general class of related classes. By direct access to the books it serves these purposes more satisfactorily than a subject-catalog, however elaborate and systematic.

In small and in special libraries classification is not only more direct but more economical than subject-cataloging. In large libraries access to the special classified collections tends to become a privilege reserved for research, and for simpler needs the subject-catalog is regarded as the proper "subject-approach." But where developed to serve both types of uses, the subject-catalog should be made more systematic, with more classification embodied in it. Many leading scientific libraries in this country and abroad have long since adopted classified catalogs, properly indexed, to serve their needs better than alphabetic subject-catalogs would. In the future systems of classification should be developed to serve both for classification and for classified subject-catalogs.

For such a system the index, relating the classified to the alphabetic order, requires for economy a comparatively simple notation, simpler and briefer than those in vogue at present.[4]

The Decimal Classification of Dewey was originally intended, as several expressions in its Introduction show, not only for classifying books but also for classified catalogs. The International Institute of Bibliography in adapting the Decimal Classification to its great bibliography on cards expanded it with elaborate detail but modified its general and formal subdivisions so as to provide for aspects and relations, which were deemed requisite even at the cost of lengthy and complicated notation, which renders it unfit for use in libraries.[5]

The *shelf-list* in its card-catalog form may combine in part the uses of the classification and the subject-catalog; that is, it may serve as a classified subject-catalog; but it is too unsatisfactory on both sides; on the one hand it has some of the incompleteness of the grouping of books, while on the other hand it combines its own lack of reference-cards with some of the objections to the subject-catalog. But the shelf-list has its proper uses as the register of the classification's correlative notation, as the repository of accession-records, and as the vehicle of inventory and of classified statistics. Only for occasional and especial requirements should it

[4] The criticisms of Diesch, Trebst, Runge, Vorstius, and others in *Zentralblatt für Bibliothekswesen* in recent years have culminated in a volume of *Beiträge zur Sachkatalogisierung*, edited by Runge, who says, as quoted and translated by Dr. Walter in his review for *The Library Quarterly* of July, 1938 (v. 8, p. 549): "In my opinion it is high time that something be done at once. Most libraries cannot wait any longer, and, if a unified coöperative solution is not found within a reasonable time, they must on their own responsibility invent their own new system, be it good or bad." This confirms Miss Kelley's view of classification in American libraries. We may instance too the economical separation of the author-catalog from the subject-catalog in the Library of the University of California, interestingly described by Miss A. F. Wood in *The Library Journal*, (v. 63, p. 723) in October, 1938.

[5] *Cf. supra*, p. 182, 213.

be brought to serve as a catalog. The subject-catalog should be adequate to meet needs even for the more general subjects.

One more difference deserves passing mention, altho too obvious for discussion: catalogs and shelf-lists apply to one library, whereas a system of classification may be applied to many unrelated libraries, tho of course the concrete collections of books belong to the individual libraries.

Most books are classified primarily with regard to their *subjects,* but they may also be distinguished by the *form* in which the contents are presented. In the schedules of classification subdivisions for relations, aspects, and forms may be requisite, but there may not be corresponding sub-headings in the subject-catalogs. It is a salient question whether there should not be — and no less various yet systematic.

2. The Problem of the Subject-Catalog

Library catalogs are in general of three forms, which may be termed and briefly defined as follows: (1) *Dictionary,* alphabetical thruout, arranging author, title, and subject entries, and all references, in one alphabetic order, the subjects, if subdivided, with subheadings also alphabetically arranged; (2) *Alphabetic subject,* the catalog of subjects being separate from that of authors and titles, and the subjects or terms, whether general or specific, arranged alphabetically and usually subdivided alphabetically, tho under some special subjects the subordinate headings may be classified; (3) *Classified* systematically tho some subdivision may be alphabetic.

The alphabetic-classified catalog, which is intermediate between the alphabetic subject and the systematic classified catalog, has also had its advocates. There are in general two forms: (4) the more general subjects are in alphabetic order, but the subdivisions are classified, also the subordinate specific subjects are classified under the subdivisions; (5) this form, while retaining alphabetic order for all subjects, both general and specific, classifies only certain kinds of subdivisions under some of the more important subjects. The first of these forms may be complemented with a subject-index combined with its alphabetic order of subjects. It should be borne in mind that subjects alphabetically arranged are in a valid sense alphabetically *classified,* for things brought together by or under a letter are thereby classified. So an alphabetic subject-catalog may be said to be an alphabetic-classified catalog. This term, however, is the more appropriate where specific subjects are classified under alphabetically arranged general subjects or classes, that is, alphabetic before classified (form 4). The nearly equivalent term *classified alphabetic subject* might be applied to the nearly similar form 5, which is alphabetic with some subdivisions classified (mentioned also under form 2). For the variant form (6) of the systematically classified catalog that has some of its subjects subdivided alphabetically[6] the hyphenated term *classified-alphabetic* (classified before alphabetic) might be adopted, if this form should become more distinctive than at present. This last distinction might add minor confusion to major confusion, all these terms and their concepts being now confused, as are also the discussions regarding them and the catalogs in their actuality.[7]

The alphabetic subject-catalog tends, the larger it grows and the more it is adapted to the needs of research, to become modified more and more by subordination and

[6] See Berwick Sayers' *Introduction*, 5th ed., p. 129-130.

[7] Even the term *classed catalog* has been used for *classified catalog*—inconsistently, if the writer's distinctions are valid. *Cf. ante*, p. 16, 17, 115.

classification of closely related details under the more comprehensive headings.[8]

The *dictionary* catalog is misnamed; it is not like a dictionary of words in one series, with subordinate items, but more like an index. A dictionary catalog lacks the simplicity and directness of a dictionary; it bats the terms hither and thither across the courts of terminology, keeping the quest on the jump. It is an uneconomic outgrowth of the economies of small public libraries in America. Before the days of card-catalogs, the subject, or classified, or "analytical," catalog was usually printed apart from the catalog of authors and titles. Often for economy the two parts were bound together. Then some people were bothered by having the two things together, and others were bothered by having them separate. So they were combined. But the uses of subject-catalogs are divergent from those of author-catalogs; prolonged Search may keep Reference waiting. If one complex catalog combines both services, the user must distinguish whether he is looking up, or looking at, an author or a subject-entry. To facilitate this, subject-cards usually have red headings and edges. Which of these three forms of subject-catalog is the simplest, the least confusing — the alphabetic, the classified, or the "dictionary"? This librarian affirms that the dictionary catalog is the least simple and the most confusing.

It has been argued that the people who come into a public library are so simple-minded, so averse to systems

[8] "There is undeniably a strong tendency in the Library of Congress catalog to bring related subjects together by means of inversion of headings, by combinations of two or more subject-words, and even by subordination of one subject to another. Yes, the tendency at times is so noticeable that it may seem as if an effort were being made to establish a compromise between the dictionary and the alphabetic-classed catalog, just as the latter was intended as a compromise between the systematic and the alphabetic plans of arrangement."—J. C. M. Hanson, "The Subject Catalogs of the Library of Congress," in the A.L.A. Conference in 1909, Catalog Section, *Papers and Proceedings*, p. 389-390.

and complexities that to have to distinguish between an author-catalog and a subject-catalog, even where these are prominently placarded, is, among other confusing things, too confusing. If so, how can those simple-minded people be expected to distinguish between the author-entries and subject-entries and the other entanglements of a dictionary catalog? The librarians who make such arguments may also be simple-minded. The users of catalogs, of whatever form, should learn how to use them and to distinguish an author-catalog from a subject-catalog.

But the dictionary catalog, developed in accordance with Cutter's admirable *Rules* and with those established by the American Association and the British, has been far less imperfect than the classified catalogs that in the past were found unsatisfactory because of confusion like that of the classifications now and because of the lack of a complementary alphabetic index and a simple correlative notation.

Classified catalogs of all forms have been disparaged by American librarians as being too intricate and indirect; for, as a classification needs an index, so does a classified catalog. The index should work usually as in this typical instance: Frost, DSM, under Meteorology; see also UAV under Agriculture, UAN under Gardening, and under UAT, Fruit. This may be contrasted with the references under this subject in the dictionary catalog of the Library of Congress: "*See also* Ice; Plants, Effect of temperature on; Refrigeration and refrigerating machinery; Thawing." Then under Ice, again "*See also*." There it is diverse, less comprehensive, less direct and satisfactory to most interests, and indeed less simple. In a catalog cross-references are indirect; in an index also.

In an alphabetic subject-catalog closely related specific subjects are widely dispersed. The subordinate subjects and references sometimes occupy the space of a column or more of a large octavo page, and they are no less complicated there than if they were classified. Agriculture is separated from Gardening; Vegetables under V, Fruits under F, but Citrus fruits under C; Mushrooms under M, Fungi under F, Lichens under L. Floriculture separated from Flowers by Flour and flour-mills; Horticulture refers to Floriculture, Fruit-culture, and Gardening. But "Flower gardens, *See* Gardens," said the old A. L. A. *List*, tho just above that stood "Flower gardening, *See* Floriculture." All this disperseness disorganizes the comparatively simple and concrete subjects of Agriculture, Gardening, and Botany. The alphabetic catalog may be simple for specific subjects and in particular instances, but for broader uses and aspects it is wholly lacking in simplicity and organization.

"As for economy of compilation," wrote Mr. Hanson[9] —and there are few so competent to judge—"it is my firm conviction that strict adherence to the principle of specific entry under minute subjects to be arranged in regular order of their names, would in the long run prove well-nigh impossible in the catalog of a large and rapidly growing library. A subject catalog compiled according to this plan must, it seems to me, resolve itself in course of time into a mere subject index in which it becomes practically impossible to guard against the ultimate dispersion of the literature on one and the same topic under various headings."

Regarding the six forms of library catalogs enumerated on p. 160-1, we may reduce them to the first three forms: (1) "Dictionary," (2) Alphabetic subject, (3) Systematically classified. The intermediate forms, (4) Alphabetic-classified, with general subjects, or classes, in alphabetic order, and subdivisions classified more or less systematically; (5) Dictionary, or Alphabetic subject, with some subdivisions classified, and (6) Systematically

[9] *Loc. cit.*, p. 390.

classified, with some details in alphabetic order: these three intermediate forms tend to merge into one another and the distinctions and terms are unclear, for subjects are classes too.

But three questions clearly persist relative to those first three forms: (1) Shall a library catalog, large or small, on cards or in books, be unitary, like most indexes, in the so-called "dictionary" form, or shall it be divided into two parts, one for authors, editors, and titles, and the other for subjects and cross-references? (2) If the subject-catalog be separate, shall it be alphabetic thruout, with a minimum of classified subdivisions for certain forms under some subjects? (3) Shall it be classified thruout, with a minimum of alphabetically arranged detail under some subdivisions?

These questions have been discussed in the past and they are being discussed again, after many years of dominance of the dictionary catalog in all kinds of libraries, especially in America. A few large scientific libraries in this country have effectively developed the classified forms. Many large scientific indexes have always separated the subject-index from the author index, most usually in German works. A notable instance in American science is *Chemical Abstracts,* the annual indices of which run to thousands of pages of fine print. But since the establishment of Cutter's admirably compiled *Rules for a Dictionary Catalog,* this form has become an American tradition, adopted in many other countries. Now it has grown to be a great and increasing burden. Economy is forced to reconsider it. The tradition is at long last shaken. The question has become a problem. What can be done to render our catalogs and classifications more efficient and economical?

A few of the most important contributions that have helped the writer to form his own opinions are cited here. Under the auspices of the International Congress of Arts and Sciences at St. Louis in 1904, Mr. William Coolidge Lane, then Librarian of Harvard University, read a valuable paper on "Present Tendencies of Catalog Practice," which treated this question especially in p. 136-7 of the *Addresses,* as published by the American Library Association. Mr. Lane referred first to an article by C. H. Hull, then of the Cornell University Library, which appeared in *The Library Journal* for June, 1890, as "the best statement that has been made of the shortcomings of subject catalogs"; and then he referred to a statement by Mr. J. C. M. Hanson, then in charge of the cataloging division of the Library of Congress, which was published in *The Library Journal* for September, 1904, and which was "in favor of the subject catalog." Mr. Hanson at the catalog section of the A. L. A. in 1909 contributed a long and interesting paper on "The Subject Catalogs of the Library of Congress," of which the second section (p. 386-93 of the *Papers and Proceedings*) deals especially with the "Present Dictionary Catalog." This, he said, was adopted "largely by a desire to be in a position to coöperate with the largest possible number of American libraries." . . . . "still to those who have been in close touch with the work it is obvious that it would have been more economical to have adopted a classed catalog with subject index, than to have attempted the compilation of a full dictionary catalog. It is also a question whether the library itself might not have been better served by a subject catalog according to the alphabetic-classed plan for which it had two excellent prototypes in those of the Harvard College Library and the British Museum." (p. 389). Dr. Rudolf Focke at the end of his address on "Classification: the general theory" at the St. Louis Congress in 1904 pronounced in favor of some combination of the classified and the alphabetic order. Dr. William W. Bishop at the A. L. A. Conference in 1906 read an excellent paper on "Subject Headings in Dictionary Catalogs," in which he went into details of this intricate problem. Recently, Miss Julia Pettee's article on "Factors in Determining Subject Headings" (*Library Journal,* December, 1929) was very interesting and not without charm. It shows how indistinct our ideas are regarding the distinctions between dictionary catalogs and classified catalogs. Mr. Martel's survey of cataloging before the Catalog Section of the A. L. A. in 1926 (*Papers and Proceedings,* p. 495 especially) touched upon this problem. Dr. Grace Osgood Kelley's study at the Graduate Library School of the University of Chicago for her degree of Doctor comprised an interesting analysis of the factors that limit the utility of minute classification, with regard also to subject-catalogs.

This challenge has since been developed more effectually in Dr. Kelley's book on *The Classification of Books.* In the Catalogers' and Classifiers' Yearbook VII (1938) Mr. Henry Black reported on replies regarding "Cataloging Problems," which he had received from 23 librarians. In the Yearbook of the preceding year he had discussed "The Problem of Subject Headings" and said: "In the future increasing reliance must be placed on subject headings." During the past two or three years several fuller discussions have been contributed to *Zentralblatt für Bibliothekswesen* by Dr. Sigismund Runge, Dr. Carl Diesch, and Dr. Juris Vorstius, and others. In *The Library Quarterly* for July, 1938, Dr. Fremont Rider has interestingly reviewed the antique question whether after all card-catalogs are altogether more satisfactory than book-catalogs.

3. Subject-catalogs for Research Also

For research it is requisite to bring closely related specific subjects together under comprehensive headings. Alphabetic order is dispersive. For a kind of convenience in hasty reference it may prove advisable to arrange details in alphabetic order subordinate to broader subjects; but for the broader subjects themselves alphabetic order may inconvenience research much more than it would facilitate reference uses. The literature of

Education is so closely interwoven with that of Teaching, of Schools, of Colleges, etc. that to disperse these subordinate subjects thruout the catalog from A to Y proves much more troublesome than to classify them under the comprehensive heading Education, marking the more important divisions with guide-cards bearing synopses of the sub-classifications. For it is easier to look up a dozen references in the subdivisions of one subject, probably in one tray of cards, than it is to pass from tray to tray in an extensive catalog, where some of the trays, when wanted, may be in the hands of other persons. If the headings are well classified under fitting terms, and the notations simple and distinctive, it should prove easier to find the materials than if they are dispersed.

Under Education in the Library of Congress *Subject Headings* are some seventy-five *See also* references, and these are followed by two or three pages of subordinate subjects and complicated subdivisions and references, running thru captions of "Education and . . . . ," "Education of . . . . ," Educational, and ending with Educators. Would an equivalent classification be more complex?

In a great university's immense dictionary catalog the subject *Education* has innumerable sub-headings bibliographical, geographical, historical, topical, and terminological, all confused in one alphabetical order as follows: Addresses, Alabama, Bibliography, China, Colorado, Dictionaries, Elementary, England, Greek, Higher, History, Holland, Periodicals, Philosophy, Russia, Secondary, Societies, Education and Society, Education of Children, of Princes, of Women, Educational Associations, Educational Psychology, Educational Surveys, etc. This is not all the complexity, but merely an abstract to exemplify complexity. There are other sub-headings, besides heading-references and cross-references. At least some of this complexity could be reduced, if sub-headings involving a terminological phrase, such as Educational Associations, Education and Society, Education of Children, etc., were brought under the principal term, or class, or subject. Why should the Associations be thus separated from Education, Societies? Then why should not the countries be in alphabetic order in a subdivision for the purpose? And should not historical subdivisions also be distinctly classified and collocated? And then the formal captions and the generalia? And would not all this be classification in the catalog?

Special aspects of research may indeed be followed thus, but books of importance are likely to be classified under more general headings. To some of these the student may not have references now; some he may never have heard of; some he knows of but has not in mind at present; he would, however, recognize them, if he saw their titles or their authors' names; and these he would come upon more readily, if the closely related subjects were classified in close proximity, or under one comprehensive heading. There may be no special bibliography that covers the subject of his research, or, if there be one, there may not be a copy in the library. So he must depend on classification and subject-catalog.

Subordination of the specific to the generic and the *collocation* of closely related subjects we have affirmed to be cardinal principles of the classification of knowledge. Since a library is purposed to function at least in part as an organization of knowledge and since the subject-classification of its books is the structural basis of that organization, those principles of subordination and collocation should be embodied in its classification and also, so far as is feasible, in its subject-catalog.

A subject-catalog should relate specific subjects to relevant general subjects in some order or system. This the dictionary catalog is supposed to do by means of references, heading and "cross." "It differs from the classed catalog," said Miss Pettee, "only in the use of the alphabetical medium." But that use is what disperses the related subjects. The references are the round-about way, not of bringing the subjects together, but of making the user go round about among them. It is "the subject-index illusion" in another guise.

This does not say that subordination should always be systematic or logical; nor does it gainsay that alphabetical subordination is often the simplest and most convenient way. With either mode there would be some subdivisions that are historical, some geographical, and some *formal.* Usually, where a subject has all these kinds of subdivisions, it is best to classify the historical together, and to arrange the geographical in another order, and the formal and collective in an anterior group, as in classification schedules. From the point of view of organization of material it seems absurd indeed to progress alphabetically from Addresses, Bibliography, Biography, etc., thru Dictionaries, Essays, Ethics, etc., to History, Periodicals, and finally Yearbooks. There is an important difference between a dictionary and an organization of resources. The stock of a department store is classified, and so are the items and advertisements of the *New York Times.* System implies an adjustment or articulation of parts for effectual functioning. For research, and indeed for reference, it is a systematic organization of knowledge that is most requisite.

But the term *research* may imply more study than the subject-catalog is purposed to serve. Most uses of library catalogs are for particular references and occasional needs. In some libraries comparatively few users are of the professional classes, professors, physicians, lawyers, scientists, engineers, and university students. Those classes know the limitations and vexations of subject-catalogs, and they often prefer special bibliographies and access to the classified collections. Yet these too have their limitations, and subject-catalogs are needed to complement them. Indeed for reference as well as for research these should be made the more serviceable by organization adequate to studious interests.

We have broadly distinguished here between reference and research; but they are not very distinct, and the two kinds of uses in a dictionary catalog continually run together and interfere. Most references particularize the author and title, and library catalogs are used most to ascertain by author and title whether the books are obtainable. Subject-catalogs are consulted sometimes when the reference to the author is lacking, and sometimes when any book on the subject is acceptable. Here, however, the subject-catalog may render a negative service by presenting the less valuable or less relevant items first. Indeed there may be no satisfactory book under the heading originally consulted. The student may then follow some of the *See also* references or subdivisions shown by guide-cards in proximity. He may discover that some of the best material on his special subject is to be found in the more general works and the collective writings. Thus reference passes on to research.

Most uses of a catalog are, we have said, for reference. A hundred people may make momentary reference, while half a dozen are following up research. These two types of users may get into each other's way — may inconvenience one another in the use of a dictionary catalog. The hasty author-reference may be impatient for the tray where subject-cards are being carefully and tediously perused by research. Then, when the researcher crosses over to look up a cross-reference, he may get cross (as some librarian facetiously wrote long ago) to find that other tray in other hands, or it may have been left lying somewhere out of sight. An immense dictionary catalog surrounds a spacious hall, where some forty trays are being consulted at the same time and perhaps forty others are lying out on the tables, left there by people too careless to replace them. Under these conditions it would be more convenient to separate the catalog of authors and titles from the subject-catalog. Their uses tend to differentiate; it is not simpler to mix up subjects with authors; it is very confusing, especially so with corporate-entries, names of countries, governments, and institutions. Rapid reference may be bothered by having the subject-entries in the way, and by finding a researcher with the tray. Research uses may be hampered both by having too many reference seekers in the way, and too many irrelevant cards in the tray.

4. Subjects and Terminology

The organization of knowledge and thought called by educators and librarians a *subject,* or *subject-matter,* is developmental in concepts rather than objective in groups, or classes, of books or other documentary materials. But by a term, or complex of related terms, the subject is denoted in subject-catalogs and subject classifications. In a good classification the subjects are related in *subordination, coördination,* and *collocation,* and then in a supplementary index the terms are arranged alphabetically, with their notations, for reference to the locations of the correlative classes in the classification. In a good subject-catalog the special subjects, or their correlative terms, are likewise subordinated to their relevant more general subjects, or terms, and under these they are *collocated,* whether systematically or practically, as closely as is feasible. A complementary alphabetic subject-index of the terms is requisite. The subjects are the "subject-matters" organized in the classes, or sub-classes, of books. They are merely denoted by the correlative terms and notations. Thus the organization of subjects in catalogs and classifications is an effectual means of access to the organization of knowledge and thought in books and in other documentary materials.

In a subject-catalog it is more direct and efficient to organize the subjects systematically, as they should be in the class of books, than it is to relate the mere terms by cross-references in an otherwise dispersive alphabetic order, in which the terms may be brought into relation, but not the classes of books. To suppose that this dispersive, indirect, alphabetic order is equivalent to a systematic classification of subjects is indeed an illusion — "the subject-index illusion."

Alphabetic order of terms is not only inherently dispersive of subject-matters; it is confused by the tangles of terminology in the vagaries of language. Subjects are developmental, as concepts and knowledge are, but the terms are both various and changeful — positively in the titles of books and confusingly in subject-catalogs.

An example of closely related developmental subjects and interrelated terms appears in the subject of Health Education, as distinguished from School Hygiene, as related to Schools. Here are two rather distinct subjects: (1) the study, may be in schools, of the ways to health; and (2) the study of the ways to make schools healthy. The first of these two subjects should come under the term Health, or Hygiene, the second under the term Schools. But in English terminologies are confused. One cannot logically know whether such terms as School Hygiene and Hygiene in Schools mean the condition or the study of it. Furthermore Health Education is part of the subject of Physical Education, tho this last is indeed not a part of Physics. The term Sanitation has more special denotation, probably not clearly distinct from Public Hygiene or from Social Health. "Social Hygiene" is quite another subject. In alphabetic order this tangle of subjects would be dispersed thus:

Education, Health, see Health Education.
— Physical, see Physical Education.
Health, see Hygiene.
Health Department, see also Sanitation.
— Education.
Hygiene, Educational, see Health Education.
— Personal.
— Public, see also Sanitation.
— School, see School Hygiene.
Physical Education.
School Health, see also School Hygiene.
— Hygiene, see also School Health.
Sanitation, see also Hygiene.

Thus there would be thirteen terms and references to five subjects: Health Education, Physical Education, Hygiene, Sanitation, and School Hygiene. This is one way of complicating alphabetic subject-catalogs.

Terminology we cannot discuss in detail here, but we will touch upon some of the more important matters pertinent to the foregoing discussions. First, subdivision of classes requires correlative specification of headings, chosen with regard to the interest and point of view. Tertiary subdivision requires three-ply terms. The subject *Teaching elementary mathematics* may have any or all of these four triple-term entries: Teaching, Mathematics, Elementary; or Mathematics, Elementary, Teaching; or Mathematics, Teaching, Elementary; or the customary phrase, Teaching, Elementary Mathematics.

In such cases the first term need not appear in the heading on each card, but only on guide-cards; but it would have to be explicit in all the references, and in the "tracings" for the catalogers, tho here abbreviation suffices. Sometimes tertiary subordination might require more terms than specific entry in alphabetic order: e.g. *Engineering, Mechanical, Design,* which is less concise than the nearly equivalent *Machine Design* in the alphabetic order.

The term *educational* is often ambiguously used, sometimes for *educative* and sometimes more broadly for that which pertains to education. Some literature, some arts are said to be educational in the former sense, but some are educational only in the sense that they are related to the interests of education. The term *educational psychology* is in this respect no less ambiguous than *educational sociology.* We have classified it under Education as Psychology of Education. By analogy the term *social psychology* should be *sociological psychology* and this subject should be classified under Sociology, rather than under Psychology; or if on the other hand regarded as psychological, the more appropriate term for the subject-catalog would be the inverted form, Psychology, Sociological (or Social).

Having instanced complexity and inconsistency in terminology, let us briefly instance the confusion that renders alphabetic approach thru English terminology so baffling to the subject-approach to library-catalogs. The subjects Agriculture, Agronomy, Gardening, Flower-gardening, Floriculture, Market-gardening, Economic Botany, Applied Botany, Plant-industries, Cultivated Plants, Plant-diseases, Fruit-raising, Pomology, etc. are all closely related, but are dispersed thruout an alphabetical catalog, with numerous references to and from synonyms such as Horticulture and Floriculture, and many related subjects such as soils, irrigation, and fertilizers.

The terminology of a subject-catalog should be adaptable and such inconsistencies should be removed. Science is continually pruning its terminologies. Economics is no longer "political economy." But it is uneconomic to build a subject-catalog on the shifting sands of complicated, confused, and inconsistent terminologies.

The English language, with its great literary tradition of comparative freedom of form and of usage, has been ill adapted to the development of precise terminologies. The sciences and the philosophies, the technologies and the business of life have suffered from the misunderstandings that arise from such inconsistency.

5. The Questions Summarized

Our main points will now be summarized. Our purpose is not to press arguments or opinions, but rather to reopen some of the questions and to consider others in the light of principles adduced in preceding chapters. Catalogs in libraries are growing too fast and too large; they overflow their trays; they fill the capacity of their cabinets; they crowd their rooms. What can be done to accommodate them or to economize them? [10] The librarians are burdened too much, and the readers are too much hindered. Shall we select and segregate the older and less used items? Shall we divide the author-and-title-catalog from the subject-catalog? These questions are recurrent in the recent published discussions. They would repay careful investigation and consideration.

But it is less a question of space for bulk than of time and convenience in use. Under many headings there are

[10] *Cf.* "California Divides its Catalog," by Amy F. Wood, in *Library Journal*, v. 63, p. 723-6, Oct. 1, 1938.

"The Changing Catalog," by A. Beatrice Young, in *Library Journal*, v.63, p. 762-3, Oct. 15, 1938.

"The Library and the Card Catalog," by A. M. McAnally, in *Library Journal*, v. 63, p. 814-15, Nov. 1, 1938.

"The Problem of Subject Headings," by Henry T. Black, in *Catalogers' and Classifiers' Yearbook*, 6 (1937), p. 91-4.

"Fundamental Principles in Cataloging," by Wyllis E. Wright, in *Catalogers' and Classifiers' Yearbook*, 7 (1938), p. 26-39, especially p. 37.

"Cataloging Problems Needing Investigation," by Henry T. Black, idem. p. 55-68, especially p. 64.

"The Possibility of Discarding the Card Catalog," by Fremont Rider, in *The Library Quarterly*, v. 8, p. 329-45, especially 329 and 332-3.

too many cards, and the headings are too indeterminate, and the references and relations too complicated. There is interference and confusion between the author approach and the subject approach.

The dictionary catalog is questioned. Is it efficient to mix authors, titles, subjects, and references in one grand mélange? Does it not cost more to compile? Is it not more confusing to handle? Is it not more inconvenient both for those who look up particular references and for those who are engaged in research? And the alphabetic subject-catalog is questioned too. All alphabetic order is dispersive of subjects that should be systematically organized. Subject-catalogs should be separate for economy in reference and classified for efficiency in research. The Alphabetic approach should enter by a supplementary Index. This is very feasible if the notation be properly economical. The immense historic undertaking to make the whole catalog combine with an alphabetic subject-index is breaking down. As Henry Black has said: "In the future an increasing reliance must be placed on subject headings." . . . . "It appears altogether probable that the problem of subject entries can be eventually solved only by a thorough reorganization of cataloging work. . . . If cataloging is to continue to grow in usefulness during the coming decades, we shall have to make revolutionary changes."

CHAPTER IX

BIBLIOGRAPHIC CLASSIFICATION

1. Some Relations of Bibliographies and Subject-Catalogs

The main subject of this volume, the organization of knowledge in classification for libraries, brings us finally thru the problems of subject-cataloging and classified catalogs to certain aspects of bibliographic classification in the more special sense. In the origins classification for libraries was but especial development of bibliographic classification. Most of the olden systems exemplify this dual utility, from Gesner to Brunet. *Catalogue raisonné* was the French term applied both to classified subject-bibliographies and to classified subject-catalogs in book form. Dewey's *Decimal Clasification* was originally intended for classified subject-catalogs as well as for classification of books on shelves. Hartwig's *Schema des Realkatalogs* was applied to classify the library of the University of Halle. The International Institute of Bibliography adopted and modified the Decimal Classification for its great bibliographic card-catalog (Répertoire) and service; and this adapted classification has been utilized to some extent in the classification of large libraries. The Library of the Engineering Societies in New York and the John Crerar Library in Chicago afford eminent examples of services combining Decimal Classification, Decimal bibliographic classification, and classified subject-catalogs. These transitions and adaptations show the reality of the relations between classified bibliographies and classified catalogs and of both to classifications for libraries.

Our purpose here is not to state these relations fully, but merely to make certain distinctions between bibliographies, subject-catalogs, and classifications for libraries. General and national bibliographies are broadly contrasted with special and subject bibliographies. The former are for particular reference, or for comparative or derivative extensive compilation, while the latter are chiefly for special study or research. There are certain intermediate kinds, some general but limited to periods of time, some for a large field of subjects. Bibliographies may be in books or on cards, and their contents may be classified or not; they may show the authorship, publication-place, price, or value, the size, the location, etc. of the books comprised; and they may also indicate the subjects or contents or scope, and sometimes they may contain annotations in other interests. Of the special bibliographies some are distinctly for classes of authors, e. g. librarians, some are for localities or for institutions, etc., some purpose selection and even annotation, while others purpose completeness. Subject-bibliographies, that is, bibliographies of subjects, special or general, may be confined to a national scope, but they usually are, and they usually should be, international. Bibliographies are essential to the collection of books.

Bibliography in the broad sense comprises cataloging, and in this sense cataloging is bibliographic, while conversely some bibliographies are called catalogs. The catalogs of The British Museum and of La Bibliothèque Nationale, published in book form, serve as bibliographies. The uses of bibliographies and catalogs are combined in the so-called *union catalogs,* which locate in groups of libraries all the copies of the books that are cataloged in them.[1] The great *Gesamtkatalog* of the Prussian State Library, comprising those of the German universities, is most complete.

Bibliographies denote all copies of the books listed, whereas catalogs represent individual libraries or collections. Catalogs or *lists* of publishers and booksellers also combine the two functions, resembling bibliographies more as they are more comprehensive or extensive and proffer larger stocks, but more like catalogs as they show smaller stocks and fewer titles.

A bibliography may, as we have seen, resemble a catalog in form. The bibliographic service of Wistar Institute of Anatomy and Biology, for the scientific periodicals it publishes, is distributed on cards. On the other hand some card-catalogs may serve as bibliographies, as does that of the Library of Congress, which is manifolded on cards in certain *depository* libraries. So the differences between bibliographies and catalogs have been outgrown on both sides.

The term *applied bibliography* is sometimes employed (in analogy to a scientific usage) for the cataloging of concrete books or collections of such, and also for union catalogs and finding-lists; and that term is contradistinguished from "pure bibliography," which would comprise all copies of the several books, or other publications, and their several editions.[2]

All the copies of a book have contents and characters in common and may therefore be regarded as a class. But

[1] Union finding-lists are carefully distinguished from union catalogs by Dr. E. C. Richardson in his chapter on "Library Resources outside Britain," in Dr. F. A. Baker's *The Uses of Libraries*, London, 1927 (See p. 281-4). "The Union Catalogue," he there defines, "contains all copies of each work in a given neighborhood, and serves as a catalogue for the local libraries. . . . The principle of the Union Finding List is to include all copies of out-of-the-way books and a few copies only of the commoner books in each locality. . . . the finding List principle of locating some copy somewhere."

[2] Dr. Richardson in restating this distinction in *The Library Journal*, February 15, 1926, ascribed it to The American Bibliographical Society.

their individual differences are seldom distinct enough or significant enough to justify *treating* them ordinarily as a class. Indeed, to speak of any aggregate of copies as a class is a little misleading. For the purposes of pure bibliographies, national, enumerative, special, or subject, the aggregates of books of identical contents, titles, characters, etc. are concrete rather than abstract — as concrete, tho not as *discrete*, as the individual copies are. We may, however, conceive of books in general, of whatever subject, class, or title, or of any extensive literature, as the subject-matter of general bibliography, which so may be termed abstract, or "pure."

Bibliographies in book form of course lack the convenience of being ever open for the insertion of additional materials, and for changes, as card-catalogs are. The intermediate loose-leaf and sheaf forms are less plastic in these respects than catalogs of cards for individual items; but they have the point in their favor that they may be run thru more readily.

Syllabi are structural organizations of study, usually educational in purpose; and they are means to organizations of knowledge. Figuratively they may be compared to skeletons, on which functional organizations of knowledge and thought develop. They usually combine classified lists of readings with the outlines of the subjects.

Books and catalogs may be economically reproduced by photographic processes; and they may then be reduced in size — on *microfilms* in reels, economically stored, transported, and again reproduced. The great questions arising here will be considered in the last section of this chapter.

2. Classification in Bibliographies

Again there is a broad distinction between classified bibliography and unclassified. In subject-bibliographies of book form classification is usually less elaborate than in libraries, tho some, highly specialized, may work out even more specific detail. As we have said before, catalogs, whether of the alphabetic or the classified forms, may feasibly be made more specific and minute than it is economical to make either bibliographies in book form or classifications for books. However, in library classification with notation it is neither practical nor economical to subdivide so minutely as has been done in some schedules; for the subjects become too difficult to distinguish or define, the order becomes less distinct, and the notation becomes too complicated and cumbersome. Still, it is obvious that in History and in the sciences, classifications may serviceably be more specific and detailed than is feasible for philosophy and for literature.

In justifying some of the elaborate detail of the later editions of the Decimal Classification Dr. Dewey has claimed that it is especially serviceable for the indexing of notes and clippings, etc. This may indeed be admitted; but we should distinguish between *indexing* minutely specific detail and classification or structural organization of knowledge for functional efficiency. When the International Institute elaborated the decimal notation for such immense detail and further complicated it with lengthy mnemonic suffixes, the economic limit of notation for libraries was exceeded in the one purpose without a compensating efficiency in the other purpose.[3] A general standard should indeed *not* be encumbered with specialized "expansions" such as those that inflate the recent editions of the Decimal Classification.

The International Catalogue of Scientific Literature is an extensive and comprehensive classified bibliography in book form. During its publication it issued yearly a volume for each of seventeen sciences. Its classification is not entirely satisfactory.[4] Nor were its subdivisions very

[3] For some particulars and specimen marks see Chapter X, section 6.

[4] We venture to make some comments and suggestions in Chapter XIII, section 3 of this volume.

specific. But to amend a yearly publication in book form is much easier than to make extensive alterations in an immense catalog with complicated headings, cross-references, and notations, such as that of the International Institute of Bibliography.

The French term *catalogue raisonné* was formerly in vogue for the classified form. Often these reasoned catalogs were more rational than practical; and often it was difficult to discover or to follow the reason.

In Edwards' *Memoirs of Libraries* were epitomized some of the most noted of the historic bibliographic classifications, and it was implied that these were also library classifications, or were suitable to library purposes. The distinction, however, is sometimes drawn more positively. In Brown's manual of *Library Classification and Cataloging* the relevant distinction is set up between "Classification Schemes for Books, without Notations" (Chapter III), and those "With Notations" (Chapter IV). In modern practice this would serve as an applicable distinction between library classification and bibliographic classification; for no modern library would be without notation. Yet notation of some kind may well be applied to a bibliographic system in order to facilitate reference to the divisions and subdivisions, as in Hartwig's *Schema.*

In the *Principles of Sociology* by F. H. Giddings is a bibliography classified according to his study of the related sciences. There under Theoretical Sociology and under Zoölogical Sociology he included books that would come under broader or coördinate classes in a library classification; but the professor knew that they combined material important to his purpose, and he cited them for the studies of his readers. The difference between subject-bibliography and subject-cataloging in such cases should interest librarians.

An example of such extension of a specialty is presented in *A Suggested Classification of Writings on Eugenics,* by C. B. Davenport,[5] wherein Eugenics is made to comprise: 1, Racial anthropology; 2, Genealogy; 3, Heredity; 4, Dif-

[5] *Science,* March 7, 1913, p. 370.

ferential selection of mates and its social control; 5, Differential fecundity and its social control; 6, Differential survival; 7, Migration and its social control; 8, Culture of the innate traits. In a subject-catalog it would not do to place all these topics under the subject Eugenics.

Classified subject-bibliographies and subject-catalogs bring together under subjects and authors the relevant and the available titles and other bibliographic data; but library classifications bring together the books themselves, arranged in the classes defined. In each of these classes are grouped all the books of that class that are available there and then. The shelf-list shows moreover all the books in that class that are possessed by the library. The catalog furthermore shows under the respective subject, and it should show also under closely related subjects, other relevant books that are in the library. But a special bibliography is likely to be still more complete as regards that subject.

The foregoing distinctions having been stated, it remains but to remark that classification in bibliographies should in general be consistent with the principles that have been brought forward in the first part of this book.

3. Bibliographic and Information Services

Bibliography extends beyond the limitations of books and libraries into great coöperative organizations of knowledge, whether in bibliographic or in catalog form or in collections of materials of whatever kind of print or manuscript. Moreover governments, institutions, commissions, associations, newspaper publishers, and information bureaus or services are compiling, classifying, and indexing collections of materials of diverse kinds relevant to their interests.[6] These aspects of the world-wide organization of knowledge, most of them considered, however briefly, in the preceding volume, are not just within the scope of this volume, tho some of them have been touched upon in the first part.

Even manuscript notes and clippings would be included in the functional organization of knowledge outlined by Dr. F. L. Hoffman in the weekly *Science* for March 10 and 17, 1922. This proposal was based largely on his experience in making an immense collection of material for the information of the Prudential Life Insurance Company, of which he was head statistician. Such too is the great functional organization of knowledge, especially economic, financial, and commercial, built up by Babson's Statistical Organization chiefly for service to business concerns. Other economic and business organizations have been making extensive collections of material not confined to books and pamphlets, and their special libraries are much engaged in these services, in which they of course employ classification, cataloging, and subject-indexing.

Very interesting in this connection is Professor Burton E. Livingston's expression of the need of "a national or international institute for the furnishing of bibliographical information on request." (See *Science,* v. 49, N.S. p. 202). The German libraries have a national information bureau under the Prussian State Library.

Certain structural aspects of such functional organizations of knowledge were discussed in Chapter V, in considering "special" libraries.

The *bibliographic service* of the Wistar Institute we have mentioned as being distributed on cards, so as to become

[6] This extension of bibliography has led the International Institute to change its name to Fédération International de Documentation. The name is still unsatisfactory as *documentation* is a term more special in its historic and linguistic usage than *bibliography*. A document is not generally a book, and a book is not always a document; and some of the materials in question are neither books nor documents; else the name might have been altered by merely adding "and Documentation." The Institute, however, may succeed in extending the denotation of the term by its influence among educators and thru intellectual coöperation. The Institute was really trying to establish a briefer term for *the objective organisation of knowledge*.

for each subscriber a bibliographic catalog. For each article in the scientific journals at present published by the Institute a printed card is supplied in advance of publication. This card gives the author's name, the title of the article, the subject-headings, and an indication of the class, also an abstract by the author. An Index is supplied annually. It is of interest that a special "biological classification" has been adopted for the purposes of the service.

Abstracts of scientific literature have for years been published in book form for several of the special sciences: Physics, Electrical Engineering, Chemistry, Biology, etc. On the functional value of these services the following opinion is quoted from Dr. E. C. Richardson's important article on "Immediate Coöperation for Bibliographical Results": ". . . . the Scientific Abstracts need and deserve to be brought into complete organization, first because this is a most valuable, if luxurious, bibliographical aid, and second because it is by far the ripest matter.[7]

In other fields the "digests" of various forms serve somewhat similarly as functional organizations of knowledge. The term *digest,* as long applied to bodies of law, implies not only condensation, or abridgment, but systematic organization of their material.

Special periodicals may be regarded as contributing to the functional organization of knowledge in the several fields. They inform their readers as to the progress of discovery, invention, formulation, theory, and opinion in the respective lines of interest, digesting reports, proceedings, etc., quoting and reprinting important contributions, and abstracting articles of interest from publications in the related fields. This may all be less coherent and systematic than it should be; but the cumulative social results are on the whole informative, educative, and progressive. A force is operative thru these publications that is indeed comparable with the "power

[7] *The Library Journal,* February 15, 1926, p. 168.

of the press," that is, the daily and weekly journals of news and opinion; but in some respects it is even more potent in functionally organizing knowledge, thought, opinion, and purpose.

The immensity of periodical literature is shown in statistical dimensions in the following data. In the *World List of Scientific Periodicals Published in the Years 1900-1921,* there are listed 24,686 titles, exclusive of those that had ceased publication prior to 1900. For all fields, literary, historical, social, artistic, and philosophical, as well as scientific, the *Union List of Serials in the Libraries of the United States and Canada* numbers 75,000.

The numerical vastness of the great bibliographic catalogs justifies the term "millionaire bibliography." The Union Catalog of the Library of Congress has now over 15,000,000 cards. Dr. Bishop estimates that there are about a million and a half author cards for the four million books of the Library of Congress.[8] The recently compiled union catalog of the Philadelphia libraries combines about two and a half millions of author and title entries.[9] Dr. Richardson estimated that there are not less than eight or ten million titles kept and cataloged in the world's great libraries, and probably very many more local publications kept only locally. . . .

"Experiments which have recently been made suggest that the union catalog as it now exists, if extended to include most of the larger libraries, will cover ninety per cent of the known titles.[10]

4. Microphotographic Reproduction

Yes, of course, photography represents and reproduces. We have long been accustomed to photographic reproduction of pictures, of medals, of charts, of docu-

[8] W. W. Bishop, "Resources of American Libraries," in *The Library Quarterly,* v. 8, p. 465 (Oct., 1938).

[9] Paul Vanderbilt, "The Philadelphia Union Catalog," in *Library Trends,* ed. by Louis R. Wilson, Univ. of Chicago Press, 1937, p. 217.

[10] *The Library Journal,* February 15, 1926, p. 169.

ments, and of "news" in theaters. If we can photostat pages, if the pages of a book may be so rapidly and economically photographed on a reel of film, why not a file of cards? Moreover photography may reduce and enlarge. Microfilms may be minute and so they may be stored in small space. Carefully protected from the heat and dust in "air-conditioned" storage, they may last longer than "news-print" and "pulp." And they may be reproduced again. They may be transported and distributed at little cost. When readers want them, they may be projected and enlarged on screens properly lighted on enclosed tables for individual researchers or on walls for groups of readers or students. Valuable, rare, or remote books and documents are thus available. Periodicals, newspapers, and serial documents may be thus stored in small space. Books and papers wanted by but few specialists may thus be reproduced and reprinted in "near-print," and distributed in a few regional libraries. Microfilm cameras, projectors, and reading-machines may move into rooms vacated by books and stacks. Catalogs may be reproduced thus and transmitted or distributed. Authors may themselves publish their small editions in "near-print." The commercial publishers and the "press" would no longer unprofitably publish such "special" scholarly publications; but they would continue to exploit their markets in informing, edifying, and entertaining the larger literate public. For libraries, for schools, for theaters, and for resorts there would be new eras — new plans, new equipment, new technics, new training, and new economies.

But we should remember that photography merely represents and reproduces. Its pictures or prints are not the original realities. We cannot live in the pictures of a house. Nor can we directly read the microfilm of a book or of a catalog. We must again reproduce the book or catalog — with some of its old imperfections and inconveniences, and some new ones from the conditions of reproduction. If a union catalog combines antiquated catalogs of antique collections, either it must be adapted or they must be modernized, or it will not exactly correspond to them.[11]

Finally the value of reproduction and transmission will depend on the interest of readers and the satisfactoriness of results to scholars. There are still questions as to legibility and eyestrain in prolonged reading, conditions of projection, inconvenience or trouble to readers, working with head, hands, and papers in the confines of a mechanical hood. The conditions must be controlled. Many readers will continue to prefer the intimate page, quite legible in the soft light of a lamp. Many scholars will continue to prefer their desk and papers and several books ready at hand. Readers will still come in the "author-approach," and researchers in the "subject-approach" will prefer to scan the cards of a subject-

[11] These probabilities are envisaged by many writers in the current journals for librarians. A few articles that have interested this writer are mentioned below:

"Resources of American Libraries," by W. W. Bishop, in *The Library Quarterly,* v. 8, p. 465 ff., especially p. 475-6, Oct., 1938.

"Union Catalogs," also by Dr. Bishop, in *The Library Quarterly,* v. 7, p. 36-49.

"The Reproduction of Materials for Research," by Robert C. Binkley, in *Library Trends,* ed. by Louis R. Wilson, University of Chicago Press, 1937, p. 225-36.

Microphotography for Libraries, 1937, ed. by M. Llewellyn Raney, American Library Ass'n, 1937. Reviewed by K. D. Metcalf in A. L. A. *Bulletin,* v. 32, p. 59-60.

"The Philadelphia Union Catalog," by Paul Vanderbilt, in *Library Trends,* cited above, p. 200-24.

"Care and Cataloging of Microfilms," by K. D. Metcalf, in *Bulletin* of the American Library Ass'n, v. 31, p. 72-4, Feb., 1937.

"Library Methods of Handling Microfilm," by R. E. Carruthers and W. E. Wright, in A. L. A. *Bulletin,* v. 32, p. 385-7, June, 1938.

"Microfilm—New Tool for Intelligence," by Watson Davis, in *Proceedings,* Thirteenth Annual Conference, Special Libraries Ass'n, v. 1, p. 29-33, 1938.

"Microphotography, Equipment and Application," by V. D. Tate, *idem,* v. 1, p. 33-7.

"Documentation for the Scientist," by E. P. Partridge, *idem,* p. 38-9.

"The Possibility of Discarding the Card Catalog," by Fremont Rider, in *The Library Quarterly,* v. 8, especially p. 335-8, July, 1938.

Microphotography for Libraries, Symposium at the 1936 Conference of the A. L. A., M. L. Raney, ed. See especially his two summaries, p. 99-121.

catalog or the contents or indexes of books classified on the shelves. So librarians will go on building and rebuilding their libraries, their collections, and their catalogs. In the new structures and new economies the processes of photographic reproduction will probably be but intermediary and supplementary. Some expensive books may thus be obtained economically. Valuable, rare, and remote documentary, historical, and literary resources will thus be transmitted for students and scholars. Catalogs and union-catalogs will thus be reproduced, reconstructed, and distributed.

All this is quantitative and extensive. Is it also qualitative and intensive? Are the services as effectual and valuable as the materials and compilations are vast? Mere accumulation, mere magnitude, without adequate system and method, result in congestion. Neither knowledge nor thought, neither research nor intelligence is satisfactorily served by mere mass production of unorganized materials; they require rather a *selection* and *functional organization* of the available *and valuable.* The efficiency of functional organizations of knowledge depends on the structural classifications in which they function. No subject-index method would suffice. Research requires subordination of the specific to the generic, with dependent collocation of closely related resources. In qualitative selection of resources, in consistent structural classification, and in efficient functional organization, would be attainable the higher development of coöperative international bibliography.

PART III

CRITICISM OF HISTORIC CLASSIFICATIONS FOR LIBRARIES

"On ne saurait apporter trop d'attention aux méthodes de classification, ...

"Peut on affirmer que les systèmes actuels satisfont assez aux immenses besoins existants pour rendre vaines de nouvelles recherches? Pour notre part, nous estimons qu'une sérieuse investigation portant sur les principes de la question et une étude comparative objective des diverses solutions qui y ont été données sont de nature à apporter des progrès considérables."

E. et G. de Grolier.

"The function of a bibliographic classification is arrangement; that of notation is merely to indicate that arrangement. In fine, the librarian who chooses a classification merely because it has a particular form of notation shows a lamentable regard for what is essential in a classification."

W. C. Berwick Sayers.

CHAPTER X

THE DECIMAL CLASSIFICATION

1. The Earlier Historical Situation

A complete or compendious historical survey of bibliographical classifications would not come within the scope and purpose of this volume. So in this Part we shall consider, critically rather than historically, the leading systems only, three American, three European, and one Asiatic. But first the early systems will be mentioned briefly here, especially the dominant French bibliographic system, which appeared in front of the classified part of the monumental *Manuel du Libraire* of Brunet.[1] Then other historic systems will be noticed. Bibliographic accounts have been compiled by several authorities: Edwards, Petzholdt, Fumagalli, Graesel, Maire, Brown, Richardson, Berwick Sayers, and Schneider.[2]

In the history of the succession of arbitrary systems we have not found any consistent growth that deserves to be called a development. So there is the less reason for grounding these introductory observations on the remoter past. In the system of knowledge, of the sciences, we did, however, find a development, relational

[1] This adaptation of the system of the Paris booksellers dates from the first edition, 1810, not from the fourth (v. 5, 1844), as incorrectly stated in Edwards' Table, by double error as 1842, the date of the first volume; nor, still more erroneously, from the fifth edition, 1860-65, as cited in Brown's *Library Classification and Cataloging*. But in the front part of v. 6 of this edition (1864) Brunet's table gives considerable more detail than in his earlier editions. Richardson correctly dates this system as 1810.

[2] These are cited (except the last two) in Richardson's book in the third section of the Appendix, 3rd ed., p. 45-8; also in Berwick Sayers' *Manual*, in the Bibliography, section III.

and probably causal, and that it is of intellectual and critical value to survey it.[3]

The systems of Aristotle, Gesner, Bacon, and Ampère did somewhat influence, we may believe, the library classifications, however crude and arbitrary, of Callimachus, Bouillaud (antecedent to Brunet), Merlin, Harris, and Dewey; but such influences were not dominant and pervasive. Practical convenience under the conditions imposed was more objective. So in the library system that the philosopher Leibniz devised the first three classes were assigned to the principal university faculties, Theology, Jurisprudence, and Medicine. The first two of these appear as the first two main divisions of Brunet's system and of those closely related to it; but the third had there been subordinated to the broader "Sciences and Arts," that harked back to Gesner's system and to certain medieval systems. There were traces too of the medieval *trivium* and *quadrivium*. Bacon had established the tri-partite division into History, Poetry (imaginative literature), and Philosophy. In later systems the caption *Literature* supplanted *Poetry*. A few years later than Bacon's, the system of Naudé, the French librarian, as outlined in Edwards' table,[4] most concisely shows this grouping of main classes, but with Medicine placed second[5] and with the addition of Mathematics: I. Theology; II. Medicine; III. Jurisprudence; IV. History; V. Philosophy; VI. Mathematics; VII. Polite Literature. The systems of Rhodius (1631), Clemens (1635), Bouillaud (1678), and Garnier (1678), as outlined by

[3] *The Organization of Knowledge*, Part IV, especially p. 399-401.

[4] *Memoirs of Libraries*, by Edward Edwards, 2 v., London, Trübner, 1859. This is the table that faces p. 811 in v. 2. The outline given there differs from that shown on p. 772 of the same volume. This later form has twelve classes in a different order.

[5] This prominence of Medicine comports with the fact that Gabriel Naudé, the learned librarian, was also Physician to Louis XIII.

Edwards there, were the chief historic variants of this grouping, the former two adding Philology, Logic, Rhetoric, Oratory and Grammar, and Physiology, as main classes, whereas Bouillaud combined several of these under Literature and Sciences and Arts, reducing his system to five main classes. This was the grounding of the arrangements of the Paris booksellers and French bibliographers and librarians of the seventeenth, eighteenth, and nineteenth centuries, most notably of Martin (1740) and of Brunet (1810). This system is briefly known as the Paris, or French, system.

The classified part of Brunet's *Manual* embodied and was preceded by a system based on that devised by Ismaël Bouillaud (or Bouillau) for the famous library of Jacques Auguste de Thou and his family.[6] This system was afterwards altered, or recast, by Gabriel Martin in 1740; by Guillaume de Bure in 1768; by Antoine Barbier, Librarian to Napoleon and author of a great dictionary of anonyms and pseudonyms, in 1803 (or 1806); by Cl. Fr. Achard for his *Cours élémentaire de bibliographie* (1806); by Thomas Horne, Librarian of Queen's College, Cambridge;[7] by J. C. Brunet, and of course by others. These changes affected both the number of main classes (usually five) and their order, which was inverted by Achard. The third class, Sciences and Arts, Horne divided into two, as shown in parallel columns below, and he transposed Literature and History. More or less similar changes were probably made by others.

BRUNET	HORNE
I. Theology.	I. Theology, or Religion.
II. Jurisprudence.	II. Jurisprudence.
III. Sciences and Arts.	III. Philosophy.
IV. Polite Literature.	IV. Arts and Trades.
V. History.	V. History.
	VI. Literature.

[6] *Bibliotheca Thuana*, Paris, Quesnel, 1679.

[7] *Outlines for the Classification of a Library*, quarto, London, 1825.

Theology was usually placed first, except in a few systems that, reflecting the radicalism of the French Revolution, put Grammar or Literature, Philosophy or Science first. With regard to the university faculties, Jurisprudence might well be ranked second, and Philosophy, if distinct from Theology, third, if not second. Literature was distinct enough from Philosophy, and History from both. The books treating of arts and sciences were again different from those studies and faculties. In several German bibliographic classifications dating from that of Ersch in 1793 to that of Schleiermacher in 1847 and Hartwig in 1888 the rising importance of Philology, or Linguistics, and Pedagogics, or Education, resulted in the assignment of a main class to one, or to both, of these studies also. These six or seven main divisions were valid with regard to the practical purposes and points of view that obtained. The purpose of organizing knowledge, or study, had not yet emerged. In the days of Brunet books were not classified on such principles. Theology should out of respect and from habit of thought come first; but it did not matter much whether History or Literature or Philosophy came last, or whether Arts preceded Sciences or not. Some librarians think the same on these matters today.

The British Museum in 1836-38, The Royal Institution in 1857, Edward Edwards in 1859, and L. P. Smith[8] in 1882 put forth adaptations of Brunet's classification; but to compare them, beyond a few remarks, would be aside from our purpose. The British Museum's resembled Horne's, differing mainly in placing Philosophy after the Sciences and Arts and in assigning the last of its ten main divisions to Philology. Edwards laid down six main classes, A to F, and subdivided them with considerable detail; he differed from Brunet chiefly in subordinating Law, including Jurisprudence, to Class D, Politics and Commerce, and in bringing Philosophy and History forward to B and C, thus separating them from Sciences and Arts in E and from Literature and Philology in F. The last of these British bibliographic classifications, that of Sonnenschein's *The*

[8] *On the Classification of Books:* a paper read before the American Library Assn., May, 1882.

Best Books (1887), with ten main classes, A to K, improved on Edwards' by placing Society forward between Philosophy (C) and Geography and History (E and F-G), but it still misplaced the sciences in H. The classification of the American librarian, Cutter, was at about the same time developed on virtually the same basis as Edwards' but with more main divisions, assigning Class K to Law and Class Q to Medicine, Class E to Biography and Class G to Geography and Travels.

This and later classifications for libraries were purposed to combine practical and logical or philosophical values. The older bibliographic classifications had practical rather than philosophic purposes, whether for bookselling or for libraries. Edwards made a point of decrying the theoretical as metaphysical, visionary, and absurd, and this was justified for most of the schemes he then had in mind. But Merlin, writing to a convention of librarians at New York in 1853, had emphasized the importance of basing a classification of books on a system of knowledge; and Cutter, forty years afterwards, brought this principle forcefully into the field of discussion. Very similar to Cutter's classification was that of the English librarians, Quinn and Brown, published in 1894. But the later *Subject Classification* of Brown (1906) differed fundamentally in placing the Sciences first after Generalia, and History last, after Language and Literature. The order was rationalized as "evolutionary" in four main stages: Matter and Force, Life, Mind, Record. We shall return to this in Chapter XIII, section 1. Then back in 1870, William T. Harris, philosopher and educator of high repute, had published a catalog of the St. Louis Public School Library, embodying a classification he described soon after in the *Journal of Speculative Philosophy,* of which he was for years editor. This classification combined philosophical with practical interests. It made Science in the broadest sense its first caption, Philosophy being subordinated to this, and Religion subsequent; but it placed the Physical and Natural Sciences, also Mathematics, after Philosophy, Religion, and the Social Sciences, as the systems of Brunet, Horne, and Edwards had done. This scheme is sometimes rationalized as the tripartite division of Bacon, inverted thus: Philosophy and Science, Art and Literature, and History. The order of its 18 main classes was the same as Dewey adopted for his nine; and it likewise had a hundred divisions.

However influential in scientific circles the philosophic systems of Comte, Ampère, and Spencer may have been, in Bibliographic circles Bacon and Brunet dominated to the end of the nineteenth century in England, France, and Italy; and to a large extent they do so still. In Italy Bacon has been especially influential,[9] but Battezzati's system, adopted by the Italian booksellers (1871), which Dewey says stimulated his study most, was an adaptation of Brunet's.

2. The Index Feature. The Last Shall Be First

This in brief was the historical situation in 1873, when Melvil Dewey in his twenty-second year, an undergraduate at Amherst, became connected with the library there and conceived the idea of making a better classification for libraries. On his graduation the next year he became acting librarian; and he served there till 1876, the year in which the first edition of his classification was published, in a pamphlet of 42 pages, only 12 being tables. His interest led him to make a study of library classifications, facilities, and economies. He soon recognized the need for an index to any classification subdivided specifically and minutely; and his practical mind rejected the complicated notations that had been variously applied. But his youthful spirit was not merely practical; he had a mind of large ideas, and of "dreams" that became ideas, and ideas that he made realities. He was a born reformer, in the better sense, and an idealist, an optimist too. He became an influential educator, an effectual advocate, a promoter of undertakings, and a

[9] See our preceding book (cited in footnote 3 of this chapter), p. 369-72.

doughty defender. The Metric System of weights and measures, Spelling-reform, the American Library Association, and the Library Bureau he put into motion there in Boston in the one year 1876. The Metric System is a simple, convenient decimal system, and it is international. So, he argued later, are the figures. Leadership developed in him and was graced with an engaging personality. The Decimal Classification moreover filled a real need in the hundreds of public libraries that were springing up everywhere in this country. The comparative simplicity of its notation for its thousand subjects and the convenience of its index commended it; and there was no better system at hand. These considerations account for the remarkable success that attended its progress.

That Dewey was intent on practical convenience rather than logical order is plainly expressed in his Introduction. The alphabetical Index he declared "the most important feature of the system, ..." But it was so obvious a necessity. Books, even those with systematic contents, had from time immemorial been indexed. Why then should not a subject-catalog, or a classification, be indexed? Of course the more confused the classification, the greater the need of an index. "Some prominent opponents of clast catalogs admit that the Relativ Subject Index, in deciding where to class a book first, and where to look for it ever afterwards, has removed their strongest objections." [10] This expressed an early stage of the "subject-index illusion." Edwards in his *Memoirs of Libraries,* which Dewey had doubtless studied, clearly

[10] Dr. Dewey was a prominent advocate and exponent of spelling reform, and his spelling is quite radical. It is consistently maintained in his Introduction tho not thruout the schedules and index. We have not felt bound to follow it, in several brief quotations, or have given the spelling of his earlier editions. The reader has doubtless noticed that we too make use of certain simplified spellings. With the movement we have long been in accord.

pointed this out: ". . . . the objections of 'vagueness' and 'complexity,' often brought against Classification, will be seen to have little validity when a Catalogue in classes is supplemented by an alphabetical Index of Topics, as well as by an Index of Authors; . . . ." [11]

But the index idea has been overworked; the index has been trusted too much. Like the famous "gold-dust twins," it was recommended to do all the house-work. It would put the library in order, no matter how disarranged. It did not matter much what order, or disorder, the subjects were in, the index would locate them. That is the wrong way in classification; it leads straight to what we have called "the subject-index illusion." It is a poor substitute for a good classification, and not much better for a poor one. It is destructive not only of classification; it is self-destructive. For in the extreme there is no use for classification at all. The subjects might as well be arranged alphabetically, as in the alphabetic subject-catalog. Then there would be no need for the index. That would indeed simplify matters; but it would not be classification. Such is the ultimate outcome of the illusion that books can be classified by an index and that, if there be an index, it matters little what the order of subjects may be.

A classification elaborated in practical service on an arbitrary basis is likely to develop disproportionate branches and to become entangled with vines of unforeseen growth. Such disproportion and disarray as have resulted would be countervailed, it was supposed, by the practical recourse to the alphabetic index. But we have confuted that subject-index fallacy. Both science and

[11] *Op. cit.*, v. 2, p. 884. The need for an alphabetic index for the classed catalog of the National Library at Berlin was in 1866 urged by one of the librarians there, Schrader. See G. Valentin in Österreichischer Verein für Bibliothekswesen, *Mitteilungen*, IX. Jahrg. (1905), p. 85-6.

education have passed beyond narrow specialization. The Relative Index and the decimal notation were, Dewey said, the main features of his system; and by virtue of these he has proclaimed — a little high-mindedly perhaps — that: "D C has becum an international laborsaver." It was indeed the product of the age of specialization. But it would save more labor, if its notation were shorter and its divisions less dispersive. One result noted is the inefficiency indicated by Dr. Kelley's study.

Classification implies division, but system implies relation and thru relations organization. Separations on the other hand impair organization and destroy unity. Science systemizes its classifications, its branches, its member sciences. Education organizes knowledge of the sciences and arts and branches of philosophy and of history. No index, however convenient or necessary, can convert an arbitrary and disordered arrangement into a systematic classification.

3. The Basis and the Main Divisions

Bacon and Brunet were the masters followed by the bibliographers of the nineteenth century, with few exceptions, even in the latter decades, when education and philosophy were adopting natural science for the ground of their humanistic intellectual survey. But the bibliographers and librarians were intent on practical arrangements of books and catalogs rather than on logical or philosophical systems, which had been disparaged; and they did not see that it was not practical to disregard the system of the sciences, even while adopting the results of science. Melvil Dewey, practical indeed, was not lacking in scientific interest. His classification has embodied a large amount of scientific detail, much of which, obtained from specialists or "experts," is scientifically correct. Otherwise it would have attained to less acceptance by scientists. But it is detail too largely lacking coherent scientific order. *Subordination* and *collocation* are manifest in most of these "expansions," but those principles were disregarded in the original, fundamental structure. It was not to be expected that in 1876 a young man of twenty-five years, however brilliant, could lay down a foundation that would provide, without change, for the future construction of fifty years; but he might have known where to find in other systems a better basis for such an undertaking. That a sounder basis existed we have fully shown elsewhere.

The scientific view, we must aver, is but one. Four principal divisions of the subject-matter of books, besides the *forms,* the *generalia,* and the arts, we have distinguished: History, Literature, Philosophy, and Science. Any of these may be made the basis of a consistent, unitary system. We should not find fault with a literary view for subordinating all scientific literature — much of it unliterary — to literature. Nor should we object, if a historian subordinate science-development to social-intellectual history; nor do we disagree when the philosopher subordinates science to philosophy. But in classification for libraries consistency with the main purpose is a leading principle. In so far as the purposes are educational and intellectual, there should be feasible consistency with one, or better, with all four of the views named.[12] This would increase the efficiency and enhance the values of the classification. In the light of these truths let us now consider the basic divisions of the Decimal Classification.

[12] How this can be attained and adjusted is shown in our preceding volume, Chapter XIII, section 2.

First the familiar outline of the Main Classes will be shown parallel with Brunet's, followed by Bacon's tripartite division inverted. It is needless to discuss such resemblance as obtains or to trace it in detail. We should, however, bear in mind that Bacon's division was unphilosophic and unpractical and that Brunet's classification was for booksellers of the 18th and 19th centuries, not for librarians of the twentieth.

DEWEY'S MAIN CLASSES

0 General.
1 Philosophy.
2 Religion.
3 Sociology.
4 Philology.
5 Science.
6 Useful Arts.
7 Fine Arts.
8 Literature.
9 History.

BRUNET'S MAIN CLASSES

I. Theology.
II. Jurisprudence.
III. Sciences and Arts.
IV. Belles Lettres (Language and Literature).
V. History.

BACON'S MAIN DIVISIONS

I. Philosophy, Sciences, and Arts.
II. Poetry (Literature).
III. History.

But Brunet did not separate Language from Literature, nor did any other influential system, except that of Harris. Why Dewey did we wonder. Can any good reason be found for it? Does any librarian defend it? It is as inconvenient as it is unjustifiably wrong.

Hardly less wry is the separation of Sociology in Class 3 from History in Class 9, whatever may be the point of view; and we have found no historical authority for that, except again Harris, and Brunet's Jurisprudence. In view of modern studies it is wholly perverse. Then the separation of Science in Class 5 from Philosophy in Class 1 is neither philosophic nor scientific, nor historical nor practical. General science, as generalized, is almost indistinguishable from Philosophy, somewhat as the philosophy of society is inseparable from the science of society, for it should be based on it.

These three major separations are enough to disqualify any system as an organization of knowledge, whatever the point of view may be. They are consistent with none of the comprehensive modern views. Two of these cardinal faults are generally recognized by librarians. By way of remedy radical changes have been proposed and by some librarians adopted. Philology (Class 4) may be transferred to the place of Class 9, or of Class 8, so as to stand alongside of Literature; but this would leave literature still separated from philology in all the languages and literatures. The French language would still be separated from the French literature, and so would the literature of Japan be separated from the language of the Japanese. If, instead, Literature were transferred to 5, Science to 3, and Sociology to 8, the last would be separated farther from Science, Philosophy, Religion, and Ethics, and the plight of Anthropology and Ethnology would be worse than before. If, as a third attempt, Literature were placed in Class 3, it would precede Philology in Class 4, which is absurd, and the several languages and literatures would still be separated in detail. These objections would no less obtain, if Philology were placed after Literature in 9 and History transferred to 4; and a large practical objection inheres in the immense detail of History, involving a large portion of the Index, if all of these items were to be changed.

If one *must* have a decimal base, despite cramping, it can be done — not too inconsistently — as follows, tho with some distortions:

Class 0: General, Miscellaneous, Collections, etc.
1 Philosophy, and Science (general), Logic, Mathematics, Statistics;
2 Natural Sciences, Physical and Biological;

3 Anthropology, Human Body, Hygiene, and Medical Science;
4 Psychology and Education;
5 Sociology, Ethnology, Religion, and Ethics;
6 Human Geography and History, Social, Ethnic, and Political;
7 Political Science, Jurisprudence and Law, and Economics;
8 Arts, Useful, or Industrial, Fine Arts, and Arts of Pastime, etc.;
9 Philology, Linguistics, and Literature, general, and special.

This outline will be found nearly consistent with that shown in the author's *System of Bibliographic Classification.*

4. Important Sciences Mangled

The separation of Social Science in Class 3 from Science in Class 5 places the study of human society ahead of the study of human nature in Prehistoric Archeology (571), Ethnology (572), and Natural History of Man (573). The first of these terms is rather antiquated. Ethnic Archæology, or Archæological Ethnology, or Palæoethnology, would be the modern terminology. Then Racial Anthropology would fit the subject-matter of 572 more in keeping with modern usage than the olden use of Ethnology. More antiquated still is the caption, Natural History of Man, where Physical Anthropology would go better with the term Somatology, added in the recent editions. This is the only one of these current terms that appears even in the index. Nor do the related terms Culture (Cultural) Anthropology and Ethnic Anthropology appear anywhere.

These three branches of Anthropology are in inverted order. The inverse order of the Baconian main divisions is by no means the only inversion in the D. C. This part of Anthropology and Ethnology shares the 570 division with a part of the subject-matter of Biology, which precedes Archeology (Anthropology) in the caption but follows it in the four sections 574-577, and in inverse order. Anthropology also comes before Zoölogy in 590. But Anthropology is not all here; indeed this great science seems to have fallen, like the Colossus of Rhodes, and to have sunk in fragments. Its psychologic member is in 150, 159, or 130, where again, reflecting an olden philosophic usage, the family name is like a cognomen suffixed to the psychological subject, Mind and Body, which is separated from other psychological subjects in 150 by Philosophic Systems (history and criticism) in 140. The folklore member appears at the end of Social Science, where it has some reason to be. Ethnography, the descriptive counterpart of Ethnology, appears only in the index. Anthropogeography, or Human Geography, the index refers only to Geography (general), which is subordinated to History, Physical Geography being referred to Physical Geology. For Physical Anthropology we must turn to Medicine under the Useful Arts, where several scientific branches are expropriated. Two of Biology's most promising children, General Physiology and Biochemistry (or Biological or Physiological Chemistry), have also been kidnapped by the art, Medicine. Medical Physiology has a three-place decimal, 612.014, for General Physiology of Cells and Organisms, which exemplifies the illogical inversion of the general into the special, in the course of subsequent expansion. The last two sections assigned to Biology are for mere attendants, Microscopy, and Collectors' Manuals, etc. Indeed this retinue of Archeology, Ethnology, Biology, and Microscopy is one of the most inverse, inexpert, antiquated, and absurd retinues that has ever travestied the stage of arbitrary library classification.

The rational and analytic branch of Psychology, lingering in its ancestral home in Philosophy, in division 150, has by Philosophic (filosofic, or philosofic) Systems (140), which might have a large historical and critical content, long been separated from its kindred, Mind and Body (130), which avows being a cousin to Anthropology, and which comprises Mental Physiology and Hygiene, Mental Derangements, Occultism, Hypnotism, Sleep and Dreams, Mental Characteristics, Child-study, Personality, Physiognomy, and Phrenology — quite a motley bunch of kids, some evidently belonging to another family, usually known as Abnormal Psychology. But these relatives have in the recent edition been brought together in an alternative classification at the tail end of the last section, where hereafter their children and grandchildren will be marked or re-marked with remarkably long tails: thus Behavior, still regarded by a prominent school of psychologists as the chief subject-matter of their science, must be forced into either 159.901943 or 159.92, neither of which is comprehensive enough to contain it. As for details, the index says that the compounded mark for such a simple subject as the Behavioristic theory of Sleep would be 159.963201943, for Sleep 159.9632, plus 01 for theory, plus 943 for behavioristic (behaviorism). The index refers Behavior, evidently meaning Conduct, to Social Ethics (177). The term Social Psychology appears only under the Philosophy of Sociology.

But it is Social Science that shows most flagrant disregard for order, both in the divisions and in the sections. Political Science (320) is separated from Administration (350) and from Law (340) by the whole of Economics, intervening in 330, except for two big stragglers, Commerce and Communication, cut off in 380 from their proper communications. Legislation is 328 and Comparative Legislation 340.5. Socialism should not be treated as merely economic in 335, but more broadly under Sociology or else under Political Science as an organization of the state to secure social-economic equalities. However, none of the theoretical topics of sociology are distinctly provided for, and few of those of theoretical economics.

Education in the midst of these disarranged branches of social and political science and economics seems prominently misplaced in 370, where it is expanded in very special detail, and where it might prove very inconvenient to have it. Education may be regarded as a social institution, but it is much less closely related to

Sociology than to Psychology, which enters into so much of its theoretical and practical investigation. Educational Psychology, or, better, Psychology applied to Education, has only a two-place decimal, and this highly specialized study is here not yet expanded, but it would be ineptly, if, as a note indicates, it were done according to the subdivisions of 150, which may apply to Psychology but do not apply to Educational Psychology.

Biology, Anthropology, Ethnology, Psychology, Education, and Sociology, these six are all large and important subjects; three of them are fundamental sciences and two others are of major importance. Yet in the Decimal Classification these great subjects not only lack proper place and adequate provision but they are dismembered, misrelated, and confused. All of these subjects were well established when this system was planned sixty-five years ago. Since then their growth has been increasingly definite and impressive. Yet they lack proper place and adequate provision. This immense deficiency is again enough to disqualify any system as an organization of modern knowledge.

5. Disproportion and Resulting Deficiencies

The apportionment of notation to classification requires both knowledge and judgment. Disproportion results in overcrowding and in lengthy marks. It was not good judgment in the Decimal Classification to assign as much room to Philosophy as to Science (Physical and Natural, including Mathematics), and as much room to Fine Arts as to History, as little to the History of Europe as to Landscape Gardening, as little to the History of England (942) as to Private Grounds (712), as little to Physics (530) as to Metaphysics (110), as little to Economics (330) as to Devotional Religion (240). This last requires but one page of schedule, whereas Economics has six, and should have more. Landscape Gardening has but nine subdivisions, and only one of these has sub-sections, and that only five. The History of Europe has more than thirteen pages of fine print with over a hundred times as much detail as Landscape Gardening. The schedules of Class 7 fill only about twenty pages, without much fine print, while the schedule of subdivision 973, History of the United States, fills over twenty pages of much greater detail.

Let us now look at the apportionment from another angle. Some important branches of knowledge that have no place among the hundred divisions of the D. C. will be named here: Mechanics, Mineralogy, Physiography, Meteorology, Genetics, Bacteriology, Physical Anthropology, Hygiene, Social Psychology, Educational Psychology, Comparative Religion, Mythology, Folk-lore, Philanthropy and Charity, Military and Naval Science, International Law, Finance, Comparative Literature, Drama and Theater. For these twenty members of the community of studies no places have been provided at Dr. Dewey's table. Several of his chosen hundred are of decidedly minor importance and they should make place for these. Others should have their antiquated captions replaced by modern terms.

Under Philosophy the captions Mind and Body, and Other Metaphysical Topics, should make room for Philosophy of Knowledge, and Philosophy of Human Nature. Under Religion the captions of 230 to 280 should be supplanted by more distinctive and comprehensive subjects, say Theology, Comparative Religion, and Christianity. Under the Social Sciences that of Administration should be subordinate either to Government or to Political Science, thus making room for International Relations, with which Military and Naval Science might well be collocated. Also the caption, Customs, Costumes, and Folk-lore, might better be changed to Folk-lore, or to Ethnography, or to Descriptive Sociology. Thirdly, Associations and Institutions should be supplanted by a broader caption, such as Descriptive Sociology. And under Philology the several languages should not be separated from their literatures, and seven divisions would thus be vacated. The Arts might easily be combined in one class. Landscape Gardening, Sculpture, Drawing, and Engraving hardly require capacity equal to that of Hygiene and Recreation, Business, Finance, and other subjects inadequately provided for. Chemical Technology (660) should be collocated with Chemistry, and Business, Bookkeeping, and Transportation should be subordinated to Economics.

The schedules of Literature and History are little more than a directory of periods, persons, and countries. For general aspects and relations and for special topics there is almost no provision, except by possible expansion of notation distinctly naughty and such as has been bewilderingly elaborated by *La Classification Décimale* of the International Institute of Bibliography. Hellenism, for instance, and the Hellenistic Influence are lacking both in the schedules and in the index. Greek Civilization and related topics might, however, be expanded under 938.001. Roman, Chinese, Japanese, and Mexican civilization, social and economic history, and antiquities, are likewise neglected. Judea and India are without any subdivisions of their Ancient history, and the subdivisions of their Modern history are merely Geographical. For Bohemia expansion would begin with the mark 943.71001, and the compounding would start from 943.71.

Following the Index are five Tables for sub-classification: (1) of subjects that may be subdivided by geographical specifications, (2) *Form* divisions, (3) Languages that may be subdivided like the English, (4) Philological divisions that may be used for the foregoing purpose, (5) Literatures to be subdivided like the English. For all of these tables suffixes of from one to three additional figures are requisite. But for History no systematic table is provided. Such subjects as Antiquities, Emperors' Lives, and Foreign Relations, which appear in the table for geographical subdivision, should not be subdivided that way but should be provided for in a schedule for subdividing history of the nations, such as was described in Chapter IV, section 4. For the several purposes there should be special systematic tables, as above, but these should not have unnecessary detail nor long marks, and they should not have to be suffixed to class-marks already too long, whether from disproportion or for other reason.

The history of Europe (in general) has only nine subsections in addition to the nine form-divisions. Germany and Austria have a page and a half of names and decimals. In contrast the History of the United States has 23 pages of minute detail, again mostly names and dates, and nearly 8 of these pages are for the War of Secession. The World War has 35 pages of expansion but the rest of Europe has only 11 pages. Spanish Literature has been expanded to five pages of detail, but Portuguese Literature is allowed only one subdivision (869), and, after all the petty Spaniards, the eminent Portuguese poet, Camoëns, receives no recognition. Russian Literature fares even worse, being cut off by the ancient Latin and Greek, and is saved from utter extinction only by a reference to the Philology of "Other" languages and by the appendical provision of Table 5. The most expansive part of Religion (according to Dewey) is the Y. M. C. A., to which are assigned three pages, one ninth of the entire class of religious interests. The whole science of Physics is scheduled in five pages, and there Electricity and applications of it have only 23 subdivisions, these running to marks of five figures. Law, with but two pages, might indeed feel slighted, if compared with the Medical art, which has 80 pages of astounding detail, most of which would be inapplicable to books even in medical libraries.

6. Notation Exceeding the Economic Limit

From disproportion result crowded classification and notation of excessive length. What we have termed the *economic limit* to the length of class-marks we have found to be four factors, whether figures or letters or combinations of both. What then shall we say to class-marks of five or six figures prevailing thruout the Decimal Classification (except in Philosophy), and in many expansions extending to seven, to nine, and sometimes even to twelve figures or more? So Forestry, being a sub-section of Fruits, Orchards, (*sic*) and Vineyards (634), National Administration of Forestry would have the mark 634.928223. Such marks result from the inadequacy of the decimal base, the disproportion, and the excessive expansion of the classification, together with suffixing, or compounding, as provided by the system. Complex specification or relation, historical, geographical, national, or for language, may require from six to ten figures.[13] A notation of letters here proves economical, suffixing for each specification only one or two or at most three letters.

For comparison, a few class-marks for subjects of importance are here chosen from the ten classes of the Decimal Classification, avoiding complex factors. The class-marks in our proposed system are placed parallel.

Book-plates	025.253	2YT
Backward Children	136.766	JES
Resurrection of Christ	232.97	PRJ
Industrial Education	371.426	JPG
English Slang	427.09	YAJ
Electrochemistry	540.37	CE
Physiological Psychology	612.821	IB
Gothic Architecture	723.5	VAP
Chaucer	821.17	YC
Roman Empire	937.06	LV

[13] Combining or compounding notations, "number-bilding," as Dewey called it, so as to "reveal the contents of the book so far as it can be expressed by means of D. C. notation," is condoned in a bright and interesting article by Julia C. Pressey in the Catalogers' and Classifiers' Yearbook, Number 6, 1937, p. 57-60. She exemplifies such combination by a number of 33 figures for a pamphlet on Fire-drills at the Newark Air-port, written in the Slovakian language. For the special subject, Air-ports, 629.136, there are only three specifications, Fire-drills, Newark, and Slovakian language. These should not require so many as 27 suffixed figures. That is expressive notation run to excess. But for contrast here is economy in notation: Aviation, BT; Air-ports, BTR; for Newark suffix bdf, for Fire-drills, P, and for Slovakian, Qm; altogether, BTR,bdf,P,Qm. If one must have such specification, it may be had thus with 12 factors.

For further contrast, we will exemplify to what extremes the decimal notation has been carried in *La Classification décimale* developed by the International Institute of Bibliography. History of France in the 18th century, written in English, is quite a simple subject, but this is the way it looks in that notional notational filigree: 9(44)"17"=2. Dr. Dewey gives this example in his Introduction.

This complex mnemonic mark is composed of nine factors containing fourteen components, where a truly simple notation would require but four letters. In our proposed system division MS is for the Periods of the History of France; for the 18th century L is added; so the mark MSL suffices for the above subject. If the language (say French) is to be designated, the letter F would be suffixed from the schedule of languages, and the whole mark would be MSLF. Now which is the simpler method? And is the filigree necessary? To exemplify the excesses of the systematic notation superposed on the D. C. in adapting it to an elaborate classification of special subjects in modern documentation, one more example that is typical will be given here. Experimental Psychology of Children is not a very special subject, but its mark in the C. D. combines ten figures and three points, thus, 612.821.3.031. Now for a very special subject, Incompatibilities of Secretaries in local administration of Public Hygiene in France, we will show just for fun what this system can do in compiling mnemonic(!) notation — 351.77 (44-2) 075.33.082.5. This was really found in a page of the C. D.

Such complicated notations, however serviceable for maintaining the elaborate order of an immense bibliographical catalog and even for indicating specifications in details of sub-classification, are utterly unfit for books in libraries, the classification of which cannot feasibly be made to follow such elaborate specifications.

In general, the notation-combinations of the Decimal Classification are too lengthy and too complex. This may be exemplified by another mark found in Dewey's Introduction: 016.891851, for Bibliography of Polish Poetry. In this the specification for Poland, or Polish, requires four figures, 9185, whereas in a simple notation two letters would suffice for Polish and three for Polish Literature, and four for the Poetry. If the bibliography of this is to be separated from that of the Literature, the figure 2 would be added from the mnemonic schedule. Which again is the simpler method?

7. Minor Sins of Omission and Commission

A system so faulty in its main structure we should not be surprised to find confused and inadequate in its details. The large and increasing literature of Business faces an unhappy situation in the D. C. Omitted from the original hundred, it must either be brought under Commerce and Communication (380) or under Communication (650). The latter has been preferred; but in either case it would be remote from Economics (330). Finance, Banking, and Money are in 332, Insurance in 368. Bookkeeping is in 657, and Advertising in 659.1.

Classical Philology, a broad historical and critical study of the classical Greek and Latin languages and literatures in relation to the social and artistic life of those realms of antiquity, lacks in the D. C. a distinct place either under Philology or under Ancient History, and the subject is referred by the index only generally to the Greek and the Latin Languages.

History and Literature are not the only classes that lack provision for special aspects, relations, or treatment of the subjects. In this the Social Sciences, especially Sociology, are an expansive vacuity. Physics, Biology, Botany, and Zoölogy have no distinct provision for the experimental and the descriptive treatment of the subjects as distinguished from the general, and the theoretical. Experimental Physics and Biology are too important to be so neglected. More particularly there is no distinct provision for the Laboratory Manuals, as distinct from the subject of Laboratories, their equipment, etc. Under Botany there is no special place for the popular books on the Wild Flowers.

Under Economics, Theoretical (330.1), relations to other subjects are provided for and there are a few special subjects, but these are altogether inadequate. For example, Capital is referred by the index to more special subjects, where it is merely subsumed. The topics of theoretical and psychological sociology are lacking, as well as those of descriptive and ethnic sociology, such as: Social Evolution, Progress, Mutual Aid, Social Coöperation, Imitation, Compulsion, Control and Community; also Crowds, Mobs, Groups, Leadership, the Relation of the Individual to Society, Matriarchy, Totemism — these are a few of the omissions of these schedules. Recently, however, they have been inserted in the Index, but referred to other subjects. They are needed to assist classifiers. Political Science has been expanded and is less deficient; but Law is no better off in this respect than Sociology. Under Religion too there are similar lacks; for instance, there is no place for the books on the Psychology of Religion.

To come back to History, the term Historiology is not in the index, nor is the term Pan American. For America in general there is no provision, nor for Latin America, tho from the term Spanish America the index refers the history to Mexico and Central America (972), and the travels to North America, 917.2. South America is separated in 980, the immense history of the United States intervening. North America and South America are separated from Europe (940) by Asia and Africa (950 and 960). There are no items in the schedules for Magna Carta, Bayeux Tapestry (which the Index refers to Art needlework), and Westminster Abbey. The Eastern Question is referred to the History of Turkey in Europe, but it does not appear there. The same is true of hundreds of other references. This is averred from statistical testing.

Placing American Literature first of the national literatures is more patriotic than historical. For the history and criticism it is feasible to separate the American from the British (820), but for the biography and the writings it is less so and may prove troublesome. Inconsistently the Scottish literature is not recognized at all, except by Table 5, which relegates it to the miscellaneous minors. But a cardinal sin was committed in these schedules of literatures. Historical classification is feasible only for large university and reference libraries and therein only for the earlier historic periods. In short it is a troublesome undertaking to classify authors historically. The alphabetic is the more convenient method, especially for the modern and the recent literature. But in the D. C. what is the purpose of all those names and dates under the several periods, if the authors' writings are not to be classified historically together with the biography and criticism? This is indicated too by the note at the head of the class. The situation is first complicated by dividing each literature by *forms,* another baffling procedure. Goldsmith appears here with the poets and then with the novelists and again with the essayists, but he is given no place with the dramatists, despite his delightful plays. These schedules fail to provide a place for Dryden's plays, and for Shakespeare's poems.

The History of English Literature in 820.9 would be separated from the History of English Poetry (821.09), of English Drama (822.09), and of English Fiction (823.09). Shall the English and Scottish Ballads (821.04) be separated from the History of English Poetry by all the general collections of English Poetry in 821.08, besides the contents of three other intervening sub-sections, while the history of the ballads is separated from the ballads in the collections?

This fault-finding section will close after mention of a few more omissions. Æther (or Ether) the index merely refers to the Philosophy of Physics. The schedule for Mechanics omits the Gyroscope, and the Meteoric Hypothesis has no place under the Sun, nor under Astrophysics, which is referred to Theoretical Astronomy, a distinctly different subject. The index does not show the very important subject Auto-intoxication, despite all the needless medical detail; nor Immunology. Endocrinology it refers to Glandular System, but that very important term is not specified there, nor its synonyms, Glands of Internal Secretion, and Ductless Glands. In the Fine Arts Impressionism is referred to Painting only, and there is no mention of Post-impressionism and Futurism, which at least should be in the index. There is no distinct place for Bacteriology in general, tho it has recently been added to 589.95, where this important sub-science is hardly recognizable, its dismembered limbs cast to the four winds. Vitamins and Hormones belong under Physiologic Chemistry, *not*, as there, under Botanical Physiological Chemistry.

Some of these lacks and faults may be remedied, as many others have been since these pages have been available to friendly readers, by additions and adaptations; but marks of excessive length too often result. Moreover, some of the subjects omitted are more general or more important than those to which they would have to be subordinated; for very few divisions have been left vacant. Forestry, remember, was subordinated to Fruits and Orchards. To vacate others would involve dislocations and alterations such as have long been discountenanced in the interests of uniformity and of copyright. When a term is antiquated, it can be supplanted; but, where a term is not comprehensive enough, and where the captions subordinated to it lack coherence, alteration is less easy and tends to issue in reclassification. With regard to the relevant question of reclassifying or reconstructing the entire system, it should be borne in mind that in many divisions the change of a single subdivision would affect or displace all the others of that division; and the same may be said of the change of divisions within the classes. So we shall first consider the confusion, and then the feasibility of remedying it.

8. Confusion Confounded

How the sciences of Biology, Anthropology, Ethnology, Folk-lore, Psychology, Education, and Sociology are dismembered in the divisions of the D. C. was shown in the fourth section of this chapter. The History of Philosophy begins in 109, but no subdivisions are there for periods, schools, *isms*, or topics; these are classified under Philosophic Systems (140). The periods and schools the classifier is led to place under Ancient Philosophers (180) and Modern Philosophers (190), where there are national subdivisions, beginning patriotically with the American. These three historical portions are interspersed by a mélange from Metaphysics, Psychology, Ethics, and Logic. It is plain that Philosophy should be reclassified thruout. If anyone doubts this, it can indeed be more fully shown.

Here are a few instances. Methodology (112) stands between Ontology and Cosmology and far from Logic, of which it is usually regarded as an extension. Theory of Knowledge is in 121, Consciousness in 126, and Soul in 128, but Psychology is in 153, and between the latter and the former group are such diverse subjects as Mental Derangements (132), Occultism, Witchcraft, and Magic (133), Hypnotism, Animal Magnetism, Clairvoyance (134), Sleep and Dreams (135), and Philosophic Systems (140-9). These four divisions certainly need internal reclassification. The Philosophy of Religion (201) is separated from the philosophical topics of 210 by the miscellaneous contents of 202 to 208; and those philosophical topics are separated from the relevant topics of Doctrinal and Dogmatic Theology (230) by the Bible and its books. The middle divisions of this class, for Devotional, Homiletic, and Institutional, should have been classified in the latter divisions of the class, so as to be closer to Sociology.

The disorder of the divisions of Social Science has already been indicated. Here we will add merely a few examples of confusion in the subdivisions. Finance (332) is separated from Public Finance (336) by the extraneous group of subjects, Land (333), Coöperation (334), and Socialism and Communism (335); and Land is separated from Capital, which appears only as subsumed under the caption of Labor, and in the sub-section 331.1, for the Relations of Capital to Labor. Foreign Relations (327) should be correlated with International Law (341) rather than with Slavery (326), which should not be separated from closely related topics of 323 and 324 by Colonies and Immigration (325). Administration (350) should not be separated from Political Science by Law (340) and Economics (330). Under Education, Public Schools (379) should not be remote from School Organization (371.2) and School Premises and Equipment (371.6). Between these captions Systems of Education (371.4) should not be interposed. The schedules have no general caption for Schools, nor for Private Schools. In short, even if Class 3 did not require reclassification because of the disorder of the divisions, it would because of the disorder of the subdivisions.

In Philology the general and comparative studies (400 and 410) should be followed by the philologic specialties, Sanskrit, Greek, Celtic, Semitic, and the non-literary languages, while the literary Indo-European languages had better follow, with the literatures from which they are inseparable. This rearrangement would involve eight of the ten divisions.

By a strange irony it is Natural Science that in this unscientific, "practical" system is least faulty. The customary classifications of the more developed sciences were readily available. But there are enough faults in Physics, Biology, Botany and Zoölogy to require their reclassification, and then Astronomy is misplaced and should come just before Geology. Geodesy belongs rather under Geology. Biology we found before to be so mixed up with Anthropology and Ethnology that it would need reclassification thruout. Zoölogy is almost wholly given over to the classificatory or systematic side of the science; and the same fault impairs Botany. Moreover there are minor faults, such as the erroneous placing of Molluscoidea under Mollusks. That the order of Systematic Botany is inverse would be enough to make most botanists reject it. The expansion under 591, Physiological Zoölogy, is incoherent and its notation is too lengthy. Anatomy and Histology in 591.7 and 591.8 are separated from Morphology in 591.4 and Physiology in 591.1. Pathology is 591.2 and Embryology 591.3. The term Genetics, strange to say, does not appear anywhere. The three biological sciences would all need internal reclassification, and Paleontology should be transferred from Geology to Biology.

The mathematical term Analysis, which has come to be preferred as more comprehensive than Calculus, does not appear in this sense, not even in the index. Molecular Physics (539) should be collocated with Gases (533) and Gases with Heat (536); and Light (535) with Electricity (537). So Physics also is a mix. Relativity and the Einstein theory are subsumed only under Gravitation, Law of, and they have no place under Kinematics, where they belong. Much of Mathematics and all of Physics would require reclassification.

Regarding the Arts, we have said that it would be more economical to reapportion them so as to combine the Useful with the Fine Arts. Dewey's classification of the Useful Arts is not practical. It is unpractical to separate Building (690) from Engineering (620). Then Communication and Business belong not under Useful Arts but under Economics. Again, Chemical Technology should not be separated from Chemistry. In the Mechanic Trades, Cabinet-making is linked with Carriage-making in 684, while Carpentry and Joinery are in 694, with Masonry and other things intervening. Even if the Arts were not shifted or combined, they would need so much alteration that there would be little left unchanged.

9. The Question of Reconstruction

We are now prepared to answer the question whether it is feasible by alteration to render the Decimal Classification acceptably coherent, efficient, and economical for libraries. It has been customary to use the term *revision* in this matter. The classification has been *revised* thru thirteen editions — mostly by additions and expansions. However elastic in expansion, the system has proved *rigid* in structure. The original hundred divisions, ill arranged sixty years ago, have been maintained almost unchanged. There have been a few revisions of headings, but in many places antiquated terms remain. And this applies also to the thousand sections. Dr. Dewey persisted in the stand taken many years before that the D. C. is to be altered as little as possible, and that radical changes are to be eschewed, lest users be inconvenienced and a desiderated uniformity be subverted.[14] But in the meantime hundreds of users have been more positively inconvenienced in making their own alterations, and conformity has become futile. Not only have the alterations consumed the time of classifiers in fussing over inadequate and ill arranged schedules, which lack many subjects they are called upon to classify, but the results are still unsatisfactory. The basis remains wrong, and expansion makes the notation long. The confusion is worse confounded.

It is much more thoro alteration that we would consider here. There are three fundamental and practical considerations: *conformity* to the natural, logical, and

[14] See especially Dewey's response to this question at the International Congress at St. Louis, September 1904 (p. 221 of the *Addresses*, printed by *The Library Journal*), where he said: "I myself believe that it is foolish to dream of recasting and remaking a classification over twenty-five years old to fit new theories." See also Dewey's article in *The Library Journal* for February 15, 1920, p. 151-6. His conservatism is most clearly expressed in his article in *Libraries*, May, 1931, p. 202-3.

educational orders; *apportionment* for economy of notation; *collocation* of closely related subjects for maximal efficiency in service. There are three ways: Specialized "revision," beginning with the subdivisions, to increase efficiency thru insertion and collocation; alteration in the order of the divisions to attain coherence; reconstruction from the foundations, the order of the main classes, the *systematic* tables, and the notation. To begin with the first is the most troublesome; to begin with the second is the most burdensome; to begin with the third is the most satisfactory; for collocation depends on coherence as well as on subordination, and coherence depends on fundamental order. So let us begin with the classes.

To attain such order it would be necessary to shift all the main classes except the first two, as was shown in the alternatives considered in section 3 of this chapter. Then the combination of the Arts in one class would leave a class free for Anthropology, Ethnology, and Medical Science; or else Culture Anthropology and Ethnology could be collocated with Sociology in Class 4, or Class 6, while Psychology, Education, Recreation, Hygiene, etc. could be collocated with Physical Anthropology in Class 3. Combining Languages and Literatures would leave another class free for the important Special and Applied Social Sciences, which thus could be classified in proximity to Religion, Ethics, Philanthropy, and Church Work. General Philosophy, General Science, Logic, Mathematics, and Natural Sciences should be brought into proximity in classes 1 and 2. Less drastic changes could be considered. We might begin with combining Philology and Literature in the 8 class; then we could move History up to the 4 class, or the 5, transferring Science to 3 and Anthropology and Sociology to 4. These or other shifts and combinations touched upon before would require from four to seven of the main classes to be shifted entire. This amounts to reconstruction. Complete reconstruction would be better still.

But suppose only two or three of the main classes were transferred. How much alteration of the divisions would be requisite for a passable coherence? In Philosophy we found 120, 130, and 150 inadequate and confused, and all the other divisions misrelated or misplaced. Only the division for General Philosophy would remain, and that is inadequate. In Religion the last three divisions should be shifted, the first two reclassified, the next two transferred, and the middle divisions shifted or reclassified. So, even if this class were not transferred *in toto,* it should be reclassified thruout. Sociology, even if not combined with the related sciences, Psychology, Anthropology, and Ethnology, we found so disordered that it would have to be reclassified from end to end. Philology, even if neither combined with Literature nor transferred, should for reasons indicated in preceding sections 7 and 8 be reclassified; but, if combined, eight of the ten divisions would be vacated. In the Natural Sciences the three biological sciences should be entirely reclassified; so should Physics and a large part of Mathematics. Astronomy should be transferred, and Paleontology too; so Chemistry would have to be shifted, and Chemical Technology should be collocated with it. The division for Science in general should be reclassified so as to provide for many special aspects and topics of general scope, as well as for the *forms* in more convenient collocation. Even if the Useful Arts retain an entire class, Chemical Technology and Commerce should be transferred, Building should be next to Engineering, and the Mechanic Trades should be reclassified. These alterations would involve all but the first two divisions. In the Fine Arts there is less need for shifting divisions than for altering subdivisions, particularly in the first and last divisions. Literature should be reclassified, for, tho historical in detail, its order reverses the historical, and it is impractical both in plan and in detail. History, even if not transferred, should be wholly reclassified so that Europe should have two divisions, those for America should be transferred to precede Asia and Africa, and Biography should be subordinated and distributed. At the same time provision should be made for general and special aspects, movements, and relations, and for description, travels, national traits, memoirs, and documents under the history of the several nations and the description of the countries. Scotland's history must have been placed first to placate the dour Scotsman for the neglect of his literature. But that compliment is spoiled by placating Ireland next. Regarding the divisions of the General class, where classification is indeed mainly for practical purposes, it would be more practical to place Journalism with Literature in General, or with other kinds of Business. It was for collections of newspapers that 070 was originally intended. Societies' publications might better be collocated with Collections, and this with Polygraphy. These changes would involve perhaps half of the divisions of this class. Similarly unsatisfactory is the analogous first division of each class. Under the general subject, the History and the Education should be collocated with the Philosophy and the Compends, while the Periodicals and the Society publications should be collocated with the Collections, Essays, and Polygraphy. These alterations would involve changing all but the first subdivision wherever this mnemonic schedule is applied.

From all the foregoing facts and considerations we must conclude that, if the principles we have adduced apply fundamentally to a classification of knowledge and therefore practically to a classification for libraries, all the main classes of the Decimal Classification except the first two would have to be shifted. If moreover a systematic coherence in the order of the divisions be indeed requisite to practical efficiency, all the divisions of Philosophy, except the first, and about half of the General class, should be shifted or internally reclassified. That means that of the hundred divisions *ninety-four* would have to be changed — not merely "revised" — and given new numbers in schedules and in index. Again, even if the main classes be not shifted, none except the Fine Arts is free from the need of reclassification not only by alteration of the order of the divisions but also thruout the details. In each of the classes this would involve from six to nine of the ten divisions. Finally, many, or perhaps most, of the subdivisions that would escape the major alterations would need more or less reclassification. To begin with such minor revision is likely to prove the most troublesome method of all. Continual "revision" had confessedly proved very troublesome to Dr. Dewey, his assistants, and his specialists; and the results are now very unsatisfactory. Expansions have only increased the burden, the complexity, and the confusion. We cannot avoid the conclusion that adequate alterations would involve nearly all divisions in all classes and would in effect amount to entire reconstruction.

10. Conclusions

This astounding conclusion rests on the facts adduced, and in it there is but a minimum of opinion. The writer himself would hardly believe it, if he had not made this investigation. Most competent classifiers will admit that the deficiencies pointed out in the foregoing pages are important and that the changes indicated are really desirable or requisite, if classification is to serve as it should.

If then reconstruction is requisite to adequacy, why should the structure again be laid upon the same constricted basis of decimal notation? It has been shown that the base of ten is too short and the area of a hundred divisions insufficient. Nine are too few main classes, because there are at least five fundamental sciences, besides Philosophy, Mathematics, Astronomy, Geology,

Anthropology, History, Religion, the Arts, the Languages and the Literatures. We must conclude that reconstruction on the decimal basis would be altogether impractical.

It has been shown that the decimal notation is simple only under the simplest conditions, and even then it is no simpler than a notation of letters; and, when it comes to complexity, a notation of letters and figures combined proves much simpler than the lengthy and complicated notation of the expansions of the D. C. Since the scientific specialists, whose assistance Dr. Dewey has acknowledged, have been brought into the service, simplicity has been overwhelmed with an imposing but unmanageable maze of complications.

The adoption of the Decimal Classification by the International Institute of Bibliography reflected no credit on that institution and little on the classification. If one will look up the history of the enterprise, one will find that the D. C. was strongly disapproved. When finally adopted, chiefly because of the Arabic notation, which was regarded as more international than the international Roman letters, it would probably have been much modified, if Dr. Dewey had not objected behind the fortification of his copyright. At all events there were cordial compromises.[15] If any committee proposed to prepare a better classification and notation in outline, to be elaborated later, as the D. C. and the C. D. have both been elaborated,[16] the enthusiasm of a few influential

[15] M. La Fontaine was very polite, when at the St. Louis Conference he intimated that despite faults and lacks the thousand sections would remain almost unchanged, while the improvements would be for the most part confined to the generalia and the *formal* and specific details of expansions.

[16] How these details were elaborated appears in an interesting article by Mr. H. V. Hopwood in *The Library Association Record* for June, 1907. He emphasized that the notation of these expansions was fundamentally changed: "the difference which exists between the two classifications is not a difference of bulk alone; it does not even rest on the revision that the original has undergone; it is fundamental; and the changes introduced are not in the main those of detail and definition, but rather those of form based on a system

persons evidently prevailed. The ready-to-hand make-shift was adopted and unfortunately established. From the viewpoint of the organization of knowledge, this was a deplorable set-back.

Those international undertakings antedated the International Congress of Arts and Science at St. Louis, which contemplated the interrelation of the branches of knowledge. Before that time the tendency to analysis and specialization was prevalent in scientific developments. It was specialization that such a subject classification and index as Dewey's was expected to serve. This is especially true of that system's expansions. But the notion that specific subjects, however confused and dispersed, may by an alphabetical index be located and brought together for reference and research we have termed "the subject-index illusion." The D. C. is still advocated by those who see classification thru the subject-index illusion.

To a librarian who still argues that the systematic order of classes and divisions is unimportant and that all practical needs may be served by specific subject classification and alphabetic index, we repeat that this stand involves the negation of the fundamental principles of classification. Such a librarian may lack understanding of the difference between the chief function of classification and the ordinary service of the specific alphabetic

affecting the classification throughout." This may be somewhat overstated, but both this and M. La Fontaine's statement are in a measure true. In *La Classification décimale* the structure of the Decimal Classification is unchanged, but the superstructure is "fundamentally" changed in details and in notations for these details. This superstructure is described in the introduction to *La Classification Décimale* and in the International Institute for Documentation, Publication No. 169, where the account fills over forty large pages, not including the geographical subdivisions. Relative to these elaborations there were interesting proposals and discussions at the Conference of the International Institute in 1932. *La Classification Décimale* has been advocated and defended by Dr. S. C. Bradford, of The Science Museum Library, South Kensington, London, in many articles and recently in Berwick Sayers' *Introduction to Library Classification*, 5th ed., 1938, Chapter XIII. On the other side see the last page of Section 6 of this Chapter.

subject-catalog. That seems to be the position of Dr. Dewey himself, as appears in some of his defensive statements, while some of his clear and succinct affirmatives indicate the very opposites of the principles we have adduced.

Two basic principles of systematic classification are *subordination* and *collocation,* but these principles have been largely ignored in the Decimal Classification. The latter principle was indeed recognized, but no statement of the former principle appears in the Introduction, nor is the term in its index. It was of course taken for granted and applied here and there as a matter of course, but not consistently and fundamentally.

The Decimal Classification is disqualified as an organization of knowledge both structurally and functionally. It does not embody the natural, scientific, logical, and educational orders. It fails to apply consistently the fundamental principles of classification. It is disproportionate in its expansions, tho elsewhere lacking in requisite specific details. In Applied Science, in Literature, and in History it is encumbered with details valueless for library services. It lacks systematic schedules to economize such details. It is too often inadequate in its specifications and antiquated in its terminology. Its index is far from complete. It is inefficient in classifying the modern literature of specific topics and special aspects of general subjects. It is confusing in its complexities. It is simple, we repeat, only when it deals with utter simplicity. Its notation is never simpler than the shorter notation of letters, or of letters and figures combined; and, with expansion or combination, it exceeds the limit of economy and becomes increasingly complicated. Its author's claims that it is simple, practical, and elastic are all denied on the strength of the facts arrayed in the preceding pages. It is simple only in comparison with systems that are extremely complicated. Nor is its vogue among librarians and even among scientists and business men especially significant, except of the fact that there was nothing else readily available, or, as some would say, nothing better. It is an antiquated and inadaptable product based on the plan of an undergraduate of six decades ago and never coherent or scientific or practical. And now it is hopelessly beyond reconstruction. Its international acceptance for bibliographical developments is offset by the finding that for a bibliographical organization of knowledge it is altogether too incoherent and unsystematic.

Radical reconstruction of the international classification has during recent years been proposed and discussed in the meetings of the International Institute. The proposed basis is interesting but of questionable validity. The inadequacy of the decimal base and the futility of less radical revision has been shown in the preceding study.

In the foregoing pages destructive criticism has been interspersed with considerable constructive suggestion; and such, Dr. Dewey has said, is welcome. It seems fitting here to repeat the following sentences from the concluding paragraph of an article written controversially many years ago: "Destructive criticism is less pleasant to the writer than constructive work. But a sense of duty dominates this purpose, and the interest in the progress of an art, for library classification, however scientific, is an art rather than a science. However strong the condemnation of the Decimal Classification may be, its compiler is above any discredit. His service to librarianship, extending to many matters besides classification, has been constructive in the highest degree."

CHAPTER XI

CUTTER'S "EXPANSIVE" CLASSIFICATION

1. THE "E. C." HISTORICALLY CONSIDERED

Charles A. Cutter, one of the most esteemed of the past generation of American librarians, originally devised this classification for the Boston Athenæum and published an outline in 1879.[1] During the next decade the system was modified and developed, and in the years 1891-93 it was published by the author as the *Expansive Classification.* The Boston Athenæum then had about 170,000 volumes. For smaller libraries the scheme was simplified. The term *expansive* implied that the system might be progressively expanded as a library increased, while the notation would merely have the prescribed additional factors suffixed.

The *First* Classification, "for a very small library," provided only eleven captions, each marked by a distinctive letter, except that English Fiction had two letters YF. The *Second* Classification occupied but three pages. Under History and Geography it introduced eight numbers mnemonic for the chief countries. The *Third* Classification assigned all the capital letters except P to main classes, adding BR to distinguish Religion from Philosophy (B). The *Fourth* Classification provided furthermore for the chief foreign

[1] In *The Library Journal,* v. 4, p. 237-40. In this article Mr. Cutter with his usual lucidity professed the principles of collocation and of the subordination of the specific to the generic: ". . . . the grouping of classes ought to bring together those which have a practical connection, so that when a reader is using any division of the library he would have on either hand the classes of books which he is most likely to wish to use at the same time. . . . . But it has had a strong shaping influence on my scheme, both in regard to the order of the main classes and of their divisions, being sometimes modified in the latter case by the usual practice of putting the most general subdivisions first and the special sections afterward." (p. 237).

languages and literatures. It covered six pages. The *Fifth* Classification filled 22 pages, was more systematic, and introduced a few marks of three factors and even of four, e.g. CBBD Bible Dictionaries, and Y39F French Fiction. The *Sixth* Classification extended to 51 pages, providing about a thousand subdivisions. While most of its marks were short, it had a rather large proportion of four-place marks (exclusive of the mnemonic numerals). A single volume of 160 pages contained the six classifications printed *seriatim*, followed by an index for all, and preceded by a brief introduction. Thus the term *expansive* applies to the classification, not merely to the notation. This feature is not, however, distinctive of the system; for the Decimal Classification had been expansive too, and other systems had used various expansive notations.

The first six classifications differed little from the original scheme, but in notation there was a radical change, also considerable alteration in apportionment, and in terminology. Originally Mr. Cutter's aim was to enlarge the capacity by utilizing all the thirty-five main classes. For geographical divisions, which were regarded as important, the 35 divisions of Class A, Geography of the East, and of Class B, Geography of the West, provided for 70 countries. Some of the letters of those divisions would become intensively mnemonic in subdivision of any subject, E for England, F for France, G for Germany, I for Italy, etc. But this must have been found more confusing than mnemonic, for the letters, each being used for two countries, were in truth not distinctive. Subsequently he gave this up, and used only figures for countries. This enabled him for the time being to say that the figures were used for countries only, and the letters never for countries. In the order of the subjects one notable change was the ill-advised removal of Paleontology from Biology to Geology.

For large libraries the *Seventh Classification* was elaborated during the decade that ensued between the publication of the system in 1893 and Mr. Cutter's decease in 1903; and it was gradually installed in The Forbes Library at Northampton, during the nine years he was Librarian there. It was published gradually in folded sheets, with several indexes, but without a general index, and without an introduction. There were, however, copious notes and instructions thruout the schedules. Tho nearly complete, the system has not — so far as the writer knows — been made complete; and no extensive revisions have been published, nor are they likely to be. Mr. Cutter was assisted by several collaborators, Mr. Richard Bliss, then Librarian of the Redwood Library in Newport, who elaborated most of the scientific classes; Dr. G. E. Wire, of the Worcester Law Library, whose classification of law was adapted, and whose classification of Medical Science, made previously for the Newberry Library of Chicago, was also incorporated; and Professor H. N. Gardiner, of Smith College then, who worked out the classification of Psychology. Mr. William P. Cutter, a nephew of the author, developed certain scientific subjects, especially Chemistry.

The Seventh Classification differed so extensively from the preceding expansions that the expansive principle was virtually forgone. The system had lost its distinctive feature. It has already been expanded into the fourth factor of its capacity, and, except where this expansion is not filled, further expansion by subdivision would involve notation exceeding the economic limit.

Advantaged by years of development, the Seventh Classification was indeed much improved. Some subjects, e. g. Botany and Zoölogy, were reclassified thruout; others, e. g. Physics and Social Sciences, were so extensively changed that the schedules, and the notations, are entirely different; still others were so much developed and improved that in comparison the Sixth Classification becomes utterly inadequate. Moreover the index to the earlier volume does not fit the later classification. The six earlier stages belong to the more remote past; it is only the Seventh Classification that we shall hereafter consider.

2. Disproportion, Complexity, and System-mad Mnemonics

The second prominent feature was the "Local List," as Mr. Cutter called his geographical schedule. His notation combined the twenty-six letters of the alphabet, for general subjects, with the nine figures, made mnemonic for "preliminaries" to any subject and preceded by a dot to distinguish them, and with the numbers from 11 to 99, without the dot, made mnemonic for countries, etc. The Local List was expanded to 31 pages and complicated in various ways: parts of countries, cities, and parts of cities might be indicated by mnemonic letters, or initial letters, or these followed by so-called *Cutter numbers*. For instance, Yellowstone Park appears in the special index with the mark 933Ye3. Mr. Cutter thus forsook the simplicity he had professed: ". . . the letters never being used to signify countries, and the figures never being used to signify any other subjects but countries."[2] And in complexity his schedules are system-mad, more complicated than those of the Library of Congress, and more excessive in the notation. Figures, or numbers, are less *intensively mnemonic* than letters. Mnemonics are not worth so much complexity.

For most general subjects, it is true, the marks are very simple and brief, and for most of the primary divisions. Such economy inheres in notation by letters. That efficiency would be greater, however, if the apportionment were better adapted and the relations of subjects more logical. Hm is a short mark indeed for Money, and it is mnemonic. But Taxation is a big subject too, and it would be cramped in the subdivisions Htc-Htm of Public Finance (Ht), while Tariffs (Hu) and Protection and Free Trade (Hv) should really be subordinate to Taxation and to Commerce. To

[2] A. L. A. Conference, 1899, *Papers and Proceedings*, p. 43. This was repeated elsewhere, and it has occasionally been quoted by others, erroneously.

avoid longer marks under HTC, local taxation should (a note there advises) be marked by the local list under Public Finance (HT). So books on Taxation in France would not be distinct from Public Finance of that nation, unless by a distinguishing letter added to HT39, which is no shorter than HTC39. This is one objection to using numbers for mnemonic marks for countries.

The longest and most complex marks in the system result from the use of such mnemonic factors. A few specimens follow. For comparison, the marks of our proposed system for precisely the same subjects are added in the right-hand column:

Western Empire of Rome	F3659 (or F36U),	LXA
Napoleon, History and Biography	F39442 (or F39FN),	MSN
Constitutional History of the U.S.	F8397 (or F83W),	NEC
History of Germans in the U.S.	F8399G (or F83ZG),	N14G
Social History of England	F4599 (or F45Y),	MUH
Municipal Government of Chicago	JW895C·A,	RVBC4
History of Modern Music	VV135,	VVQ
History of the Drama, General	ZYDD,	YX8
Bibliography of French Drama in the 18th Century	ZWZYPHAD (or ZWZY39AHD),	XSDS2
Bibliography of History of Elizabethan England	ZWF45EZ (or ZW45F49),	MVK2

Sometimes the more general subject thus has a longer mark than subjects logically subordinate to it: the general sub-science, Mechanics, has the mark LHE, while the special subject, Dynamics of a Particle, has LI. The important general subject, Electrical Engineering, is forced back into TDZ, while the following division TE is assigned to the specific subject, Electric Current Generation. Worse still, TD is for Steam Engineering, to which it is absurd to subordinate Electrical Engineering. Folk-lore is too important a subject, with too many topical and geographical subdivisions, to start its expansion from the cramped corner PZW, with its mark a letter too long. Similar disproportion appears elsewhere in short marks being allotted to unimportant subjects. Divisions SD to SI are given to Construction and Building, SF being wasted on Outside Covering for Buildings and SH for Openings, Doors, Windows, etc. Then, while Chemical Technology is cramped in RZ, and

Electrical Technology in Ry, the divisions Ro to Rx are lavished on Domestic Economy, Rr being squandered on Collective Housekeeping and Rt on the Care of the House — important subjects, to be sure, but not to be equalized with the immense requirement of Chemical Technology.

The more general subjects should have the shorter, more distinctive marks; they should be basic to future subdivision and subordination; but it is evident that Mr. Cutter did not consistently carry out the fundamental principle of subordination. It was a lack of principle that no classification can live down in the face of authentic criticism.

Some important subjects have insufficient subdivision, for instance, History of Education, Sociology, Social Psychology, Socialism, Charity, Commerce and Business. In some of these contemporary development is manifestly lacking. Other subjects, particularly in Mathematics and the Natural Sciences, have entirely too much detail of little use, and consequently their notation is too lengthy. Mathematics has 40 pages of schedules, Geology and Paleontology 17 pages, Botany 29, and Zoölogy 88 pages. In contrast with these, Economics is allowed but eight pages, and there Banking has but three subdivisions. Sociology, Criminology, Charity, and Insurance are similarly undeveloped. Tho Education was allotted sixteen divisions of Class I, hardly enough, the great subject is merely outlined in six pages, and this outline does not fit the immense literature that has arisen since. These subjects would require reclassification, and for large libraries they would require expansion, for which the provision seems inadequate, especially for Sociology. Yet the schedules for Mathematics and the Natural Sciences (Classes L to P, inclusive) [3] have large wastes of elaborate detail useless even for large

[3] These classes were elaborated by Mr. Richard Bliss, of the Redwood Library, Newport. It is not likely that his library — nor Mr. Cutter's — had embodied so many very special subjects in collections of books and pamphlets. It seems more likely that those schedules were compiled from the contents-pages and paragraph captions of scientific treatises. But from unpleasant criticism of Mr. Bliss the writer would refrain, considering that he bears the same family name.

and special libraries. Classifications for libraries need not be so elaborate as specialized classifications for notes, clippings, etc., nor so complicated as classified subject-catalogs. For example, tho a place is needed under Mathematics for Determinants (LDD) and perhaps for Special subjects subordinate to that, there is not practical need for the schedule to specify Centrosymmetric Determinants (LDDK), and certainly not the particular brand, Zeipel's (LDDLF). Under Hydraulics there is not likely to be a group of books on Overflow on a Dam (LIWN), but, even if that were possible, it were very impractical to specify such details as Incomplete Overflow (LIWNI). This is altogether too much overflow of classification. Again under the technology of Railroads it may be requisite for a special library to provide for Parlor Cars (SVR), but hardly to distinguish Corridor Cars (SVRC) and Observation Cars (SVRA).

The apportionment of the classification to the notation is certainly less economical than it should be. This is not merely a matter of detail but also largely of structural plan.

3. Less Scientific and Practical Than Supposed

Cutter's Classification has enjoyed the reputation of being admirably logical in its scheme and adequately scientific in its structure. Dr. Richardson, years ago, declared it to be the most logical and scientific of modern bibliographic schemes, and this was then probably true.[4] Mr. Berwick Sayers a few years ago re-echoed this praise, and he added, with regard to his own findings, that: "It has all the virtues we have premised in a good classification of suggestion and elucidation in relation to other schemes; and it answers the soundest canons of construc-

[4] *Classification, theoretical and practical,* 1st ed., 1901, p. 206-7. There tribute is beautifully and deservedly paid to Mr. Cutter's scholarship, intelligence, modesty, and altruism.

tion in a remarkable degree."[5] The first statement seems too sweeping, while too vague to criticise; but the last statement is positive. We deny it positively, and this denial rests on all that we have written in our chapter on the principles of classification for libraries and in this chapter of criticism. The remarkable thing is that this classification should have been regarded as sound or scientific or practical. What is meant by these attributes? They are merited tribute, not discerning criticism.

This reputation of the Expansive Classification was not justified, and we shall see some of the reasons. The scheme divides serially into four main divisions: Philosophy, History, Science, and Art. But these divisions, while basic and valid, should each parallel the whole series of subjects graded by speciality, as we have shown;[6] and this should imply a cross-classification. Tho the order of the main classes was indeed logical and philosophic, it was not correctly scientific even for the science of its decade, and the less so for the present. It logically carries out to unscientific conclusions the division of science from philosophy, which has been found untenable and impractical in handling the problems, the studies, and the books. Psychology is no longer a mere branch of philosophy but has joined hands with Physiology, taken up its abode with Anthropology, in the domain of Biology, with which it has attained to equal rank as a fundamental science. And this was established a half-century before by Comte and Spencer.

[5] *Manual of Classification*, p. 155.

See also p. 158-60. On this last page there is a curious error in ascribing to a notation of letters a capacity—". . . . in mathematical expression a power of 26^{26} as against 10^{10} in Dewey." Now the former number vies with some of the recent cosmophysical dreams of Eddington and Jeans, and the latter is just a cool ten billion. What was meant was of course only 26^2 and 10^2, as the author showed in his next sentence, by giving the figures that those squares represent.

[6] See our preceding book, p. 252 and the Synoptic Table on p. 302-3.

Education is no longer a branch of Sociology but is largely applied psychology, and is closely related to Anthropology. Religion too is no longer merely philosophic, or theologic, but has essential historical, anthropological, and social relations. The Social Sciences should not so precede the natural sciences but should follow as dependent on them as well as on history and on philosophy; for Sociology depends on Anthropology and Ethnology, and these on Biology, which depends on Chemistry and on Geography. Geography does not belong thus on the human and economic side to History alone, but on its physical side it depends equally on Geology. Statistics does not, as there, apply to the Social Sciences only, but is a general method of science of recognized importance to physics, astronomy, biology, and anthropology. These relations have become scientifically manifest in the books and in the studies.

From those major divisions many illogical separations resulted. For example, Chemical Technology, and Electrical Technology, were widely separated from their respective sciences. Such separation is now untenable. The History of Ancient Rome is inconveniently separated from the History of Ancient Greece by the History of Modern Italy, and the History of Modern Rome is likewise separated from the History of Modern Italy by the History of Ancient Rome. The History of the United States in F83 is separated much too far from the History of England in F45. The separation of the several literary languages in Class X from their respective literatures in Class Y, and again the separation of these from their *histories* under the "Book Arts" in Class Z, is structurally inconsistent and must prove functionally inconvenient.

For the chief countries Social History is marked by adding 99 to the mark for the country, but there is no provision for the Economic History, nor for the Constitutional History of the country. The auxiliary sciences are treated inadequately and some of them are not recognized at all under History. Paleography is subordinated only to Writing, under the "Book Arts" in Zd. Diplomatics too is mentioned there but not under History. Rhetoric is under the "Book Arts" instead of under "Expressive Arts," and to it is subordinated Journalism rather than to Publishing (Zl). Mining as one of the "Extractive Arts" is separated from Engineering as one of the "Constructive Arts." Bacteriology is subordinated to Microscopy. In Physics the order, Optics, Heat, Electricity, is antiquated, or unscientific. Mineralogy and Crystallography should not be separated from Chemistry by such unrelated subjects as Meteorology, Microscopy, Bacteriology, and Astronomy.

There are alternative or duplicated positions for many subjects, but the schedules are complicated, and clear references are not always provided where requisite. For instance, under Mathematics there is a caption for Life Insurance (Leg), that is, for the mathematical and actuarial branch of the subject, but that lacks reference to the main subject in Iil, which is not subdivided and which has no reference to the branch Leg. Statistics (Lb) has no reference to Mathematical treatment of Statistics (Lef). Then Theory of Functions under Algebra is placed in Lda and under Analysis in Lfan, while the studies of special functions appear on other pages, Analytic Functions in Lfm, Algebraic Functions in Lfr, Elliptic Functions in Lfu, etc., but all without references either way. Of course, if Mr. Cutter had lived to complete the compilation and indexing, he would have discovered and corrected most of these lacks and inconsistencies. Incomplete and imperfect as they are, the schedules need thoro revision by those who use them.[1]

More important is the lack of provision for new subjects which were already well-rooted in Mr. Cutter's day and have since grown to the full stature of sub-sciences. Educational Psychology was utterly unprovided for

[1] This need was painfully manifest in the home of the classification (not its birthplace), when an inquisitive examination of the shelf-list for Sociology and for Education revealed classification so inadequate for such a library that, for these subjects, it was little better than none at all.

either under Education or under Psychology, yet Stanley Hall in Worcester was contemporary with Cutter in Boston and Northampton, and not so very distant. Eugenics was not provided for either under Anthropology or under Biology; yet Galton too was contemporary with Cutter. Biochemistry was not recognized under Biology, tho Physiological Chemistry has a place under Zoölogy. The important subjects of Industrial Economics, Business, Commerce, Immigration, Social Amelioration, Philanthropy and Charity were treated so inadequately in comparison with the impractical over-elaboration of certain scientific and technical subjects that on this ground alone the system may be declared inadequate to the modern requirements of libraries serving the interests of serious readers.

It is evident that Cutter's Classification is neither so scientific nor so practical and economical as his appreciators have supposed it to be. Scientific detail does not make a scientific system. Nor does logical division always make a consistent and efficient library classification. This system, even if it were extensively revised, modernized, and simplified, would still have fundamental and pervasive faults which are ineradicable by mere revision. Reconstruction had better be grounded on less faulty foundations and carried out on sounder principles.

4. A Tribute, A Judgment, and An Epitaph

There is much to appreciate and admire in Cutter's Classification, and in its compiler's devotion; but that is another matter, and our conclusions are affected but little by those considerations. It is over half a century since the system was planned. It is more than a third of a century since its author's decease. Tho incomplete and inadequate, it has had its day and has enjoyed a reputation greater perhaps, as now appears, than it has really deserved. Its distinctive *expansive* character was soon forgone. That was a questionable advantage anyhow, for by the time a library had grown from the third to the sixth classification, it would have needed more thoro reclassification, which would have cost little more than changing the marks on books and cards. The mnemonic features became too complicated. Its author set too much store by mnemonics. Neither systematic nor intensive mnemonics are worth such complexity, and in such complexity they are not worth much. From disproportion and from mnemonic complexities the notation proves uneconomical. The classes for Mathematics, the natural sciences, and certain technologies were over-expanded with detail that, however scientific, is impractical and burdensome, and now much of it antiquated. The classes for the social sciences, economics, and education are very meager and inadequate. There is too little provision for subjects that were new in that decade, and for those of the present there is of course much less provision. The classification has not been kept up to date, improved, or revised, nor is it likely to be in the future. It is not in conformity with the order of the sciences as conceived in the consensus. It does not embody the principles of classification for libraries.

Yet, here lies the library classification that has embodied *some* valid principles and has served as a stepping-stone to the future. Those principles, tho imperfectly embodied, have been in a sense prophetic, and they have aided to redeem the problem from the "subject-index illusion." High respect and gratitude are due from those who have followed.

CHAPTER XII

THE LIBRARY OF CONGRESS CLASSIFICATION

1. Some General Grounds

Cutter's classification, we have said, is a thing of the past, tho still living in its influences and its tradition. The classification of the great Library of Congress is preeminently a thing of the present. But it is present in a historical situation. This classification was planned for the Library of Congress, and it has arisen from the historical conditions of that great library. It is the leading classification of the present, not only because of prestige and service, but because on the whole it is less unsatisfactory than the others are. Tho the Decimal Classification still holds its place in thousands of libraries, few large libraries and hardly any college and university libraries have adopted it since the Library of Congress Classification became a fairly complete compilation rendering national service.[1] This classification has accordingly been adopted, entire or in part, by many libraries, and it will continue to be accepted until better coöperative classification is realized.

When we say libraries have adopted the Library of Congress Classification, we mean they think they have, that is, their librarians do. No library, no librarian has adopted, or can or would adopt it. It is in the Library of Congress itself and there only. Its schedules and tables are what librarians adopt, as they are what the

[1] *Cf.* "Library of Congress Classification for College Libraries," by J. C. M. Hanson, in *Library Journal* for February 15, 1921.

Librarian of Congress himself has adopted. This may seem a bit of sophistry, but it appears to be necessary to remind librarians, who in regard to the Decimal Classification have been so prone to confuse notation with classification, that there is a real distinction between a classification of a library's books and the schedules provided for continuing and expanding that classification. It is the D. C. original thousand, more or less adapted, that have been so extensively adopted by small and medium-sized libraries; and its several special "expansions" have been adopted more or less adaptively by individual special libraries. Whether the Library of Congress itself now uses or will ever utilize all of its detail is a question open to doubt. But, without question, no other library can or will utilize all of it. Librarians understand this on taking thought, and in taking parts of the classification or details from the schedules they are not unmindful of it; but some of them seem to forget it when they speak of adopting the Library of Congress Classification. What they really adopt is a schedule, an aid, a means.

This elaborate classification contains an immense amount of accurately compiled detail in careful arrangement. This is a great credit to the collaborators; and its publication has been an important bibliographic service on the part of the national library. It stands as a repository on which other classifications are drawing and may well continue to draw in the future.

The International Institute of Bibliography has rendered a similar service in publishing its *Classification Décimale*, apart from its great bibliographic catalog and other bibliographic services. That compilation, more elaborate in parts than even that of the Library of Congress, has been superposed on Dewey's classification, which, despite its faults and unfitness, has been faithfully maintained. It is impressively rich in materials that are available for other compilation, tho without the ingenious notation, which with all its amazing complexity is inadaptable to library uses. It should not be supposed, however, that the details of these classifications, mostly compiled a decade or two ago, are adequate without alteration and addition in new classifications.

But detail, elaboration, schedules do not make a system of classification, nor a classification of books. Whether the Institute of Bibliography and the Library of Congress could have made better systems and been served better by them is not the question before us; but whether libraries in the future could be served better by other classifications, that is the very question for us to consider as we proceed.

The fundamental principles of classification and the developing organization of knowledge have been too little regarded by librarians — and indeed too little by scientists. But now that the principles have been recognized and the tendencies to organization and coöperation have become manifest, we find that we are immersed in a historical situation. The specializing scientists are in danger of being overcome in the jungles of their specialties. The general readers are in jeopardy of being submerged in the floods from the commercial presses. The librarians are in peril of being swamped in their alphabetic-subject-index illusion. Educators are entangled in the maze of interrelated but dispersed subjects. Thinkers, writers, and talkers are distraught in a Babel of confusions.

Yet the situation is not hopeless. We need go to neither extreme. The interrelated branches of knowledge and study are reducible to comparative order and system.

On the principles of logical *subordination* and consistent *collocation* there may be construction, if not unification, and organization with adaptability. That system will be most thoroly practical, most efficient in service, most satisfactory to users of libraries, and most valuable educationally, which is most consistent with the recognized orders of nature, of science, and of education.

It is from this broad view that we shall proceed to survey the main structure of the classification of the Library of Congress. We shall then pass on to details, and to the problems that emerge from the historical situation.

2. The Unscientific Order of the Main Classes and Sub-Classes

We have seen that this classification resembles Cutter's and that his was apparently based on Edwards' and thus indirectly related to Brunet's. When in the last years of the past century the new Librarian of Congress was considering the problems of reorganizing his great library, Dewey's classification was passing its prime without having lived down the criticisms that had been brought to bear upon it, and Cutter's classification was riding its wave of merited esteem and rising influence. The committee that determined the plan was probably affected by these considerations. The faults of Cutter's scheme had not been brought to light; no better system was then available; no classifier was prepared to outline a sounder basis for the committee, on which Mr. Cutter was well represented; there seemed no positive need for seeking this; the purpose was practical; and the situation probably required results without too labored undertaking and unnecessary delay. A promising opportunity was missed. Consequently an extensive structure was reared on a foundation that we shall show to be faulty and unscientific without being practical or economical. The elaboration has been nevertheless immense, and the delay has been proportionate. This delay, however, has had its compensations, and the elaboration has become a monument to the labor of love of those who have devoted some of the best of their lives to this highly valued service.

The order of the main classes followed Cutter's in part and was partly determined by conditions in the Library of Congress and other practical considerations. It is nothing like the natural and logical order of the sciences and studies. "The system devised," said Mr. Martel, "has not sought to follow strictly the scientific order of subjects. It has sought rather convenient sequence of the various groups, considering them as groups of books, not as groups of mere subjects." [2] But convenient sequence, or collocation, of groups or classes or subjects depends on order consistent with the scientific and educational orders, and on logical subordination. Such order and collocation of subjects on shelves prove convenient to most readers who come in the subject-approach, whether for reference or research. The distinctions between group, class, and subject do not materially affect these principles. The order in question is as follows:

[2] Advocating the Classification before the A. L. A. Catalog Section, May, 1911 (*Proceedings*, p. 230-2), also in the *Report of the Librarian of Congress for 1901*, p. 234. Mr. Martel more fully presented the case in *The Library Journal* for August, 1911, p. 410-16. The system has been ably defended by Mr. J. C. M. Hanson, who had much to do with planning it, in *The Library Journal* for February 15, 1921, and in other articles. Mr. Hanson tells there of a preliminary plan considered by him and Miss Olive Jones in 1896. Mr. Berwick Sayers in his *Canons of Classification*, Chapter VI, and again in his *Manual of Classification*, Chapter XVI, is appreciative in some respects but gives some very discerning criticism, showing the resemblance to Cutter's system, finding fault with the fundamentals, the unscientific order of the main classes, the lack of coherence, the unnecessary repetition, the resulting bulk, and the uneconomical notation.

A General Works — Polygraphy
B Philosophy — Religion
C History — Auxiliary Sciences
D History and Topography (except America)
E America (General) and United States (General)
F United States (Local) and America except the United States
G Geography — Anthropology
H Social Sciences
J Political Science
K Law
L Education
M Music
N Fine Arts
P Language and Literature
Q Science
R Medicine
S Agriculture
T Technology
U Military Science
V Naval Science
Z Bibliography and Library Science

Five of the letters, I, O, W, X, and Y, have not been assigned subjects. That three of these come at the end does not matter much, for the whole series is unsystematic. There are three mnemonics: G for Geography, M for Music, and T for Technology. They may not have been purposed; but neither are they important.

The main practical objection is the lack of "convenient sequence," but this may not make much difference in the Library of Congress. In smaller libraries there would be little convenience in passing from Law to Education, from Literature to Science, from Medicine to Agriculture, from Religion to History. Moreover, in the scientific and educational views, it is illogical to place the Social Sciences before the Sciences.

The difference between the order of the main classes of this system and that of Cutter may be summarized briefly: if Anthropology and Ethnology were removed from Geography and restored to their proper place after Zoölogy, if Education were brought back from Law to follow Social Sciences in Class I, if Classes M, N, and P were made again to follow instead of preceding the sciences and technologies, if Sports and Games, Athletics and Recreation were brought from under Anthropology and Ethnology in GV and replaced under the Arts ahead of Music, the differences that would remain would be subordinate or minor.

But the following objections are not minor. Biology is similarly subordinated to Natural History, and Psychology to Philosophy, whereas both should be treated as fundamental sciences, and they have a better right to this than Sociology and Economics. Then Paleontology belongs to Biology rather than to Geology, tho there is difference of opinion regarding this relation. Physics should not be separated from Mathematics by Astronomy, despite the olden relation between these boon companions, for the modern relations to mathematical physics are undeniably closer. Chemical Technology and Electrical Engineering can not feasibly be dissevered from the respective sciences as both these systems have done. Both separate Physical Geography from Geology, but in the Library of Congress the distance is much the greater, GB to QE, in a stack of many tiers. The relations of Psychology to Anthropology, to Sociology, and to Education are much more important than those to Logic and Metaphysics, Æsthetics and Ethics (BF to BC and BD, BH and BJ). Moreover Religion, in its relation to human life, human nature, and society and ethics, should be placed in relation to Anthropology, Ethnology, and Psychology rather than to Philosophy, tho Theology has indeed a good claim to companion with Philosophy. Mythology should not, however, be separated from Folk-lore by such distance as that between BL and GR. Physical Anthropology in GN should not be separated from Zoölogy in QL and Human Anatomy and Physiology in QM and QP. Hygiene in RA should not be so remote from Recreation in GV. Ethnology and Prehistoric Archeology in GN should not be so far from History of Civilization in CB, and had better precede this subject as well as descriptive sociology. In fact placing History ahead of Science produces this distortion, whether Anthropology, Ethnology, and Social Sciences are regarded as sciences or not. In the Social Sciences it would be practically more convenient to have Ethnography, Human Geography, Descriptive Sociology, and Political Science all precede Economics, in order to effectuate the manifold relations of this "dismal science" to the industrial and household arts. Moreover Sociology, General and theoretical (HM) is here inconsistently separated from Social Sciences, General (H), by some 300 pages of the schedules of Economics; but Sociology is usually regarded as a fundamental science to which the special and applied are subordinate.

In a broader aspect the separation of Science in Q from Philosophy in B involves such unscientific and unphilosophic consequences as severing the Philosopy of Science from the Philosophy of Knowledge, and more particularly separating Logic (BC) from Mathematics (QA), despite the claims of both logicians and mathematicians that their studies are inseparable. Even less logical is the severance of Æsthetics in BH from Fine Arts in N. We have shown how the special branches of study have their philosophic and scientific sides, which should usually be correlated in classification for libraries, as should the special histories of the subjects. Thus the philosophy of mathematics would have place under Mathematics. So the philosophy of Art, or Æsthetics, should be given its place under Fine Arts.

To summarize these faults: General Science is separated too far from Philosophy, Logic from Mathematics, Physics from Mathematics, Geology from Astronomy, Geography from Geology, and Geodesy from both. Paleontology is misplaced under Geology, and so is Mineralogy, which really belongs under Chemistry. Four of the seven fundamental sciences, Biology, Psychology, Sociology, and Religion (if we may venture to name this with the sciences in the broad sense of the term), which should have been assigned main classes, are subordinated in divisions, and Biology is even subsumed. Chemical Technology is separated from Chemistry and Electrical Technology from Electricity, which is not distinct in a division. Education is dissevered both from Psychology and from Sociology; and Psychology in BF is remote from Physiology in QP. Anthropology is on the one hand parted from Zoölogy, and on the other hand Ethnology is severed from the Social Sciences, which it really overlaps; and all these are on the wrong side of History. Mythology is not near Folk-lore; Religion and Ethics are not collocated with the social studies most vitally related to them, particularly Philanthropy and Charity, Social Welfare and Amelioration. History in general and History of Civilization (ethnic, social, and political) are separated from Ethnology, Prehistoric Archæology, and Sociology by the immense detailed content of national and local history. Economics should follow, not precede, Sociology and Political Science. Æsthetics, the philosophy of the Fine Arts, should be under the Fine Arts rather than under Philosophy. In short, the fundamental sciences are not assigned main classes and are misplaced, and many other important subjects are misrelated.

3. Some Appreciative Considerations

There are distinctive merits and comparative superiorities in this classification that to some extent are assets set off against these heavy liabilities. We shall mention some of them here, and others as occasion offers. To do justice to them, however, would require a longer section of this chapter, and there is not space for it. That meed of appreciative criticism and also some more constructive criticism remain for another occasion or for other critics to bring forward.

Apart from the rest of the system, the six classes Q to V are well grouped and are for the most part well subdivided, despite the faults pointed out above and the inconvenient separation of Therapeutics, Pharmacy, and Nursing (RM-RT) from Pathology and Practice of Medicine (RB and RC). Besides, there are placings that we would avoid, such as that of Domestic Science (TX) just ahead of Military Science (U). But in the Library of Congress the actual location may differ, as it did in 1922, when the last "Outline" was published, TX then being on the 11th deck of the South stack and U on the 13th deck. This exemplifies how the notation fails to be strictly correlative to the location, as in theory it should be — and in practice, as nearly as is possible under the conditions. But problems presented by Domestic Science, Photography, and Bacteriology have been met by defensible decisions, tho we differ. Domestic Science we would give a distinct caption under Arts. Bacteriology is broader than its human, or medical, relation, tho practically QR is a defensible place, coming between Physiology (QP) and Medicine (R). The most important relations of this sub-science are, however, those to Pathology (RB) and Botany of Bacteria, which would come in QK after 635; these are more general and more important than such special relations as those to sanitation, milk, water, soil, fertilizers, plant pathology, animal, and chemical industries.

The difficult problem of classifying the literature of Education is handled well, as shown in the convenient outline, tho it is not satisfactorily solved — if indeed it can be. It seems feasible to draw a clearer distinction between theory, philosophy, and principles on the one hand, and practice, teaching, and schools on the other hand, tho we admit that in handling the literature there must be frequent crossing of hands, as in much of piano music. But the sociological aspects, the moral and religious, and the "Types of Education" are on the whole more philosophic or theoretic in treatment or discussion. Then it would probably prove inconvenient to have sub-classification by countries under History of Education (LA), including Higher Education, and another still more extensive sub-classification by countries in the appendical divisions for Individual Institutions (LD-LG). But this is part of the Library of Congress, and other libraries need not follow it. The schedule for History of Philosophy is an excellent, thoro piece of work; but Logic should come next to Methodology. In English Literature, History and Collections (PR 1 to 1400) much well selected detail is presented and much of it is well arranged. Regarding the plan and treatment of Literature, however, we shall have to render less favorable criticism. To repeat, it is detail that we appreciate in this classification, and again correct detail, selected and arranged by competent specialists. But the structure that incorporates this available detail has, we have seen, too many serious faults.

4. Some Faulty Details and Omissions

Before proceeding to more distinctly practical considerations, let us consider the internal classification of some of the more important subjects. This is not mere fault-finding, but frankly it is finding faults, not in an impartial thoro survey, balancing faults against good points, but more thoroly than has been done before — yet not unfairly, considering our question whether this Classification is scientific and practical enough to justify its general acceptance by librarians despite its faults, objectionable features, complexities, and uneconomical ways.

Tho the classification of Psychology was fairly commendable when it was made twenty years ago, it fails to provide for the established divisions, Individual Psychology, Abnormal Psychology, and Psychology of Types. The term Differential Psychology, subordinated under Comparative Psychology, is not just equivalent to Individual Psychology and it has not become current. The subjects Individuality (697) and Personality (698) do not properly come under Comparative Psychology (BF 660); and they should not be so far from the psychology of Character (818). Then the psychology of the Unconscious, including Sleep, Dreaming, Hypnotism, etc. belongs not under Psychic Research — there appearing under the unusual term, Metapsychology — but rather under the psychology of Mental States and Abnormal Psychology. Psychiatry and the more inclusive subject Psychopathology should not be relegated to Practice of Medicine, but the nearly equivalent term Pathologic Psychology refers from BF 173 to that and to other places for the details. Psychoanalysis and Analytic Psychology are lacking both in schedule and in index, tho the former term appears in the schedule for Nervous Diseases (which is a little joke on Freud). Behavior and Behaviorism are both lacking from schedules and from index; and so are the terms Social Psychology, Folk-psychology, and Anthropological Psychology, all of which were coming forward in 1910 and have become very important since then. Social Psychology has, however, a place under Sociology in HM 251 (published in 1920), where the term Psychological Sociology is preferable. In this same analogy, the term Psychological Anthropology appears under Anthropology in GN 270, but this term again is not quite equivalent to Anthropological Psychology, which should be under Psychology, which indeed is subordinate to Anthropology. Most of the terms omitted — if not all of them — appeared regularly from 1910 onwards in the *Index to Psychology,* which is mentioned in the Prefatory Note to Class B as having been consulted. So this classification of Psychology, tho commendable in part, is not only misplaced (as was shown above) but is inadequate and dispersed.

Under Logic there should be a place for Formal Logic, but this is lacking from schedule and index. There is of course no provision for such recently developed subjects as "Humanistic" Logic. Manners, Etiquette, and Social Usages belong under Sociology, not under Philosophy after Ethics, in BJ.

On the general treatment of Anthropology and Ethnology we made some remarks in preceding pages. Tho anthropological anatomy and physiology, or Somatology, are usually differentiated from the studies of anatomy and physiology as related to Medical science, there are many special studies that are common ground for both branches. The Library of Congress, however, has Anthropology in GN and Human Anatomy and Physiology in QM and QP. Many subjects have place in both schedules. Pelvis, for instance, is GN 151 and Hip bone and Pelvis is QM 115. For Organs of Digestion there are three places, GN 206, QM 301, and QP 145, etc. Whether such special subjects are to be distributed under the several branches or unified under one of them, the branches, Physical Anthropology, Human Anatomy and Physiology, and Medical Science are too closely interrelated to be thus separated in GN, QM, QP, and R. Still closer is the relation of organ to function. The anatomical study of the organs of digestion is not distinct from the physiological; yet Stomach is marked QM

341 and QP 151, while Gastric Juice is in QP 193. Such special subjects are monographic and should not be duplicated; they should be classified under a caption: Digestion, Organs and Functions, Anatomy and Physiology. Physical Anthropology appears only in one place, subsumed in a parenthesis; this term and the following are lacking in the index: Culture (Cultural) Anthropology, Taxonomic Anthropology, Ethnic Sociology, Paleoethnology and Paleoanthropology, or Ethnic and Anthropological Archæology, which have to a large extent supplanted the term Prehistoric Archæology. Human Infancy, Longevity, and Vestigia are anthropological subjects that are better entitled to have place in this schedule and index than many that are duplicated there. Vestigia does not appear in QM either. Prehistoric Archæology should precede, not follow the ethnographic materials. Folk-lore should come between Ethnology and Ethnography, instead of being separate in GR, while Manners and Customs are in GT, and Manners and Etiquette again separate in BJ. Sports and Games, including Physical Training, in GV are less significantly related to Anthropology and Ethnology than to Hygiene, Recreation, and Athletics. Hygiene, the purpose of which is to obviate medicine, should not be subordinated to Medicine. Anthropogeography should be subordinated to Anthropology, not precede it in GF.

The separation of Sociology (HM), general and theoretical, from Social Science, General (HA), has already been noticed. The succeeding division (HN) has the caption "Social History. Social Reform." The outline of this division (p. 25) puts us into a quandary, which the full schedule (two pages) does little to remedy. This division seems intended for studies of social amelioration, applied social science, but the only special captions there are: "The Church and Social Problems," "Religious Denominations," and "Social Ideals in Literature." The former might better be with Church History and the last subject would seem to belong to History and criticism of Literature. Social History belongs rather in History, which comprises descriptive material, regarded in sequential relations, from which the special social sciences are drawn, with regard to the abstract principles of Sociology. The historical material may indeed be brought under the several social sciences, but, if so, the branches, Social, Economic, and Intellectual History, would be distributed inconveniently. The more special subjects have of course their historical backgrounds, which it may be well in most cases to collocate with the subjects as under Economics in this schedule; in other cases alternatives should be provided, and this should be done for Economic History, General; but it would seem better to place the economic history of the several nations under the history of those nations. So, if Social History be transferred, Social Reform would indeed be out of place between Social Theory and Social Groups, that is, between theoretical and descriptive sociology. This subject should have been collocated with Social Pathology, Philanthropy, Charities and Corrections (HV). The social work of the churches is so important that it justifies classifying Religion in proximity to social Ethics and ethical social amelioration. Socialism, Communism, Anarchism (HX) are properly collocated in the Library of Congress between social amelioration and Political Science (Class J).

Certain deficiencies will be noted here to show that these schedules are not always adequate, not even in the second edition, in this case dated 1920. Under Socialism there are only four special subjects besides the historical, the formal, the geographical, and the relations to other subjects. There are no items for Marxian Socialism, State Socialism, Agrarian Socialism, Nationalization of Land, Syndicalism, Guild Socialism, International Socialism, and Collectivism, nor references, except that in the Index the last is referred to Socialism in general, and the other subjects are referred to Labor in Economic History (HD). Euthenics is not in the index. Police should not be subordinated to Penology, for Police is for protection, not for punishment, and it should be under the Functions of Government in Political Science.

In the schedule for Economics the distinction between *social* economics and *private* economics is not recognized; nor is the term National Economics (German *Nationalökonomie*) in schedule or index. Corporations should not be subordinated to Industry, for there are other than industrial corporations, for instance, the insurance, the transportation, and the beneficent corporations. Nor should Land, as an economic subject, be subordinated under Agriculture, but rather should be collocated with Capital under Theoretical Economics. Statistics (HA) is a general method of science and should not be wholly subordinated to Social Science. Vital Statistics, subordinated to Demography, is misplaced under Economic Theory in HB 881-3700. Communication has social-economic aspects indeed, but the Postal Service should be with other services of the state in Political Science, or in the branch of Economics termed State Economics, where Telegraph and Telephone also belong, if not classified under Special Business, or under Electrical Technology, as they should be in a scientific or technological library. Thus there are three ways of classifying public services depending on technology: (1) as services rendered, or regulated, by the state (or by the government), so under State Economics, (2) as special business, (3) as technologies. But in few cases should these three special aspects be distributed under the four general subjects, Political Science, Economics, Business, and Technology. Nor do Telegraph and Telephone belong especially under Economics, save as other special public services belong either under that branch we have termed State Economics or else under the caption Special Business. In other words, these services are to be treated either like other special business depending on technology and rendering public service or as services rendered by, or regulated by, the state. In a scientific or technological library, however, these subjects should be subordinated to the respective sciences or technologies. So three methods of classifying these subjects, whether unitary or distributed, should be provided. On the whole, however, the latter half of Economics (HE-HJ) seems to provide some of the most satisfactory classification of the entire system, save for certain objections generally applicable to these schedules of which we will treat in a subsequent section. So we see that the schedule for Social Science is not only too cumbersome and complicated thruout, even in the parts commended here, but in other parts it has too many faults, and, considering its detail, many important subjects are omitted.

In Political Science the writer finds much more to commend than to criticise. The collocation of International Law (JX) with Law (Class K) and of Local Government (JS), Colonies and Colonization (JV), and Emigration and Immigration (also JV), this is all very good. Only ten of the subordinate letters of J are assigned. International Relations and International Law have grown so important that they should have two divisions, JX and JY. To make room in the other direction, Local Government could be moved to JR, which is now unused. Under the caption International Relations there should be provision for many other subjects besides Foreign Relations, Diplomacy, and International Arbitration. *Chauvinism,* so important in these interests, does not appear even in the index, nor do the terms *militarism* and *armaments.* The index to Military Science, however, refers these terms to Cost of Armaments (UA 17). This suggests that Military and Naval Science should not be classified apart from Political Science, for they are really functions or services of the state.

The schedule for Education too is commendable in certain respects, as we remarked before. It has, however, too few main captions, only ten, and three of these are for such minor subjects as Student Periodicals (LH), Student Fraternities (LJ), and Text-books (LT). The classification under Theory of Education may be criticised for including such practical matters as Education and Training of Teachers, School Government, School Architecture, School Hygiene, etc. The collocation of Pedagogics, Educational Psychology, and Child Study is commendable, but the sociological aspects (LC 71-245) and Moral and Religious Education (LC 251-951) might better be classified under the theoretical division (LB). There should be provision for many topics now lacking, for instance, Education for Democracy, for Efficiency, for Social Adjustment, etc., which are not well provided for under Sociological Aspects, nor under Types of Education (LC 1001-1261). Many subjects of more recent interest are lacking both from schedules and from index, for instance, Mental Ability, and Intelligence, Tests and Measurements, Individual Differences, Proficiency, Super-normal children, etc. Nor is there a clear distinction between Defective children (LC 4001-4801) and Backward or Deficient children, Laggards, and Sub-normal children. Teaching, or the Art of Education, should be distinguished from the Theory. The familiar term *method* is conspicuously absent, except in the term Methods of Study (LB 1049), which is a different and more special subject. In brief, this schedule of Theory, Principles, Practice, and Pedagogics (LB 1025-49) is very inadequate. Under School Government, School Architecture, School Hygiene, School Gardens, School Life, etc. (LB 2503-3625) many details are well classified; but there is no provision for the subject of Schools in general, except that in the index it is referred to Education in general; nor for different kinds of schools as distinct from different stages of education, e.g. High-schools, Continuation schools, Intermediate schools, Trade schools; nor for Colleges and Universities as distinct from Higher Education. These are distinct subjects with extensive literature. The several terms appear only in other subordinate details of these general subjects, except that under Education Extension there are distinct items for Evening Schools, Vacation Schools, and Correspondence Schools, as there should be. Coeducation the index refers only to Higher Education for Women. Three more special lacks that we happen to notice are Vocational Guidance, Visual Education, and the Montessori Method. On the whole the schedule for Education is too complicated and for the more recent literature it is very inadequate.

We now come back to the schedule of Science (Class Q). In the schedule for Mathematics there is much to praise; it is one of the best parts of the system. This subject of manifold relations is most difficult to classify — almost defies classification. The writer feels quite incompetent in mathematics. He thinks, however, that it were better not to interpose Descriptive Geometry and Trigonometry, which diverge into the special and applied, between Analysis and Geometry on the one hand and Analytical

Geometry on the other hand; for there are many interconnections between these two branches, all in the realm of pure mathematics, for instance, Infinitesimal Geometry and Differential Geometry, which depend on Analysis as well as on Analytical Geometry. More positively inconsistent is the placing of Foundations of Geometry, Non-Euclidean Geometry, and Hyperspace at the very end of the subject (QA 681-699), whereas these subjects should be at the beginning, under the general subject (QA 445) and collocated with the Philosophy of Geometry, which is in neither place, nor in the index. Geometrical Constructions too is lacking both from schedule and from index. Modern Geometry and Synthetic Geometry should have place just ahead of Projective Geometry (471). Here Geometry of Position, another distinct subject lacking, might well be placed; and then the Non-Euclidean and the Hypergeometry (sometimes called Metageometry) might follow. Among other important omissions we may note: Assemblages (*Mengenlehre*) or Aggregates, or Theory of Sets of Points, Combinatory Analysis, Nomography (graphical methods, tables, solutions, etc.), Barycentric Calculus, and Diophantine Analysis, which should be allocated to Diophantine Problems, which is subsumed under QA 242 but which should have a distinct place. There should also be a caption for Special Algebras, e.g. Double Algebra. As regards arrangement, it might be better to place Theory of Numbers, with the special subjects subordinate to it, ahead of Theory of Equations and of the algebra of Permutations, Combinations, Groups, Substitutions, Departments, Forms, etc. But arrangement is not very significant for these interrelated subjects, as the relations are not very distinct.

Analytic Mechanics, Kinematics, Statics, Dynamics, and Elasticity, Hydrostatics, Hydrodynamics, and Aërodynamics, tho their theoretical treatment is indeed mathematical, belong rather with Mechanics as a sub-science under Physics and with the respective branches of Physics. Kinematics, the geometry of motion, should precede both Statics and Dynamics, because it is the more abstract subject. Under it should come the Relativity of Motion and the relevant Theory, or Doctrine, of Relativity, invented by Einstein, about which there has been so much discussion during recent years. Tho we may differ as to the value of this theory and discussion, yet it is most obtrusively prominent, even in popular and newspaper publicity, and it has a large literature, mathematical, physical, metaphysical, and nonsensical; moreover it is important, at least historically. It should have a distinct place under Kinematics, or under Physics, and Einstein's name should be added both there and in the index. But the Library of Congress schedule for Physics seems more conservative about this theory than anybody else. It was ignored in the second edition (1913) and in the third edition (1921) it is merely subsumed under Philosophy of Physics (QC 6), that is, the term Relativity is. The problem that brought about this theory a quarter-century ago, tho the question reaches back a half-century or more, the question of the *entraînement,* or "drag," of the æther by the Earth moving thru space, and the famous experiment of Michelson and Morley in 1887, besides other relevant subjects, have no place either in this schedule nor in its index, not under any of the terms used so much; and there is not even a cross-reference from æther to ether.

These mathematical, analytical, theoretical studies in QA should not be separated thus from the respective branches of Physics, where the special descriptive studies are classified. Elasticity, for instance, is a general property of matter, and under the physics of Matter the entire subject, including the mathematical theory, belongs. Sound (QC 222-246) it were better to collocate with the special mechanics of Waves, etc. (157), and Heat (QC 252-338) with the Properties of Matter. Thermodynamics (311) should be closer to Kinetic Theory of Gases (175). Radiation and Radio-physics, or Radioactivity, have come to be regarded as very general subjects and they should precede both Light and Electricity. Radioactivity has here been brought in at the end of Electricity, where it seems misplaced. The term Radio-physics does not appear anywhere. Radiation in general there is no proper provision for; and the special subjects, Emission, Transmission, Reflection, Refraction, etc. it would be more scientific to subordinate under Radiation, for Light is but special effects of radiation. In a similar sense Electricity, or rather the special subjects that are brought under that caption, are special, tho some of them are less so than the respective subjects under Light. In this sense we may say that Light is a more special subject than Electricity. But both should follow Radiation as more general. The Quantum Theory, which has troubled physicists for about twenty-five years, and which has its formidable literature, has no place in this schedule or its index. The Theory of Ether (QC 177) does not companion well with Theories of Gravitation (178) and Kinetic Theory of Gases (175) and Radiometer (176) and Molecular Dimensions (179). These subjects have not their convenient and proper collocations; in other words they are somewhat mixed up. The classification of Physics is less scientific and less commendable than that of Mathematics, and it would hardly be adequate for the science of the last two decades, not for any library that is really expected to classify scientifically.

Mineralogy, with the introductory or complementary study Crystallography, is properly a branch of Chemistry, more closely related to it than to Geology, tho it is in one aspect a branch of Geognosy, the descriptive science of the Earth's materials, and tho it is closely related to Petrology and to Economic Geology. But these subjects should not come in between Dynamic and Structural Geology on the one hand and on the other hand Geographical Geology, nor should this last precede. In this schedule for Geology we miss the customary main division of the science into Physical (including Dynamical, Structural, or Tectonic, and Chemical) and Historical (including Stratigraphical, Paleontological, and Geographical). Then, as we have remarked before, Paleontology belongs to Biology rather than to Geology, even tho it contributes so greatly to Geology. Paleobotany should accordingly be placed under Botany and Paleozoölogy under Zoölogy, tho with respect to the geological interests there might well be alternative provision under Geology.

Under Chemistry, as under Geology and Astronomy, the Theoretical and Physical (QD 453-651) are separated from the General. More particularly under Chemistry, while there are some details for Chemistry in general, as a study, profession, etc., other subjects, such as the Importance of Chemistry to Man, to Civilization, to Legal Prosecution, etc. are lacking; and the term General Chemistry, which has recently come into prominent usage, is not distinguished from Recent Treatises (QD 31) under the general caption of the class. Then the Physical and Theoretical Chemistry follows instead of preceding the Analytical, Inorganic, and Organic branches; and at the end comes Crystallography (QD 901-999), cut off from Mineralogy in QE 351-399, to which it is most closely related.

In Astronomy there is more reason for placing the Practical and Spherical ahead of the Theoretical and in this schedule many good collocations result; but a more consistent classification with equally good collocations may be obtained with the order as follows: General, Descriptive, Theoretical, Spherical, Practical, Observational, Cosmical, Astrophysical, Special Bodies, culminating in the Earth and leading to Geology and Geodesy. Cosmical Physics (QC 806) should be collocated with Astronomy (QB), and Terrestrial Physics, including Terrestrial Magnetism and Meteorology, should be collocated rather with Geophysics and with Physiography as branches of the science of the Earth. The same is true of Geodesy (QB 281-341), which belongs not with Astronomy but with Physical Geology or with Mathematical Geography.

The inconsistency of placing the general and theoretical after the special, particular, and descriptive recurs under Botany and Zoölogy, where Morphology, Anatomy, Embryology, Histology, Physiology, and Ecology follow the geographical, topographic, and taxonomic — more concretely descriptive branches. Placing the geographical ahead thruout the descriptive natural sciences is an objectionable feature of the system; and the order of the branches of Zoölogy is wholly inverse. This has one advantage, the collocation of comparative anatomy and embryology of animals with the relevant branches of human anatomy and embryology. But here Ecology, under the unusual and ambiguous term Ethology, not only precedes Anatomy but is separated from Geographical Distribution, with which it should be collocated. A similar separation impairs the schedule for Botany. Here the order, Morphology, Anatomy, Embryology, Histology, Physiology, and Ecology, is correct; but all these illogically follow the taxonomic classification of special morphological forms, and this is itself unscientifically and inconsistently inverse. In the details to instance that the taxonomic classification is not perfect, we note that Bryophyta, the name of one of the great divisions, or phyla, of Cryptogamia, is omitted from the schedule.[8] The classification for the biological sciences is very unsatisfactory. The index lacks the terms: Ontogeny, Taxonomy, and Organization.

The details of Technology and the Arts space does not permit us to particularize, so we will merely remark that in these two classes we have found much to commend and little to criticise. We have objected before to the separation of Chemical Technology from Chemistry, and of Electrical Technology from Electricity. Here we notice similar separation of Economic Geology and Mineralogy from the mother subjects in QE; also the separation of Sanitary Engineering in TD from Sanitation in RA 421-607, Water Supply having a schedule in both classes. This tendency to duplicate and to distribute appears thruout the system. To minimize the disadvantages of this often unavoidable result is a real problem of library classification which is aggravated by an unscientific order of main classes such as impairs this system.

We will note here a few details omitted: Appreciation, Enjoyment of Art; Expression, Imitation, Morality, Sublimity, the Comic in Art; Commercialism, Imposition, Counterfeiting in Art (but Forgeries appears in N 8790). And in the schedule of Class S, Agriculture, Plant and Animal Industry: Arboriculture, Care and Salvage of Trees, and Nurseries. In citing these lacks in schedules and indexes the writer remembers that the publication is tenta-

[8] Some faults of the Library of Congress Classification of natural science are gently touched upon by Miss Monica Cant in a commendable article, "Some Notes on Botanical Classification," in *The Library Assistant*, v. 19, p. 54.

tive, "printed as manuscript." Some of these items may be inserted in later editions, as a few were in the past. But it seems advisable to show that these schedules are really incomplete, lest their immense detail should lead the unwary to overvalue them in this respect.

The History of Civilization and Culture in CB is separated too far from General History in D. To instance confusing duplication, Historiography and Biography of Historians appear first in CB 15 and then in D 13 and recurrently under the nations' history; and Philosophy of History is CB 19 and also D 16.7. Historiology does not appear even in the index. The subdivision of CB for nations implies that the history of the civilization and culture of the nations is to be separated from their general and political history; but under the several nations in the schedules of D recurs the caption, "Social Life and Customs. Civilization." In some places the term Culture is added. Under Greece and Rome (ancient) this caption is "Civilization and Culture," subsumed under Antiquities. Clearer and more adequate provision is not made for such important subjects as the Civilization of Ancient Greece and Rome as distinct from the social and private life and institutions as studied in the antiquities. The important related subject, Hellenism, Hellenistic Influence, is nowhere to be found; nor are the Greek Colonies, nor the Greek City, or State, nor the famous Constitution of Athens, nor the Olympic Games; nor is there any provision for the literature on the Influence of Greek and Roman Civilization on European, unless under the "General special" — that tantalizing term.

The divisions of Class D are for the several nations, beginning with Great Britain. The order might as well have been alphabetic, for it is not historical, nor geographical. Germany (DD) is separated from Austria (DB), while Switzerland is in DQ next to the Balkan states in DR. Classical Antiquity (DE) is severed from Ancient History (D 51-90). Russia (DK) is neighbor to Netherlands (DH and DJ). But the order in Asia (DS) is very good. Aside from such faults and lacks the schedules for Class D seem systematic and thoro. Under the several nations a caption for Ethnography recurs; but under Anthropology, Ethnology and Ethnography, a subordinate heading, "Customs and Institutions (Primitive)" is subdivided for "Special Races" and both for Ethnographic and Geographic subdivisions (GN 537 and 550). Classifiers must find this duplication confusing, for references are lacking, nor are distinctions defined.

In the Library of Congress bibliography is kept all together in Class Z, and there classified into General, National, Subject, and Personal. It is more convenient to distribute subject-bibliographies under the subjects. National bibliographies may well follow general bibliographies, but bibliographies of the nations as historical subjects, etc., should be distributed as subject-bibliographies. Under the main caption, Books in General, are included Paleography and Writing, including Calligraphy, Typewriting, and Shorthand, which would imply that those arts exist chiefly for the making of books. Paleography is so closely related to Diplomatics and Epigraphy that it seems to belong rather with those "auxiliary" sciences of historical studies. Writing and Printing should be under the Arts, so should Shorthand and Typewriting. But Stenography, which does not appear in this schedule nor in any of the indexes, does appear under Economic History, Labor, Employers' and Workingmen's Associations, where it would have the mark HD 6948.S58, which seems longer than short-hand.

The schedule for Philology (P-Pa) is more impressive even than those for History. We admire its erudition and marvel at its elaborateness. We shall never have time to study it adequately, nor even to make use of it; and we would turn it over to the catalogers, to whom the Prefatory Note hopes it will be a "source of useful information." The bibliographers and scholars too would probably find much in it to appreciate. But to classifiers it is, one thinks, an *embarras de richesse*. Why, there are over twenty pages, closely printed, of schedule for Aristotle alone, and fourteen for Homer, and ten for Plato. Is it conceivable that the literature, however extensive and various, could require all that complication? We would echo the acknowledgement in the Prefatory Notes to the printers in the Government Printing Office. It is now apparent why we have had to wait for it for twenty years. The schedule for Literature (PN-PZ) was published in 1915. It is much less complicated, but hardly less admirable and interesting to the cataloger and bibliographer. For classifying we regard it as utterly impractical. In preceding chapters we set forth some of our ideas regarding the classification of Philology and of Literature. The main thing is that the several chief literatures should not be separated from their respective languages. In criticising the Decimal Classification we repeated this stricture. Another principle is that alternative modes of classifying literature should be provided for, as simply as possible, if different libraries are to be served. Thirdly, for individual authors (except for a few of the greatest) it is wrong principle to use class-marks or numbers other than those of Cutter order-numbers or some other order-notation. In other words individuals should not be specified as classes; they should be *classified* in classes and *arranged within* these classes. It is still worse to have individual writings treated thus. Class-notation should not be extended into such details and particulars. Then under authors subdivision by table should be simple for most authors and elaborate only for the most important authors, and then within practical and economic limits. Moreover it is inadvisable, if not impractical, to separate British from American authors and furthermore to have several alphabets under each division for periods.

In the broadest view these schedules are altogether too historical and otherwise too complicated, even for specialized studies and for the largest libraries. They would prove more troublesome than advantageous. Those who think they have really adopted them must have simplified and adapted them beforehand or after trying them. But, if literature and its history are to be classified historically in adequate detail, this should not be complicated by three main divisions for History, Collections, and Individual Authors, repeating, or paralleling, the historical classification, further complicated by subordinate divisions for countries and periods, and again by forms, so that there are four or five series of divisions superposed and interlaced with cross-references. The biography is as inseparable from the history as the criticism is from both biography and history. But there the History of Elizabethan Literature, for instance, is placed in PR 836-839, while the criticism and biography would be under the individual authors in PR 2200-3198 and the collections would be distributed among those of other periods in seven places ranging from PR 1207 to PR 1369. The user of this classification would be lost in the mazes of this system, and so would the classifier too. How translations of foreign literature into English poetic, dramatic, or other forms are to be treated would be learned only with difficulty from the schedules and index, and probably with resulting confusion.

In this long section many items have been pointed out or criticised as fairly as requisite brevity has permitted. They are regarded as matters of fact rather than of opinion. Tedious tho the matter be, the cumulative effect should substantiate our concluding criticism that the classification of the Library of Congress is impaired thruout by too many inconvenient separations of closely related subjects, by dispersion of the parts of many subjects, by too many unnecessary complications, and by too many important omissions and deficiencies.

5. The Notation and the Apportionment

From disproportion and excessive elaboration result notations of uneconomical length. In this system five letters are unused for main classes, and thus the base is shortened. The unused letters are not just reserved for prospective future use, for new subjects are usually subordinated. Then within the twenty-one main classes too few sub-classes, or divisions, are distinguished by subordinate letters. To distinguish important subjects by distinct class-marks is very advantageous both for the uses of the classification and for certain economies in mnemonic notation. The number of sub-classes is tabulated below:

Class	Sub-Classes	Class	Sub-Classes
A	10	A-N	111
B	14	P	18
C	9	Q	12
D	19	R	17
E-F	2	S	6
G	9	T	17
H	16	U	9
J	11	V	10
K	unpublished	Z	1
L	11	—	——
M	3		201
N	7	For K estimate	10
	——		——
	111		211

This would make an average of ten to the class. The initial letters, when expanded (as under D) are here counted as sub-classes. If twenty sub-classes were used, the reserve would probably suffice for future requirements. The feasible *area* would then be 420 divisions. If three more main classes were added, the area would be 480. The maximum for 24 letters is 24 x 24 + 24 = 600. So we may say that this notation uses about half of its *feasible area* and a little more than a third of its *maximum area*. That is indeed uneconomical.

We will particularize a few of the resulting deficiencies. Books and Bookmaking, Writing and Paleography, Libraries, and Bibliography are fairly distinct subjects and should be regarded as four sub-classes in Class Z; yet they have not distinctive class-marks. Biology is subsumed without distinctive mark; so are Mineralogy, Meteorology, Paleontology, Geometry, Mechanics, Educational Psychology, Teaching, Hygiene, Labor, Corporations, Banking, Insurance, Greek, Latin, Italian, Spanish, French, and German languages, Scandinavian, Celtic, and Semitic languages, and the respective literatures. In contrast with these subjects lacking distinctive marks are the following comparatively unimportant subjects that have letters to distinguish them: Cavalry (UE), Marines (VE), Roads and Pavements (TE), Nursing (RT), Chronology (CE), College Fraternities (LJ), University, College, and School Magazines (LH).

Disproportion underlies the following more important strictures: Philology and all the languages and literatures are confined to the capacity of one main class, whereas History expands in four, and American History has two of these. With a literal base there are letters enough to distinguish each of the fundamental sciences with a capital letter in a main class; but in this system only one, Social Science, is so distinguished. Yet the arts and technologies, Medicine, Agriculture, and Military and Naval Science occupy seven main classes, a third of the whole base. Philosophy and Religion together have but one main class. As little room is assigned to Physics (QC) and to Chemistry (QD) as to Sculpture (NB) and to Engraving (NE); as little to the English language and literature (PE) as to Cavalry (UE); as much to Heraldry (CR) as to History of Great Britain and Ireland (DA). Evidently in this system there has been no purpose to provide distinctive class-marks for all important subjects; and the value of mnemonics has been disparaged.

This notation does permit of expansion, but it runs into excessive length. Any division, whatever its content, any subject, whatever its scope, may have hundreds of subdivisions marked with numbers of three or four places, not consecutive but intermittent, with a large proportion of unused numbers for future insertions. Except at the beginning of each sub-class, numbers of three or four places, besides the two letters, are required for important subjects and for much used books. That is, this notation normally requires five or six factors where an economical notation would require but three or four. Indeed figures used decimally are less uneconomical than when used intermittently. But sometimes the consecutive numbers prove insufficient, and decimal extension becomes necessary. In such cases and wherever additional marks from *systematic* schedules are affixed, the notations become altogether too unwieldy. A few examples will enforce this objection.

Biography of Disraeli	DA 564.B3
Crete, Archeology and History	DF 221.C8
Hannibal's War with Spain	DG 247.59
Provence, Description and travel	DC 611.P958
Child Labor Laws in the United States	HD 6243.U5A4
Primates, Lemurs, Monkeys, Apes, etc.	QL 737.P9

These subjects are indeed special, tho not *very* special. The last would have to be subdivided for Apes, for Lemurs, for Chimpanzees, etc. The above marks are composed of from eight to twelve factors, where an economical notation would use but three or four, or at most five. And now we will compare the marks of some *general* subjects in an economical notation with those of the Library of Congress:

Educational Psychology	JE	LB 1051
International Arbitration	RIR	JX 1938
Railways, General, Treatises	TJE	HE 1031
Radiotelegraphy, General, Treatises	BRK	TK 5741
Journalism, General	YV	PN 4731
History of Greek Literature, General	XE	PA 3001

6. Excessive Bulk and Complexity

The Library of Congress Classification applies systematic tables for certain subjects, notably for History of Europe and for the Literatures; and there are different types of these presenting somewhat different specifications for countries, languages, literatures, and authors, graded according to their relative importance or the requisite detail, some requiring fewer, others more numerous subdivisions. Each history, each language, each literature, and each author has distinctive features, but requisite economy should reduce these, at least in part, to types and to systematic schedules; and these should be few and not too elaborate. This is found to be feasible. So many specifications recur, those for relations, aspects, methods, treatment, forms, those bibliographical, geographical, historical, scientific, and philosophical, that typical systematic schedules are usually applicable, tho of course not invariably. Even so, they prove to be very effectual economies both in lessening the details of schedules and in facilitating their use; and in this respect the more mnemonic they are the better. Our views on this matter were presented in Chapter IV, section 5, and they are positively divergent from those embodied in the schedules of the L. C. and expressed by their defenders. Those schedules we find needlessly and excessively complicated. From the lack of such economies the system has become extremely cumbersome.

Further bulk and complexity result not only from duplications and alternatives, with the requisite cross-references, but moreover from certain subjects being classified in some detail in two distinct classes. For example, History of Science is regularly classified under Science (general) in Q 125-7, which is subdivided by countries alphabetically; but then sub-class AZ also is assigned to History of the Sciences in General, Scholarship, and Learning. For another instance, Constitutional Monarchy is classified in JC 401-408, under Political Theory, but under Constitutional History (JF) Constitutional Monarch is marked 253, without reference in either place to the other. More often, however, there is reference to the preferred location; and the indexes usually provide the proper indications.

The twenty classes published thus require over 4,000 pages for the schedules, without counting the indexes. Estimating an average of about 35 places to the page, the total would be about 140,000. This is about three times as many as we have estimated as likely to be used in the largest libraries. The History of Europe fills 420 pages; the Social Sciences (Classes H and J) occupy 749 pages, without counting the synopses and outlines, tables and indexes. Technology requires 255 pages for the schedules alone. The complexity of the schedules is proportionate.

To exemplify the dispersion of subjects, two simple cases will be instanced and then a subject that is very problematic. Copper appears in four places, the chemistry in QD 181.C9, the technology in TP 245.C8, the metallurgy in TN 780, and mining in TN 440-449. These last three places should be collocated under Technology and that should not be separated from the chemistry. Similarly Radium has its chemistry in QD 181.R1, while a monograph on its atomic weight would have the mark QD 464.R1, and one on its production would be marked TP 245.R2. These studies should be united under Radium in Chemistry.

The study of children involves many subjects in several branches, but the related subjects should not be so confusingly distributed as here under five classes. Children (care), Child Study, Child Life, Youth, etc. are classified under Social Groups in HQ 769-799. Children, Adolescents, appears under Anthropology in GN 63-64; Hygiene, Feeding, etc. of Children are in RJ 101-253, under Pediatrics; Child Study under Education is classified in LB 1101-1139, repeating such subjects as Adolescence (1135) and Anthropological studies (1125), Psychophysical studies (1121), and Psychical Development of the Child (1131); but Child Psychology appears also in BF 721 under Psychology.

There should be a division for the main subject, with references to alternative locations; and there should besides this be a distinct division for Psychology of Childhood, and another for Pediatrics; and these three divisions should not be too distant from one another; they would not be, if Anthropology, Psychology, Education, and Hygiene were in contiguous classes.

The schedules too often lack clearness in caption and indention. We have to search for the general subjects, and for the main divisions, and too often these lack distinctive literal notation. These objections would remain, even if there were less bulk and complexity.

7. Is this Classification Adaptable for Centralized Classifying?

We have found many faults, tho we have tried not to be unfairly fault-finding. We have taken pains to show facts rather than to set forth arguments. But now we must conclude with an argument. For there is a marked tendency among librarians to accept the classification of the Library of Congress with all its faults, because there is no better system worked out and published in detail and because centralized classifying is a feasible economy in assisting individual classifying. There are reasons on both sides of the question. Let us consider them.

First, as to the satisfactoriness of the system: we have found the order of the main classes unscientific and uneconomic, resulting in inconvenient separations. History, the Sciences, the Social Sciences, the Arts, and Literature are incoherently misplaced. Three fundamental sciences, Biology, Psychology, and Sociology, are subordinated. Psychology is separated from Science, and Education from Psychology, and from Sociology too. Anthropology and Ethnology are misplaced with regard both to science and to history. Physics is separated from

Mathematics by Astronomy, and Geography far from Geology. Chemical Technology is remote from Chemistry and Electrical Technology from Electricity. Many other subjects are improperly placed, with resulting separations of closely related studies. In this view the system seems wholly inadaptable.

We have looked into the schedules more in detail; we have found many merits, much to commend, much to accept with appreciation and thankfulness; but we have found more faults and deficiencies than we could attempt to describe or even mention, faults in scientific relations, in adaptations to changing conditions, and in practical library economies. They seem to justify the conclusion that to amend and adapt this system to practical conveniences would be as difficult probably as to fit it to the scientific and educational organization of knowledge. This would require reconstruction from the foundations; but that adaptation would require hardly less extensive alteration thruout the immense structure.

Thirdly, we have considered the notation and apportionment. Five initial letters and too many subordinate letters are unused; yet many important subjects are without distinctive literal notation. This disproportion and waste reduce to about a third of its capacity the base and *area* of the literal notation; and subdivision by consecutive numbers, fewer being assigned than unassigned, is much less economical than a notation of numbers used decimally; and that we have found uneconomical. The resulting notation is expansive but of excessive length, requiring regularly, five or six factors where an economical notation requires but three or four; and, when decimals or suffixes from *systematic schedules* are added, the notations run to eight or more factors, far beyond the economic limit. In a word, the notation is uneconomical.

Fourthly, the system is altogether too complicated and cumbersome. It is not in a single book, but in some twenty, with as many indexes. Even if these indexes be sometime consolidated into one, it will be, however valuable, very bulky and complicated. This complication of schedules and index would largely offset the economy of centralized classifying. Unless the libraries take the notations from the cards without adapting them to their individual classifications, the schedules would have to be handled and studied and altered; and the time and trouble would greatly reduce the savings of the centralized service. It might prove easier and more economical to make your classification for your individual library, in consistence with established principles and approved standards, than to labor over these complicated schedules in classifying your daily accessions. The writer cannot say positively, but he can proffer a little smile all around in saying that he would rather try it than not, — that is, than the other alternative.

If the classification of the Library of Congress is inconsistent with the organization of knowledge and the economies of library classification, the centralized service, however liberal and efficient, does not really much enhance the value of this classification to other libraries. A faulty system conforming to the conditions of an immense and rapidly growing library is too much weighted with the handicap of its own ponderosity. It is the less likely to be altered and adapted to new requirements. In this system, now over a quarter-century old, faults long since recognized have not been remedied, and they will probably not be removed in the coming quarter-century. A massive system adopted by many large libraries is thrice bound by conservatism, by the *cost* of reclassifying *large* collections in *many* libraries. Alterations in the mother system would impose on the daughter libraries the unhappy alternative of following in the mother's footsteps or of being left behind in the limbo of the past. So, while the daughters cling to the mother, she clings to them all. For fear that some may not be capable of progress, all are likely to remain where they are. Have we not observed this maternal conservatism in the Decimal Classification and its large family of daughters?

The economies of centralized coöperative classifying need not, and should not, depend on the classification of a national library, nor on that of any one library. Standards, whether in products or in methods, must be as adaptable as is feasible to changing requirements; and economies must yield somewhat to values, which may be intellectual. It is of paramount importance that a standard classification for libraries should be not only practical and economical but also scientific and educational. For economy, the subject, or class, or class-mark, should be plainly indicated in the book, or on a card that represents it. As we have suggested elsewhere, such indication could well be given by the author and publisher concurrently in the preface and under the copyright notice; and this might be confirmed, modified, or altered by a board of classifiers, whether of the national library or of the national library association. Such a method of classifying should not only be centralized and coöperative but truly economical and at the same time adaptable. The subject indication, or standard class-marks — for there might well be three or four of them on each card — could then be translated into any consistent and adequate library classification by the simple use of its index, which indeed might have one of the standard notations in a parallel column beside its own. We will return to this doctrine in the concluding chapter.

Notation and index are but means. Schedules are none the less requisite. For standard classifications they should be as simple as adequacy permits and as adaptable as is feasible under the conditions. For the individual classifications they should be consistent with the standards so far as is possible and they should be specialized and elaborate only where requisite. Thus true economy may be attained. Such classifications may be coöperative in plan, in elaboration, and in specialization; and classifying by them may be coöperative and centralized. In order to partake in coöperative centralized classifying we need not adopt a faulty and complicated classification, and on the whole it probably does not pay to do so. It would probably cost more in time and trouble to translate the subjects and class-marks of a cumbersome and confusing system and to adapt them to local and individual requirements than it would to adapt a simpler standard classification, even if the expansions, where needed, would have to be developed according to the requirements. Herein lies a need and an opportunity for the classifiers of the future and for the schools for librarianship.

The Library of Congress classification is very commendable in much of its detail, historical, scientific, and technological, and good use can be made of this detail; but the system is too cumbersome and complicated; it has too many faults, and it is on the whole inadaptable. The advantages and economies that may be gained by adopting it are overborne by the disadvantages, inadequacies, and wastes of the system. As an organization of knowledge it is unscientific and inadaptive; as a library classification it is uneconomical; as a standard it is disqualified.

CHAPTER XIII

THREE EUROPEAN CLASSIFICATIONS AND ONE ASIATIC

1. Brown's "Subject Classification"

The three leading American classifications have been criticised and found unsatisfactory. Let us now turn to four important systems that have been developed in older countries. *La Classification Décimale Universelle* (which is international but not "universal") will not be considered in detail here, because as developed for the purposes of a great bibliographic catalog and more broadly for "documentation," it is hardly adaptable for the organization of knowledge in libraries, tho much of its detail would be available for classification of large research collections, if the notation could be simplified within economic limits. As its basic structure remains almost unaltered — the faulty historic American *Decimal Classification* — it is on the whole, despite an elaborate superstructure of mnemonic notation for recurrent specifications, subject to the same criticism that has been rendered in Chapter X, concluding that it was always inadaptable for standardization and now is antiquated and unavailable for economical reconstruction.[1]

[1] Its complexities in mnemonic notation have been mentioned in preceding chapters. A committee of the Institute is said to have undertaken extensive "revision," but the writer does not yet know how radical that will be nor what results have thus far been accomplished. A trenchant German critique is that of Dr. Carl Diesch, *Katalogprobleme und Dezimalklassifikation, eine bibliothekswissenschaftliche Untersuchung und Abwehr*, Leipzig, Harrassowitz, 1929, 66 p. See also Carl Walther, "Probleme der Dezimalklassifikation" in *Zentralblatt für Bibliothekswesen*, Jahrg. 48, p. 289-99 (June, 1931). Briefer criticisms appear in Milkau's *Handbuch der Bibliothekswesen*, section 155, and in Georg Schneider's *Handbuch der Bibliographie*, 3rd ed., Leipzig, Hirsemann, 1923; translated into English by R. R. Shaw, 1934, Columbia University Press.

Let us first examine the English library classification which many librarians seem to regard as less objectionable than the three American systems. It has at least the merit of being in some respects simpler. The title[2] signifies the author's intention, or "main principle, the placing of subjects under concrete or specific heads, ... For example, books on the human heart are all together at one place, whether treating of that organ from an anatomical, physiological, pathological, or therapeutical point of view. All through the scheme the same principle has been observed, as far as the complications and intersections of human knowledge would allow, while ample provision is also made for general as well as special aspects."[3]

Two other principles are: ". . . to place each subject as near as possible to the science on which it is based. . . . . Practical use has been considered all through the scheme, and it has been sought to obtain this by dispensing with conventions, distinctions, and groupings, which are arbitrary rather than scientific." (*S. C.*, p. 17-18).

These principles are good, if not carried to extremes, and to contravention of other principles no less important to library classification. But they were carried to extremes by Mr. Brown. When the subject Numismatics, which should be auxiliary to History, is subordinated to Finance and Money, as a branch of Economics, and is there collocated with the economics of Currency and Cash Registers; when the whole literature of Music —

[2] *Subject Classification, with tables, indexes, etc., for the subdivison of subjects*, by James Duff Brown, London, 1906, 423 p.

[3] *Library Classification and Cataloging*, by James Duff Brown, London, 1912, p. 79. This book comprised two *Manuals*, one for Classification and the other for Cataloging. In our subsequent references to it we will use merely the term *Manual*, and for the *Subject Classification* merely the initials *S. C.* With the above quotation compare the following: " . . . . all through the classification the endeavour has been to maintain a scheme of one subject, one place." (*S. C.*, p. 11).

history, theory, and technology — is thrust between branches of physical science; when between General and Theoretical Physics, Molecular Physics, and Dynamics on the one hand, and Electricity and other special branches of physics on the other hand, over nine pages of details in *applied* mechanics and engineering thru all the various branches are made to intervene — Mechanical, Civil, Sanitary and Municipal Engineering, Architecture and Building, Railway Engineering and Administration, Vehicular Engineering, Transport and Communication, Post Office, Shipbuilding, Seamanship and Navigation, Shipping, Naval and Military Science, — when arts and technologies thus intrude into the studies of sciences and philosophies, we may indeed object that Mr. Brown has gone to extremes in "dispensing with conventions, distinctions, and groupings," extremes that are neither practical nor scientific and which will prove very inconvenient. Neither the sciences nor the technologies are properly served by this colligation. Nor is it more practical to subordinate all the applications of biological and sociological science "directly" under the fundamental sciences from which they may in a sense be derived. Moreover technologies and arts depending chiefly on one science may be composite of elements from several other sciences and thus dependent on them too, as is, for instance, Photography.

Is there practical reason for placing books on Yachts and Yachting (B669), books on Parcels Post (B629), books on the Art of Travel (B602), books on Freight Rates (B535), books on Plastering (B340), books on Sewage (B262), and books on Hand Tools (B154) in Class B, Physics? It would seem that Mr. Brown reacted against the tendency we criticised in the Library of Congress system to distribute, or disperse, the several branches or aspects of a subject, or the "standpoints," as he calls them. But, in reducing this problem to a pervasive rule, he attempted a simplification that is altogether impractical. For some subjects it is convenient to separate certain branches; for instance again, the chemical branch of photography may in scientific libraries best be placed under Chemistry, or the physical and chemical side altogether under Physics, while the artistic side may be classified under Fine Arts. The Chemistry of Foods may be placed under Chemical Technology, while other studies of Foods belong rather under Hygiene and under Domestic Economy. Regarding Bacteriology, however, there may be some doubt whether the medical branch should be differentiated from the botanical and agricultural branches, etc. If the Library of Congress is often wrong in distributing branches that belong together, it is sometimes right in distributing other subjects. Mr. Brown, in applying his two principles not only to special subjects but to general, subverted the practical principle of collocation for maximal efficiency in service. Moreover he distorted feasible subordination. He even failed to carry out his principles in all subjects: for instance, Education he neither subordinated to nor collocated with Psychology, nor Æsthetics with Arts, nor Metaphysics with Philosophy, nor Folk-lore with Ethnology.[4]

Mr. Brown no less explicitly than Dr. Dewey professed the purpose to be very practical, and he no less plainly disclaimed any broad scientific purpose. But in avoiding the scientific he likewise missed the practical, and, strange to say, he did this most inconsistently in subordinating the practical — too much of it — to the scientific. Like many other librarians, he labored under the negation that there is no accepted scientific order. "Classification has become," he said, "a mere battlefield for theorists, from which nothing of a very definite or permanent kind has emerged." (*S. C.*,

[4] Mr. Berwick Sayers mentions several other inconsistencies and separations. Those who are interested should read his valuable chapter on this system. (*Canons*, Chap. III, or *Manual*, Chap. XVII). Tho we differ in certain opinions and conclusions, we agree in others. This agreement is the more to be considered because it is nearly independent. Tho the writer had read Mr. Berwick Sayers' *Canons* soon after it was published in 1915, his re-reading it was postponed by circumstances till three months after this chapter had been rewritten and revised; and that was before the *Manual* was published (1926).

p. 8). Yet he professed that his classification was "based on the principle of placing all topics in a logical sequence." (*Manual*, p. 80). " . . . . every class is arranged in a systematic order of scientific progression, as far as it seemed possible to maintain it; . . . ." (*S. C.*, p. 11).

Let us examine the classification with regard to this claim. But first let us show the Table of Main Classes.

A	Generalia	
B-D	Physical Science	Matter and Force
E-F	Biological Science	Life
G-H	Ethnology and Medicine	
I	Economic Biology	
J-K	Philosophy and Religion	Mind
L	Social and Political Science	
M	Language and Literature	
N	Literary Forms	Record
O-W	History, Geography	
X	Biography	

This scheme does in part crudely resemble the established order of the sciences, and credit is due to Brown for placing the Physical and Natural Sciences ahead of Ethnology, the Social Sciences, and History, as Edwards, Dewey, Cutter, and the Library of Congress had *not* done; but he deserves more credit perhaps for the practical measures of combining Languages and Literatures, then History and Geography, as those predecessors had moreover not done. Brown's outline is thus commendable as more scientific and less inconsistent than Edwards' and Cutter's and as avoiding the basic separations of Dewey's; but it is far from faultless; it separates Philosophy from General Science and from Logic, and places it next to Domestic Arts. Then Education and Mathematics have hardly more right to be brought under the caption Generalia than have Language, History, and Philosophy. Psychology, a fundamental science, should have been given a distinct place in the series, and so should Anthropology. But Ethnology is a term of various usage in more special fields, with little claim to be distinguished as a main class, and Economic Biology, with still less, flouts Brown's leading principle.

As regards the philosophical concepts superposed on the scheme and the logical consistency praised by Mr. Berwick Sayers and others, they are no less inconsistent than Bacon's misconception that History may be divided from Science as memory may be distinguished from reason. Life has its mind as well as its matter and its record; and matter has its record in history as science has its history in record. Those distinctions or divisions are not merely vague but invalid.

Let us now proceed to examine the order of the special subjects. Psychology is separated on the one hand from Physiology and on the other hand from Education and Sociology. Æsthetics is remote from the Arts. Philosophy, the most general subject, in J3 is distant from General Science (A9). Folk-lore, with Mythology and Religion (J5 and J4), is dissevered from Anthropology and Ethnology (G). Human Anatomy and Physiology (G2) are separated from special anatomy and physiology (G6 to H4) by Pathology, Materia Medica, Pharmacy, Surgery, and Therapeutics (G3 to G5), and consequently these more general branches of medical science are separated from the special pathology of diseases and special practice by all the details of special anatomy and physiology. But worse is the separation of Chemistry in D7 from Physics in B by all of Engineering, Astronomy, and Geology, Meteorology, and Metallurgy intervening in unconscionable confusion. Physiography and Meteorology come in between Astronomy and Geology, tho they should be subordinate to the latter. Hydrostatics, which belongs under Physics, is misplaced under Hydrography, subordinate to Physiography; and the index refers Hydrodynamics to Hydrostatics. Crystallography and Mineralogy are separated from Chemistry by Metallurgy and Mining, which, to accord with Mr. Brown's scheme, should be subordinated to

Chemical Technology and to Economic Geology respectively. General and theoretical Physics is separated from Mathematics, with the Graphic and Plastic Arts and General Science intervening. In the Arts there is the same disregard for "conventions and groupings," convenience and consistency. Gardening (I220) is separated from Agriculture (I000) by Live Stock, Dairy Farming, Veterinary Medicine, and Milling, and these are separated from Vegetable and Animal Products by Woodworking, Furniture, Textile Manufactures and the Clothing Trades, the former two of these subjects evidently being regarded as *applications* of Forestry, to which they are subordinated. Commerce and Trade (L8) are separated from Political Economy (L1) by all of Political Science and Law. In Law the subjects of Criminology and Criminal Law, Police, and Penology are interposed between Torts and Contracts. Paleography and Bibliography are brought together with Typography in M7 between American Languages (M6) and Practical Printing, Paper-making, and Bookbinding (M8). Paleography and Diplomatics and Archives are usually regarded as accessory to History. Into the details of the subdivisions it is needless to examine. Any competent classifier should see how bad this classification is. It not only disregards "conventions" and convenience, but it ignores established scientific relations, and conceptual or logical relations that are no less important.

The notation was intended to be very simple and economical. Comparatively simple it is, but not economical. It employs a broad base of twenty-four letters, discarding Y and Z. It does not, however, use the letters distinctively, except in five or six cases, M for Language and Literature, L for Social and Political Science, W for America, and X for Biography. Most of the other letters are grouped: Physical Sciences are grouped under B, C, D; Ethnology and Medicine under G, H; and British Islands under U, V. Philosophy is not J but J3; Chemistry is D7; Political Science is L2. Half of the base, twelve letters, is apportioned to the main division "Record," that is, to Philology, History, and Geography. The other twelve letters of course do not suffice, and distinctive marks are therefore lacking for some of the most important sciences and studies. The notation is not mnemonic. The divisions and subdivisions are marked by consecutive numbers, intermittent, as in the Library of Congress, but also permitting of intercalations on the decimal principle. The decimal-point is to be used only before the numbers suffixed from the Categorical Table. It would have been more economical to have used a two-letter base, or *area,* as the Library of Congress has done. A three-letter notation is still more economical. There are 154 pages of schedules, with about 80 numbers to the page. Mr. Brown has estimated that about 14,000 numbers are assigned.

The economic limit would be exceeded the more often because of the disproportion, which is not only basic but results in minor subjects having major marks. As much room is given to Wales (history and geography) in U2 as to Biology in E0; as little to Education (A1) as to Logic (A3), as little to Finance (L9) as to Skin and Hair (H4), as little to Civil Engineering (B2) as to Woodworking, Furniture, and Basket Making (P3), as little to European languages and literatures (M4 and M5) as to Denmark and Norway (T5 and T6). In the last only 14 of the hundred numbers are specified.

The system has two means for economizing the schedules, and possibly their use. The first provides that the numbers for countries in the History-geography schedule may be affixed to any subject. Thus, Arabia being marked Q260 and Climate D240, the Climate of Arabia would be marked D240Q26, the final cipher being omitted. This lengthens the notation, as it does in the

Decimal Classification and in Cutter's too; for letters are more economical than numbers in supplementary notation for systematic schedules.

The other auxiliary schedule is called the "Categorical Table," that is, "a table of forms, phases, standpoints, qualifications, etc., which apply more or less to every subject or subdivision of a subject." These are numbered consecutively from .1 to .975, the numbers not being used decimally but set off by the point to indicate that they are taken from the Table. Thus .19 would follow .2. There is an alphabetical index to the list. This includes a few historical but not geographical subdivisions. The first, those having the shortest numbers, are perhaps the commonest in use, but Laboratory work is .69, Methods would require .767, and Law .811. Experiments and Experimental method are lacking. The list does not seem complete or definitive. The truth is, the attempt to simplify *all* repetitious subdivisions in *one* systematic schedule applicable to *any* subject is a mistaken notion and breaks down of its own burden. Most of the specifications are useless under most subjects. A generally applicable systematic schedule should provide only for the most commonly required subdivisions and should reduce these to a few captions with short literal notation. For History, Language, and Literature special systematic schedules should be provided, and such prove economical in use and in notation. The Management of Factories in Saxony would require the absurdly long mark L121.767S745. This is what the Library of Congress avoids at the cost of immensely bulky expansion in its schedules; and, in avoiding that bulk, this is what Brown's cumbersome means would come to. Neither system solves the problem economically. A series of systematic schedules with literal notation would economically solve it. An economical mark for that subject, precisely as specific, is TFIgh, which is analyzed thus: T for Economics, F for Industrial, I for Factory Management, gh for Saxony.

One more important test we have still to apply. Does this classification provide properly for subjects that were rapidly developing in the decade of its compilation? Biochemistry would have to be subsumed under the old term Chemical Physiology (more usually termed Physiological Chemistry). Then Ecology is erroneously subordinated to Evolution, and there are no places for its subdivisions, e. g. Littoral Life, Aquatic Life, Alpine Life, etc. Under Psychology there is no provision for the special branches, Comparative Psychology, Animal Behavior, Folk-, and Social Psychology, nor for Individual Psychology, Psychology of Types, of Children, of Character; nor is the term Physiological psychology there, but many of its older subjects are subordinated to Nervous Diseases, as are also Dreams, Hallucinations, Psychiatry, and Insanity. Genius is misplaced under Ethnology. Under Education there is no provision for Educational Psychology, unless it be compounded with a long mark (.626) from the Categorical Table to be suffixed to Pedagogics (A110); nor is Philosophy of Education distinguished from plain Education. The schedules of Sociology and Economics do not explicitly provide for any of the theoretical topics. Without going further into details, we may say that these schedules are very inadequate.

We must conclude that Brown's Subject Classification, tho simpler on the whole than the three American systems, is not distinctly better as regards the order of the main subjects nor as regards the relations and collocations of the specific subjects; nor is it conveniently complete; nor is it readily adaptable. As regards apportionment and notation, when the marks from its Categorical Table are suffixed, or from its geographical schedule, its notation becomes excessively cumbersome. Brown's classification is no more practical and no more scientific than the other systems we have criticised, and no less disqualified.[5]

2. The Classification of the University of Halle

The Germans, as everybody knows, are very systematic; so it is not surprising to find that the classified catalog of the library of one of their universities is in its plan systematic and consistent with a logical synthesis valid at the time of its compilation. Wundt's *Eintheilung der Wissenschaften* appeared a few years later, in 1889, but it had been embodied in his *Logik,* first published in 1883. Hartwig's *Schema*[6] was planned in 1879, but was not carried out until the years 1884-88; so it may have been influenced by Wundt's system; or it may have been drawn from the scientific atmosphere of the time. It is regrettable that more of it did not come to America and get into the Cutter system; then the Library of Congress would have drawn upon something worth while adapting.

There are broad similarities between Hartwig's Scheme and Wundt's system; but then there are basic differences. Wundt's purpose was logical; Hartwig's was primarily practical. He was indeed a librarian. He first broadly distinguished between books of scientific

[5] An excellent review of Brown's classification, by Dr. W. W. Bishop, appreciative, discriminative, and also destructive, appeared in *The Library Journal* for December, 1906, p. 836-8. Dr. Bishop made many points not covered in the foregoing pages. In recommending this review, however, one need not endorse all the opinions for praise or for blame. Mr. Berwick Sayers is more appreciative in his chapter on this system.

[6] Hartwig, Otto, *Schema des Realkatalogs der K. Universitäts-bibliothek zu Halle a S., Zentralblatt für Bibliothekswesen,* III, Beiheft, 1888, 350 p.

content on the one hand and on the other hand books chiefly of literary and artistic interest — somewhat as DeQuincy distinguished between the books of knowledge and the books of influence.[7] Being a librarian first and evidently not too much of a logician, he put this literature first, and all the languages and their respective literatures he placed in that same forward position (Classes B, C, and D), and then the Fine Arts (Class E); but foremost in Class A he placed the General subjects: Bibliography and Library Science, Printing and Publishing, Introductions to Science, and History of Science and of Learned Societies and their publications, and also Periodicals and Encyclopedias of general scope. For a university library and indeed for any large reference library this provision may have been quite practical. The most notable objections from the knowledge point of view are that Classical Philology (Class C) and Ancient Art (division Eb) are thus separated too far from Ancient History (Nb) and History of Ancient Civilization under Class H.

From Wundt's *Eintheilung* this scheme differs fundamentally in placing the natural sciences after the mental and social sciences and history (ethnic-social-political-economic), and in making transition from the mental to the natural thru Geography,[8] whereas Wundt treated Psychology as being at once the culminating natural science and the fundamental mental science. That is to say, Wundt's scheme embodied the naturalistic view of the fields of knowledge, whereas Hartwig's in a manner represented the correlative

[7] "Man könnte daher auf die Idee verfallen, die Bücherschätze einer Bibliothek in zwei grosse Massen zu sondern: 1. wissenschaftliche Werke; 2. Werke, die ihrer Form, ihrer Sprache, ihres künstlerischen Werthes u.s.w. wegen aufbewahrt werden." (p. 13).

[8] "Alle wissenschaftlichen Disciplinen . . . . hat man Recht in Geisteswissenschaften und Naturwissenschaften getheilt." (p. 14).

"Den Uebergang von den Geisteswissenschaften zu den Naturwissenschaften lasse man durch die Geographie bilden, ... " (p. 15). **In his schedule this is Erdkunde.**

humanistic view. In Wundt's system Philosophy was a third main division, and in this the last caption was for the philosophy of the history of civilization. Wundt's first main division was for Formal, or Mathematical, Sciences, distinguished from Real, or Empirical, Sciences, which he divided into Natural Sciences and Mental Sciences; but in Hartwig's Scheme the Mathematical Sciences are subordinated to the Natural Sciences, Mathematics was separated from Physics by Astronomy, and this was thus separated from Geology; and Biology was not distinguished as a fundamental science but was subsumed — what there was of it at that time. Geology in SaIII was placed too far from Physical Geography in Oa; and this last was separated from Meteorology under Q.

In the Mental and Social Sciences several no less inconsistent separations are incidental to the inversion by which these sciences precede the Natural Sciences. Anthropology and Ethnology in HaII are remote from Zoölogy in Sc, from the related Medical Sciences in U, from Sociology in Le, and from History in N and Geography in O. The History of Civilization and Ethnology (under Class H) should not be so far away from History (ethnic-social-political-economic) in Class N. Nor should Theology in Class I be so distant from Philosophy in Class F; and under Philosophy the fifth special branch, Psychology (FbV), should not be entirely separated from Physiology, nor should the Philosophy of Religion (FbVII) be dissevered from Theology in Class I; nor should Logic be separated from Mathematics. Nor should Education in Class G be severed from Psychology (FbV) by Natural Philosophy, and the Philosophy of Religion, of Æsthetics, of Ethics, of Law, and of History. Indeed with so many salient and inconvenient separations this scheme savors of the departmental university curriculum rather than of a coherent logical synthesis of knowledge, by which a university library should serve to unify the university.

As a classified catalog, rather than a classification for books, Hartwig's *Schema* comprised much to appreciate and to adapt. Some of the faults noticed here are referable to the period of the compilation. The system has unfortunately borne the reputation of having a cumbersome notation, tho that with which it was published is said to differ from that actually used in the library at Halle.[9] There this classification has probably been altered, modified, and kept up to date. If this improved and developed system could be published, it would doubtless serve as an important contribution to library classification and it could more advantageously be utilized by the makers of systems less objectionable in their fundamental structure. As published, the scheme is disqualified by its age, its inadequacy, its disproportion, and its inconsistency with the modern scientific synthesis.

3. The International Catalogue of Scientific Literature

Here we have before us a classification that, except for a few faults, is fundamentally consistent with the synthesis of science as maintained in the consensus of the present. This great classified bibliography for the annual output of scientific literature was published yearly from 1901 to 1914, when the publication lapsed from lack of financial support. Annually seventeen volumes were issued, one for each of seventeen sciences, the content and requirement of which determined the practical division. While the relations are consistent, the divisions should not be supposed to be fundamentally coördinate. The series of main classes is shown on the opposite page.

[9] "The practical usefulness of it for this purpose would have been greatly enhanced if the notation actually in use had been printed. It is often erroneously supposed that the various letters and figures employed in the scheme to differentiate the rank or subordination and coördination of divisions and subdivisions form combined the notation." — Martel, *Library Journal*, v. 36, p. 414.

A Mathematics
B Mechanics
C Physics
D Chemistry
E Astronomy
F Meteorology
G Mineralogy
H Geology
J Geography
K Paleontology
L General Biology
M Botany
N Zoölogy
O Human Anatomy
P Physical Anthropology
Q Physiology
R Bacteriology

In this order there are items that are not just in agreement with the order of the sciences as conceived in the consensus — that is, as we have discerned it. Mechanics is usually regarded as a branch of Physics, to which it is propædeutic and basic, the most general, abstract, and exact branch. That Mechanics may be treated mathematically and more abstractly than the special branches of Physics should not mislead scientists to admit the claims of some mathematicians that Mechanics is merely a branch of Mathematics. That is not true even of Rational, or Analytic, Mechanics, which of course should not be dissevered from the sub-science as a whole. As well might the mathematicians claim that Elasticity, Thermodynamics, Electrodynamics, Acoustics, or any other branch that admits of mathematical treatment, is merely applied mathematics. Mathematics is indeed applied in them; they may even be dependent on mathematics; that is a reason for placing them after Mathematics in the order of the sciences as graded in speciality. But, in so far as studies are distinct from one another, these sciences, or branches of physical science, are distinct from Mathematics as a group of abstract studies. In the classification in question Mechanics is placed ahead of Physics probably for the reason that its prospective bulk seemed to require a separate volume and so it seemed best to treat it as intermediate between Mathematics and Physics. But it is doubtful whether the literature has proved, or will prove, bulky enough to justify separation for convenience or proportion.

Meteorology, another sub-science, is dependent on Physics for theories and for methods, but it is one of the earth sciences and is more especially related to Physical Geography and thru this to Geology. It is not intimately related to Astronomy, tho it has sometimes been traditionally confused with the science of meteors, as it has etymologically. There is not good reason for placing it between Astronomy and Mineralogy. There is good reason for subordinating Mineralogy to Chemistry, even tho it is closely related to Geology, which depends much on this sub-science. If it needs must be separated, it were better placed next after Chemistry. And Geology should immediately follow Astronomy.

Paleontology is properly a branch of Biology, or of its branch Morphology, tho it contributes greatly to Geology, especially to the historical and stratigraphical branches of this science. Here is another indication that the "International Committee . . . . appointed to settle authoritatively the details of the schedules" was more considerate of practical bibliographical concerns than of scientific consistency.[10]

Bacteriology is another sub-science which might better have been subordinated to its fundamental science, Botany, which it should rather have followed, if sepa-

[10] "Ultimately, after prolonged discussion, it was decided to adopt an arbitrary combined system of letters, numbers, and other symbols, adapted in the case of each branch of science to its peculiar needs."

This and the phrase quoted above appeared in the Preface to the first volume (Mathematics) of the first issue. Certain questions had been discussed for years at successive conferences. From the Preface again the following is quoted: "Although the question of the method to be adopted in classifying the subject matter of the several sciences was discussed at great length, no decision other than one adverse to the Dewey system was arrived at. The Royal Society was requested to appoint a Committee . . . ." They were probably discouraged both by the incoherency of the Dewey system and the incoherency of the discussions from attempting to set up a consistent or logical classification of the sciences and their sub-sciences.

rated. Physiology (Q) here included not merely the human but also the comparative and the zoölogical, and should have followed General Biology (L) and have preceded Physical Anthropology (P); but the order of these last four subjects seems to have been a concession to the medical profession rather than to the biological view, for which it would have been better to have classified the comparative physiology of animals with General Physiology under General Biology, and to have put Human Physiology in the same volume with Human Anatomy. Zoölogy in class N is treated descriptively and taxonomically, without details for the theoretical, physiological, and morphological subjects treated comparatively or generally. So, if Bacteriology were moved to N and Zoölogy to O, Physical Anthropology in P would appear as transitional from the natural sciences to the human sciences, and Human Anatomy and Physiology might then be classified together in Q. Then, if Psychology should later be added to the scope of this Catalogue, it would occupy the next place (R) in proper collocation with the two anthropological sciences with which it is most closely related; and, if furthermore Sociology were admitted to the series, that science too would be properly collocated.

In thus criticising this order, we have perhaps regarded it as more important than did the Committee, which, as was said above, was evidently more intent upon bibliographical convenience than upon scientific consistency, the lack of which appears more speciously in the order of the divisions and subdivisions of the several sciences. It is needless, however, to enter into these in detail. When the next conference in the interests of the International Catalogue of Scientific Literature is convened[11] and the resumption of the publication is considered, it is likely the classification may be improved.

To justify our animadversions a few instances of inconsistency will be noticed here. Mineralogy (class G) has four divisions: General, Mineralogy (descriptive and systematic), Petrology, and Crystallography. This last, which is comparatively abstract and theoretical, should precede the second, not be separated from it by Petrology, which is the special branch for the study of rocks. Similarly in the science of Chemistry the division for Theoretical and Physical Chemistry should precede that for the Chemistry (specific) of the Elements, and so should that for Analytical Chemistry as a general branch of the science; and this should not be separated from Laboratory Procedure by the division for Organic Chemistry.

In Biology, the special branch Cytology should be collocated with the caption Origin and Development of the Organism, and more specially with Embryology, rather than with the captions, Life of the Individual and Ecology. In Botany, however, the caption Morphology, Anatomy, Embryology, and Cytology, properly brings these subjects together, tho the order would be better if Cytology preceded Embryology, that is, it would proceed from the more general to the more special. In Physiology the first division, Physiological Chemistry, should rather be combined with Biochemistry and classified under Biology, which lacks this branch. It should be unnecessary to duplicate this subject in Chemistry.

Hydrography should be subordinated to Physical Geography rather than to Mathematical, and the Tides

[11] There were to have been international conferences at least once in each decade, besides those of a Council. At the Second International Convention (1910) a committee was appointed "to revise the schedules and to make such other alterations as may be necessary in the form of issue of the Catalogue." (*Science*, v. 33, p. 718).

should be transferred to the former branch, mauger the mathematical theory of this special subject, which might be placed under Hydrodynamics. Petrography should not separate Dynamic Geology from Tectonic Geology.

We should remember that this classification was intended for a bibliographical catalog, not for libraries. A library classification should according to modern standards be divided much more specifically and minutely. Here, for instance, in the division for Cultural Anthropology the caption, Religion, Magic: Religious and Magical Beliefs, Observances, and Customs, is not subdivided, tho in the year 1914-15 there were under it fourteen pages of entries averaging about forty to the page, or about 500.

The duplication of certain large subjects, such as Physiological Chemistry, increases cost of publication. There are many lesser duplications that, as in the Library of Congress classification, are confusing and uneconomical in dispersing related materials. For example, Variable Stars has place under Theoretical Astronomy in E 1850, again under Descriptive Astronomy in E 7600, and still again under Stellar Spectroscopy in E 8300.

The notation was professedly "arbitrary," initial letters for the sciences, followed by intermittent serial numbers for the divisions and subdivisions. It resembles Brown's, which may have been misled by it. In the schedules the numbers are regularly of four places, but in some smaller schedules likely to require fewer subdivisions two-place numbers suffice. Indeed two-place numbers would suffice thruout, for there are comparatively few subdivisions and the numbers for the most part have useless ciphers in their latter halves, and, being used intermittently, not decimally, are very widely spaced.[12] That is to say, the notation is very

[12] In the schedule for Geology, however, where two-place numbers are used, certain subjects have their details marked with decimal notation, tho not very consistently. Thus the mark H 07.05 is given to the more general subject Description of Earthquakes, while the mark H 07.70 wastes a cipher on Earthquakes in relation to Geodynamics, etc., a more special subject.

uneconomical. At the head of each general subject there is a recurrent table of generalia or *preliminaries*. To apply these in subdividing a special subject, or to combine the numbers of two related subjects, would require from six to eight figures to be added to the letter of the science. Geographical subdivision may be marked by affixing the respective lower-case letters that form the notation of the first half (Topographical) of the Schedule of Geography: thus, d for Europe, db for Russia, and dbb for Southern Russia. The table of preliminaries is not remarkable for order or collocation. The general treatises are separated from the philosophy of the science by the periodicals and from the lectures and addresses by other items.

Bibliographical classification concerns us here less than the problem of classification for libraries; but we have criticised the International Catalogue of Scientific Literature because it is likely to affect library classification in the future.[13] It has failed, however, to embody satisfactorily the system of the sciences as regards the synthesis or organization of knowledge. It has failed to rise to a great opportunity and to serve a great purpose. In the future let us hope that its publication will be resumed, its classification improved, and its notation economized.

4. The Colon Classification of Ranganathan

This interesting and ingenious system, developed during the past fifteen years in the library of the University of Madras and published in 1933, so as to be available

[13] It would seem that certain schedules of the Library of Congress may have been affected by the International Catalogue rather than by Cutter's system or that of Hartwig — for instance, in placing Pharmacology in the last portion of Physiology rather than with Pharmacognosy under Materia Medica, where only a certain part of the subject is provided for. Another instance is the placing of Theoretical and Physical Chemistry after the divisions for Analytical, Inorganic, and Organic Chemistry, which we have before declared to be objectionable.

to other libraries in India and elsewhere, should be described and criticised more adequately than space and time now permit. The system is constructed on valid principles and on a not-too-incoherent order of main classes. The "basic" classification is logical in most of its divisions, scientific in its details, and scholarly in its elaboration. It is of course especially adapted to oriental collections. The oriental mind may comprehend it, tho the occidental would hardly essay to undertake it. But it is important in its main principle, and we should profit by some study of it.

The main principle is that of *complex*, or *composite*, classification.[1] This principle is more than fundamental in this system; it is pervasive. Ranganathan has developed it with admirable ingenuity and consistency. All kinds of specifications, relations, and topics are provided for, with correlative auxiliary notation. Here is an elaborate extension of Dewey's principle of "number-bilding" — more elaborate than the notational devices of *La Classification Décimale*. It may be reminiscent of Cutter's device of employing punctuation-marks to indicate combined notations. From so using the colon the name Colon Classification derives. That the system is so complicated is a reason why we have not time and space to criticise it adequately. If we fail to do justice to it, if our attitude seems unfriendly or unkind, the reader may consider that we are intent on disapproval of

[1] In the first edition of this book, in Principle XXII (p. 43) the reviewer termed it *complex classification*, but in this second edition the term *composite* is introduced, with regard to auxiliary *systematic schedules* and correlative mnemonic notation, as stated in Principle XXVIII. This term appeared in the statement and discussion of "Theoretic Principles of Bibliographic Classification," a paper contributed by the writer to the XIV Conference of The International Federation for Documentation, held at Oxford in September, 1938. (See the Appendix to this book on p. 331). It was brought forward also in reviewing Ranganathan's *Prolegomena to Library Classification* for *The Library Quarterly* of April, 1938 (See v. VIII, p. 303, the concluding paragraphs). Ranganathan prefers the term *synthetic*, but that has different connotation and is differently defined in our Principle XVII (p. 42). The two terms will be found together in *The Prolegomena*, in the second paragraph of page 137.

a too complicated elaboration of the important valid principle of *Composite Classification.*

Ranganathan's mind comprehends the immense diversity and intricacy of objects, aspects, and relations in nature and in life; and he would synthesize this complexity adequately in a system of bibliographic classification. Here adequacy countervails simplification. But is such complex specification feasible and requisite? Is it requisite for libraries? Is it feasible even for bibliographic documentation? Miss Kelley argues that it is not, and that it is inefficient.[2] The writer has indicated the "Limitations" of classification and the "economic limit" of notation.[3]

In the Decimal Classification and also in that of the Library of Congress the schedules specify subjects and topics in unnecessary and impractical detail, assigning "ready-made Class-numbers," as Ranganathan calls them. But the Colon Classification, instead of doing this, combines and constructs "Class Numbers for all possible topics. . . . In this volume the function of the colon (:) is like that of the bolts and nuts of a Meccano set."[4]

La Classification Décimale is ostensibly a system for extensive bibliographic *documentation.* The Colon Classification probably surpasses this in capacity for composite specification, in inherent elaboration of details and in complication of systematic and pseudo-mnemonic notation. Notation is pervasive and predominant in this system. The Colon Classification is most interesting as an applied notation.

[2] Grace O. Kelley, *The Classification of Books,* The Wilson Company, 1937, "Conclusion," p. 126-9.

[3] *The Organization of Knowledge,* p. 147; and in this book p. 49 and 51.

[4] *Colon Classification,* by S. R. Ranganathan, M.A., L.T., F.L.A., Madras Library Ass'n., 1933. *Vide* Preface, p. xiii.

That notation is subsidiary to classification has repeatedly been emphasized. Notation should denote and locate classes, not specify them as terminology does, nor attempt to designate the terms severally, nor to be mnemonic of them. Within limits it may be mnemonic, but beyond those limits it becomes too complicated; it ceases to be mnemonic, and it renders even a good synthetic system uneconomical.

The "colon device" is only one of "Eight Devices," which are described in Chapter 6, and which appear in a table under its heading: 1 "The Colon Device . . . . consists in separating by a colon the parts of a Class Number, which relate to the different characteristics forming the basis of a classification." 2 The Geographical Device ". . . . for the further subdivision of a class which is capable of geographical division. . . ." 3 The Chronological Device ". . . . for the further subdivision of a class that is capable of chronological division. . . ." 4 The Favoured Category Device, which assigns the shortest subordinate numbers, 1, 2, ... 9, to nine specific subjects selected for importance. 5 The Classic Device ". . . . for bringing together the different editions of a classic in a class . . . . its commentaries, ... subcommentaries, and so on. . . ." 6 The Subject Device ". . . . for the further subdivision of a class . . . ." —that is sub-classes. 7 "The Alphabetic Device consists in using the initial letter, or the initial letter amplified, of the name . . . . of a class of substances or entities." 8 The Bias-number Device ". . . . for bringing together . . . . the books in a class . . . . written . . . . from a special point of view that can be associated with some other class, or for the use of a special class of readers whose primary interest of study is in some other class, or as have some other special relation to some other class. The class to which the book belongs may be termed the 'Basic Class' and its number may be termed the 'Basic Number.' The other class may be termed the 'Bias Class' and its number may be termed the 'Bias Number'." This is the only definition quoted here with any fullness. The other devices are defined with similar complexity. Indeed they would serve as models of redundancy. They exemplify the complexity of the author's thought on these complicated subject-matters.

But these devices are not especially original. It is the complexity and the ingenuity with which they are defined and applied that is distinctive. Antecedents more or less equivalent to the Geographic, Chronologic, Subject, and Bias-number devices may be found in the auxiliary signs and notations for "common subdivisions" in *La Classification Décimale*. For the Chronologic, Classic, and Alphabetic devices antecedents may be found in the Library of Congress schedules. The subject device seems but an extension of the principle of Subordination. The Favoured Category Device seems but a high-toned name for the practical apportioning of notation so as to have "distinctive marks for main subjects"—as it was indexed in the first edition of this book and remains in this edition, referring to the top of p. 52, the top of p. 77, and the bottom of p. 268. The Geographic, the Chronologic, the Subject, and the Classic devices are not very different from the *systematic schedules* for Countries, Historic Periods, Subclassification for certain special subjects, and for Chief Authors and Philosophers, in the writer's *System*. All this similarity probably leaves only the Colon Device *per se* as especially and creditably original.

Correlative to three of Ranganathan's eight devices are tables: 3 Geographical Divisions, 4 Language Divisions, and 5 Chronological Divisions. Preceded and indicated by the colon, the composite devices may be suffixed to the notations of the schedules of the basic classification, in which here and there indications for them are given. They thus tend to economize the bulk of the schedules, which occupy only 118 pages of two columns.

The notation is supposed to be mnemonic. There may be minds in India and elsewhere that can remember and apply these complications. There might consequently develop a profession or cult, as there has for the Decimal Classification. The introductory Part I, "Rules of Classification" is an elaborate code of definitions and instructions, which probably can be mastered. But the writer doubts whether he could do it. He would rather not try. He holds that such mnemonics are rendered impractical by their extreme complication.

Simple subjects indeed have simple notation in the basic classification: thus Photography is N6, Education of Women T55, and Teeth L214, under Medicine. The Index of 61 pages does not indicate Dentistry, nor Dentition, whether of infants or of animals. Such subjects are relegated to the mnemonic system somewhere and somehow. The comparatively simple *basic classes* may be specified, or "amplified," by various *characteristics*, O for organ in Medical science, N for natural group in Botany, P for problem in Geology, and so on, the characteristic letter being suffixed to the *basic* factor. We should note that "number" means letter too, as for so many American classifiers. The first definitions in the book are of "Call Number," "Class Number," "Book Number," and "Subject Digit," all of which combine *letters and* numbers. Indeed the definitions of this system often are as peculiar as they are redundant.

By various combinations of characteristics, divisions, and devices this notation becomes exceedingly lengthy and complicated, even for comparatively simple subjects. An interesting instance appears on p. 42: Critical studies of Shakespeare's Plays, in the English language, would have the mark O:2J64:90P111, which in an economical notation needs only YFA. That long mark is obtained thus: O for Literature, 2 for Drama, J64 for the date of Shakespeare's birth, 1564, (applying the chronological device) and :9 for Criticism, then by the Bias-number device OP introduces the language-number for English, 111. To specify something more, e.g. the Diction, other devices suffixed J:30B28, so that the entire mark for that specification exemplified there has 21 components, O:2J64:90P111:J:30B28, where a simple, economical notation would require for all that specification that is needed only four or five, the date and the language being unnecessary. That is the excess of the Colon notation. There is no practical need for such complicated notation.

Having thus criticised the dominant feature of mnemonic notation, we may conclude with a brief view of the basic classification. In outline it is logical, from the naturalistic-humanistic point of view, proceeding from Science in general thru the Physical and Natural Sciences, and the technologies derived from them, to the Arts, Philology, Religion, Philosophy, Psychology, Education, Geography, History, the Social Sciences, and finally Law. But the following objections obtain. Class G, Natural Science, General, and Biology, should have been termed Biology, the fundamental science, as all the subdivisions there should come under that term. Natural Science should comprise Astronomy, B9, which should not be included under Mathematics. Geology, H, should not separate Botany, I, from Biology in G; nor should Geology be so far from Geography in U, nor Philosophy in R be so remote from General Science in A; nor should Psychology in S be severed from Physiology under I, K, and L. Education in T does not companion well with Geography in U, nor Religion in Q with Philology in P. Anthropology appears only under History in V6, with Folk-lore, while Ethnology appears nowhere, not even in the Index.

The importance of the *Colon Classification* is neither in its colon nor in its classification, but in its exemplification of the valid principle of *composite classification,* systematic and synthetic, for specification of complex subjects of two or more characteristics, and for recurrent subdivisions. This system, however, fails to economize its systematic devices, and its complicated pseudo-mnemonic notation is too much of a burden for any bibliographic classification to bear.

Yet we must repeat, as we did in reviewing the *Prolegomena,* that the erudition, industry, insight, and ingenuity of the author are truly admirable. The system is well worth study by those who contemplate constructive developments in bibliographic classification.

CHAPTER XIV

THE SITUATION SURVEYED

1. Systematic Classification the Proper Basis for Specific Classification

Great credit is due to American librarians for their extensive and effectual development of services to many classes of readers. To those services and the requisite economies many efficient methods have contributed. Among the most important are classifications and catalogs. But these developments, however estimable in their day and their way, however serviceable in the present situation, are, and have been, far from satisfactory. This is largely because the established systems have lacked adaptability and have therefore become antiquated too soon, but fundamentally it is because, in the purpose to be practical in the particular historical and local situations, in the several libraries where they originated, they have disregarded the essential principles of classification for organization of knowledge.

Classification is affirmed to be an essential method for the organization of knowledge. It avails most when it is systematic — organized. An incoherent or arbitrary array of subjects is unsatisfactory and entirely dependent on an alphabetic index. Without an index it is a labyrinthine maze; and the index serves the classifiers, not the users of the books at the shelves.

A classified collection of books is itself structurally analogous to a book. The classes and sub-classes of books are analogous to the chapters and pages and paragraphs of the individual book. The schedules of the classification may be likened to the contents-pages of the book; they furnish a conspectus of the subject-matter, the captions, their divisions and subdivisions, their order, and their relations. The subject-index to the classification is equivalent to the index to the book; it locates the items. The notation correlative to the classification serves like the pagination of the book. To learn the contents or find where to read on a subject of present interest, we scan the contents-pages. To refer to an item, we open from the index. A good book is well arranged for reading or study, and also well indexed. A good classification is a structural survey of the fields of knowledge, thought, and interest; it is a synthetic organization of the special subjects of study and their analytical details. It is constructed on a basis of general classes in an order consistent with the scientific and educational systems. On this basis it proceeds by coherent division and gradation of subjects and by subordination of specific and again analytically more specific subjects, collocated, wherever feasible, by intrinsic relations or interests. Where requisite, interrelated subjects are systematically referred to chosen and to alternative allocations. And to all this complex system of subjects the index is the alphabetic reference by means of the notation. Thus good classification as a structural organization serves the functional organization of knowledge.

As interests, studies, and inquiries are ever various, this structure should not be regarded as rigid and unchanging. To function in the service, to live, and to keep alive, it must be adaptable to growth and to change. The need for change will be least where the provision for growth is most liberal. And, where the structure is basically and organically adapted to the predominant needs, educational and scientific, cultural and intellectual, the system will fundamentally be the most permanent.

2. The Subject-Index Illusion

The notion that any order of subjects will serve well enough, and that for practical and incidental uses (disregarding research) the divisions and subdivisions need not be classified logically or systematically — this notion we have given the sobriquet "subject-index illusion." It is short sighted in ignoring the fundamental principle of subordination of special classes to the relevant general classes, from which they are derivative by division and analysis; and it is but dimly perceptive of the valid principle of *collocation*, on which efficiency depends.

For locating specific subjects the alphabetic index may be the first recourse in classifying as in subject-cataloging; and this simple means may at any time serve for particular reference to a subject; but to relate specific subjects to the relevant general subjects and to coördinate subjects of kindred interests, we proceed more broadly from the conspectus or the schedules to the shelf-list or the shelves; and this procedure avails also for the uses of research. In actually classifying books we should look both ways — tho of course not at the same time. To work always from the index comports with narrow specialism, and with the subject-index illusion. On the other hand, to refer each case to the schedule and also compare it with the shelf-list would take too much time. This might moreover result in occasional inconsistencies which the index might obviate. There are reasons for having the map of the country and of the city streets; and for seeing the city with this guide and at the same time walking for exercise; but, when you know the city well enough, and when you would save time, it is convenient to have a directory tell you the number and a taxi set you down at the door. So a classification for a library should have an index for passing from the alphabetic order by means of the notation into the systematic order of subjects.

How the index may mislead the unwitting classifier into the wrong avenue appears in the following instance of error: in a certain college library two books on the production and utilization of natural gas were classed under the physics of Gases, because the subject-index under Gases referred to that place, and it had omitted the terms Gas, Natural, and Natural Gas.

The truth is that an alphabetic index neither classes nor classifies — not even backwards. Alphabetic order is dispersive, not synthetic; it contravenes logical order,[1] or any other order. An alphabetic index is merely complementary to a classification; it is, we repeat, a method of locating the subjects, by means of the correlative notation, in the system of classified classes. To substitute the index for the classification is as foolish as it is to confuse the classification with the notation; yet both have been done too much during the past decades, even in the serious literature of the subject; and many catalogers and classifiers are not yet clear of the confusion.

3. The Established Library Classifications Are Inadequate and Disqualified

These terms may sound rather harsh and trenchant, applied thus to systems that have been highly esteemed; so we shall hasten to justify them. The classifications in question are inadequate and disqualified in that they

[1] For fuller discussion see the writer's article, "L'Illogisme de l'ordre alphabétique," in *Revue du Livre*, 3. année, 1935, p. 16-19, followed by a translation into English.

have disregarded fundamental principles that we have found essential, or at least they have embodied them inadequately; and, tho much new detail may have been incorporated into them, they have nevertheless lacked requisite adaptability to the broader progressive developments. They are inadequate because they were not planned and constructed in consistency with the scientific and educational systems. It is not that these systems are comparatively new, nor that those library classifications are too old in years, for it is fair to say that they have all grown up together; and the library systems, if properly adaptable, might have conformed to the scientific and educational systems, or might now, or in the future, be brought to do so. But they have not been built that way. Their unwisely planned structures remain basically unaltered and unalterable, with all their misplaced rooms, doorways and windows, stairways and passageways. Their purposes were "practical" rather than scientific or educational, and their builders did not see that these aims should not be so divergent. Their main divisions and major subordinations are too largely arbitrary and unauthentic. That they have failed to provide liberally for alternative views and locations increases the resulting inconvenience. They have made but inadequate and ill-adapted provision for the multiplicity of new subjects and for the various aspects of old subjects in new relations. They have not consistently collocated subjects that are closely related in study and research. This inefficiency appears not in a few places merely but, as our preceding chapters have shown, thruout their expanded schedules. A quarter century to a half century old, they have progressed only in adding details and "expansions." They have now grown much too cumbersome with unnecessary details. Their schedules should have been reduced a third or more by economized *systematic schedules.* Their notations usually exceed the *economic limit.* Their terminology is too often antiquated. All these faults have become bristling realities to open-minded, experienced classifiers; but many individual attempts to remedy them have been on the whole unavailing. The magnitude and difficulty of the problem have now become manifest to those who bear it as an administrative and professional burden.

4. The Historical Situation

That classification is indispensable to library service is a principle not merely advocated but espoused by the profession of librarians. Their professional happiness, self-respect, reputation, and success depend on the virtue, fitness, orderliness, and efficiency of their spouse.

But there is much dissatisfaction; the problems of classification have not yet been acceptably solved; and the criticisms have been amply justified, as we have seen in the preceding chapters. If those systems were less unsatisfactory, librarians would be more respected for this part of their service.

If there really were a satisfactory or standard classification for libraries, we should not speak so trenchantly or so disrespectfully of it, nor thus of the conservative historical situation. But there is no library classification constructed on valid principles and standardized.

We have called the situation "historical," implying past conditions, conditioned acceptance, and traditional estimation. The established systems are maintained by professional conservatism in the midst of professional progress. This is customarily justified on economic grounds no more valid than the historical situation is economic. Together the historical and economic conditions have too long delayed a fairly feasible solution of the problem, or even remedial measures. The situation has now become a social and intellectual one. An intellectual need arises from the confusion and inadequacy of the library systems in the great social movement of the organization of knowledge.

For library service to be harnessed forever to antiquated conveyances, to crude, arbitrary classifications that were never consistent with fundamental principles and with the scientific and educational systems of knowledge — this would indeed be an unfortunate historical situation and intellectually discreditable to librarianship. Let us hope that the opportunity will prevail over the economic obstacles to realize a larger and more edifying coöperative economy and service.

It has long been averred that, if better classifications had been published, they would have been more generally adopted. The arbitrary makeshifts that we have criticised have been accepted and elaborated because they were ready at hand, and to construct other systems better would have required more time and talent than were available. But what may have been beyond the knowledge and resources of individual librarians might have been accomplished coöperatively by librarians, educators, and scientists.

5. Progressive Reclassification

This historical situation, like others, is motivated by conflicting urgencies. The economic cost of reclassifying a library is to be weighed against the resulting economies in the use of the books and the estimable enhancement in professional, educational, and intellectual values. Where these prevail, the desirability and feasibility of reclassification is likely to be recognized and realized. But the historical situation like a heavy mortgage burdens the costs of reconstruction.

But let us take not undue alarm at the prospect of reclassifying our libraries. That will come not in a revolution, but gradually, as progressive changes usually come. Here and there, in this library and in that, in this class and in that, changes will be made as the need becomes manifest and the conditions permit. Sometimes new systems or special classifications will be adopted; sometimes old systems will be modified or adapted. New standards are likely to be established. Yet the situation will not be chaotic; it will be less so than at present. American librarians, however conservative in the historical and economic situations, are not likely to continue long to abide by the structures already recognized as antiquated; and few will cling to them till they show signs of crumbling to pieces about them, like the "wonderful one-hoss shay."

In classifying for libraries there is constant waste in fussing over schedules that fail to provide properly for a large percentage of modern books, and in revising the schedules and in discussing the revisions. A certain amount of addition, alteration, and adaptation is essential to any live classification of books, inevitably so; but in an antiquated system this adaptation becomes increasingly difficult and complicated. Revision thus may eventually take more time, may cost more than reclassification, and the resulting product may be much less satisfactory.

There are, it seems reasonable to assert, many librarians, especially in university and in college libraries, who, finding their classifications inefficient, confusing, and discreditable, would adopt an improved modern system, if such were known to be economically available. Some of these might reclassify only certain portions of their collections, in concession to the more urgent needs. In general the progressive change would of necessity be gradual.

Reclassifying libraries can and will be economized. Methods and routines for re-marking books and cards will be devised and practiced. Marks in books and on shelf-list cards should be with pencil, not with ink. On catalog-cards and on backs of books it is usually harder to take the old marks off than to put the new marks on; but an electric eraser may facilitate this step.

The American method of using the notation of classification not only as a means to locate the groups of books but to designate them in records and in applications — the dear old "call-numbers" — may now prove to have been an economic blunder. On catalog-cards a similar symbolic abbreviation for the author and subject, or title, might serve as at present and permanently. This would be on the upper corner of the card. New class-marks would be added in pencil in the lower corner. Reclassifying then would not involve erasing typewritten class-marks on cards. On the backs of the books, above the old marks the new class-marks only would be gilded or labeled, and within the book recorded with pencil. In most cases the permanent marks need not differ from the alterable class-marks. On shelf-labels for every class, section, and sub-section, if requisite, the class-marks, together with their class-terms, should be prominent. Then within each group the books could be arranged by their call-numbers, or book-numbers, or *internal* notation. Thus there would be two notations, one permanent for designation and record, the other for classification by subject and more readily and economically alterable. This duplexity would be no more complex than that of the antique and uneconomic *accession-numbers.* Classification would thus gain in efficiency by reclassification and by having more shelf-labels plainly indicating the subjects in their systematic order.

The literature of the past, whether superseded, antiquated, or historic, may be separated, without reclassification. This would be likely for special subjects in science and technology, and to some extent also in history and philosophy, and even in philology and literature. The recent books would then be classified according to modern standards. Where thoro and elaborate change is in process, means would probably be found for minimizing confusion between the new classification and the old. These are but problems to try the mettle of librarianship; they should add zest and expertness to the profession and its schooling. There are general problems, and problems of individual libraries in their particular conditions.

Some libraries are now classified so unsatisfactorily that reclassifying thruout in the near future will be deemed requisite for efficiency. These should be free to break away from the tradition. For them, the longer reclassification is postponed and the larger the increase of the collections, the more burdensome the undertaking will be, when at last it becomes an economic necessity or a desideratum deemed educationally worth its cost. New libraries should clearly, emphatically, be untrammeled by the historical situation.

Systematic classification avails not only for readers consulting books on the shelves but for readers' consultants, or advisers, and reference librarians, to whom readers may come in the subject-approach, when the dictionary catalog proves too complicated or too inadequate. Much in the preceding pages that has been affirmed regarding the classification of books applies, with certain differences, to classified catalogs and bibliographies.

6. Centralized Coöperative Classifying

If there be so much inefficient classification and if these needs and values be recognized, what should we do? Centralized coöperative classifying and cataloging together, as indicated in the plans proposed in 1927, seems feasible. The report of the special committee of the American Library Association, appointed that year to consider the question, led to the appointment of another special committee of eminent librarians to raise a fund for a more thoro investigation of the large problem. A fund was then raised; another committee also was appointed to investigate, to develop an experimental project, and to continue and extend the services already undertaken in coöperation with the Library of Congress and other libraries. The results so far are encouraging, but they are mostly in the field of cataloging for large research libraries. There appears moreover the evidence of financial support, of the feasibility of selection, and the willingness of coöperating libraries to contribute materially. The service has increased and the return from the sales of the cards has now made it almost self-supporting. It is valuable to the coöperating libraries in supplementing the liberal and highly appreciated service of the Library of Congress, developed during the past three decades.

For coöperative classifying what is further requisite is, briefly, that the subjects of books should be plainly indicated in them and on the cards that represent them. This might be provided by the author and publisher in the preface and in connection with the copyright notice; and it could be confirmed or modified by a corps of classifiers in the central library. The standard cards, bearing subject-headings and class-notations, could be printed and stocked in the central bureau in anticipation of estimated demand. From stocks with sufficient reserves the cards might be distributed wholesale to publishers and booksellers or retail to libraries directly on request. The publishers and booksellers could supply the cards together with the books, when requested by the purchasers.

Such centralized coöperative service need not be dependent on a central library's classification and catalogs, which may be impaired by objectionable features or even be basically disqualified. These disadvantages might wholly offset the advantages of proximity to a comprehensive collection of books. It might be better to develop a new standard more or less coöperatively too.

7. A New Coöperative Standard Proposed

It is not necessary to adopt a faulty or cumbersome classification in order to participate in the economies and benefits of coöperative classifying. It should prove feasible to maintain such a service on the basis of a standardized general classification consistent with the principles of classification for libraries and with the organization of knowledge as maintained in the consensus of scientists and educators. In consistency with this there could be a system of standard special classifications for the several distinct types and groups of libraries. The class-marks of the standard classification could be given on the printed cards; and this might be done also, as now, for two or more of the classifications in use. There should be room on the cards for three or four class-marks, if not too lengthy. Other classifications could by means of their indexes translate the subjects there indicated into their own class-marks, of course with proper adaptations.

A system of classification for libraries consistent with the principles adduced in this book and exemplifying their application has been published in condensed form. It is offered in educational interests as a contribution to the solution of the problem that this book deals with. Even in this condensed form it is available to small and to medium-sized libraries. Give the new life a chance to grow, and you are likely to find it valuable in the future.

But now this system is being expanded and the first volume (Classes 1-9 and A-G) will probably in a few months be ready for printing. This will comprise the preliminary numeral classes, Philosophy, Mathematics, and the Natural Sciences, besides an extended Introduction and an Index to all the terms and synonyms. If this volume should be well received, the second and third volumes will be prepared coöperatively, and the final fourth volume will follow, a Cumulative Index to the entire Classification.

An eminent librarian of the older generation wrote me some years ago that to him it then seemed "unfortunate to launch a new system of classification on the library world." He meant of course that it would be unfortunate for the new ship and its crew and passengers. The mental attitude that the problem of classification for libraries was once satisfactorily solved for all time, or at least for the twentieth century in America, exemplifies one phase of the conservatism of the historical situation.

But the newer generation of librarians may regard it as rather *fortunate* to have a new ship in the offing, when the old ship becomes too leaky to bear them expeditiously. In the future, however, it will be only by their coöperation that such a new ship can be constructed, maintained, and manned. If reconstructed, it would thus become their ship. Such a coöperative standard classification should prove not only more efficient than merely arbitrary and "practical" classifications, and more valuable educationally and intellectually, but also more durable fundamentally because it is relatively permanent in its general classes; for the main branches of knowledge and the main concepts and relationships of superpersonal science are more stable than the various practical, personal, and notional interests of men, which pass with the minds that sustain them.

BIBLIOGRAPHICAL NOTES

A few books and articles that seem especially relevant to the interests and arguments of this book are briefly mentioned here, without any approach to completeness. Most of them are in English and of the recent period. The notes are not meant as criticisms, but merely to indicate the present writer's impressions of their value and relation to the subject-matter of this book. For convenience here titles of articles are cited in italics as well as those of books and periodicals.

BACON, Corinne. *Classification: preprint of Manual of Library Economy, Chapter XVIII,* published by the American Library Assn., 1916; revised ed. 1925. 37p. A convenient guide, with selected bibliography. It quotes from some of the leading contributors up to that time, and gives bits of discerning criticism.

BISHOP, William Warner. *Subject Headings in Dictionary Catalogs,* a paper read at the A. L. A. Conference in 1906; mentioned on p. 164 *supra.*

BLISS, Henry E. *A Modern Classification for Libraries, with simple notation, mnemonics, and alternatives.* This is the first outline of the argument, and of the system then proposed, which has since been much modified. In *The Library Journal,* August, 1910, v. 35, p. 350-8.

——. *Simplified Book-Notation,* and *A Simplified Alphabetic-order Table,* two brief articles in *The Library Journal,* December, 1910, and February, 1912, give more details of certain matters than this book's chapter on "Notation," where they are mentioned.

——. *Practical Considerations regarding Classification,* a paper read before the College and Reference Section of the American Library Assn., June, 1913 (*Proceedings,* p. 309-15). This treated the problem broadly, brought out some of the ideas developed in this book, and made some comparisons, and some pointed suggestions.

——. *The Problem and the Theory of Library Classification,* a paper read at the A. L. A. Catalog Section, June, 1917. (*Bulletin,* v. 11, p. 200-2). A very succinct statement was given of the writer's position, since then developed and adapted to changing conditions.

——. *More Adequate Coöperative Classifying and Cataloging,* a definite plan presented before the Catalog Section of the A. L. A., June, 1927. (*Bulletin,* v. 21, p. 252-5).

——. *Standardization in Classification for Special Libraries.* This epitomized an argument and mentioned an application to a library of Chemistry. In *Special Libraries,* March, 1929, v. 20, p. 74-6.

———. *The Organization of Knowledge and the System of the Sciences,* New York, Holt, 1929, 433 p. This precursor of the present book furnishes the scientific, philosophic, and logical grounds for the study of bibliographic classification, and the educational foreground. This second volume depends on it and often refers to it; and so may the reader well do.

———. *Billionaire Bibliography,* in *The Library Journal,* v. 56, p. 435-9 (May 15, 1931). Animadversions on bibliographic projects of immense detail and complexity, referring particularly to *La Classification Décimale universelle,* and Dr. S. C. Bradford's advocacy of it as an international standard.

———. *Scientific is not Philosophic Classification;* a reply correcting an unfair criticism; it appeared in *The Library Association Record* for May, 1931 (p. 174-5).

———. *Classification for Bibliography of Science—a problem;* again replying to Dr. Bradford's advocacy of the Decimal Classification as an international standard, this communication suggests standardization of a new classification developed thru international coöperation of scientists, scholars, and bibliographers. In *Nature,* v. 127, p. 889-90 (June 13, 1931).

———. *What do you Mean by Practical Classification?* This brief leading article in *Special Libraries,* v. 24, p. 35-7 (Classification Number, March, 1933) stresses that practical classification should subordinate and collocate relevant subjects, not merely index them as specific.

———. *Comment la Classification bibliographique peut être standardisée,"* in *Revue du Livre,* 2. année, 1934, 109-114 and 147-150, followed by a translation into English.

———. *L'Illogisme de l'Ordre alphabétique,* in *Revue du Livre,* 3. année. 1935, 16-19, followed by a translation into English.

———. *Special, related to General, Bibliographic Classification,* a paper read before the University and Research Section of The Library Association (British), at the Conference at Scarborough, England, June, 1937, and printed in the *Library Association Record,* June, 1937, Supplement, p. 318-322, and Discussion, p. 322-326.

———. *Consistent Classification for Special Libraries,* in *Special Libraries,* v. 29, p. 78-84, March, 1938.

———. *Theoretic Principles of Bibliographic Classification,* a paper presented before the XIV Conference of International Federation for Documentation at Oxford, England, September, 1938, and published in the Transactions of the Conference, v. 1, p. 57-65.

Brown, James Duff. *Library Classification and Cataloging.* London, 1912, 261 p. Chapters I-V are on Classification and Notation; Chapter VI on Classification and Cataloging; and chapters VII-IX are relative to Cataloging. Chapter VI is of especial interest in relation to two of our chapters, VI, "The Art of Classifying Books," and VIII, "Relations to Cataloging." Mr. Brown rightly emphasized the close relation of subject-cataloging to classification.

But he erred in supposing that subjects in classification are to be treated as separate, as they are in an alphabetic subject-catalog, and in his *Subject Classification*. The principle of collocation of related subjects he apprehended, but he overlooked its relation to subordination. Yet one of the most patent faults of his system is the overworked subordination of applied scientific studies to the relevant theoretical sciences, etc. It is his view that "The main divisions of classification schemes are liable to much change; the subdivisions are also liable, but specific subjects may be regarded as beyond change in relation to one another, though various circumstances may combine to make their transference to other subdivisions or main classes desirable." (p. 98). But we have argued to the contrary conclusions that general classes are the less changeable and impermanent. These chapters deal, however, with historical and practical matters rather than with theoretical principles.

BURGESS, Lawrence A. *Canons of Classification, a revaluation.* This interesting article in *The Library World*, v. 34, p. 3-6 (July, 1931), courteously but rather trenchantly disparages the theoretical value of the principles and canons of both Dr. Richardson's volume and Mr. Berwick Sayers' *Canons* and *Manual*. In prior articles in the same periodical, v. 27, p. 91-6, 124-7, 197-200, and 214-15, Mr. Burgess had offered some sound opinions on classification scientific and bibliographic. He distinguished between "differentiative" (specific and dispersive) and "correlative" (synthetic or collocative) classifications. He also outlined a scheme of his own, which seemed very estimable.

COULSON, Thomas. *Outline of the Theory of Classification.* Two concise articles in *The Library World,* v. 14, p. 37-42 and 67-70 (1912), compact with valid statements, some quoted from authorities, but many of them probably original, we commend to those who would have a very brief account of some of the logical grounding of a theory of classification. They are, however, far from complete. They are too concise to be clear to those unversed in the subject. But Mr. Coulson is to be credited with having well compacted much in small compass.

CUTTER, Charles A. Eminent among the classificationists of the formative period of American library economy, and one of the most intelligent and scholarly, Mr. Cutter, in his many papers, addresses, notes, etc. on classification and notation, was intent upon promoting and explaining his own *Expansive Classification,* and upon critical and controversial aspects, in which he was effective and instructive; but he nowhere, so far as the writer knows, brought together the general ideas and principles on which a theory and a system should be based.

DEWEY, Melvil. Effectively controversial too, as well as practical, were Dr. Dewey's contributions during the same period. But more recently his positions have been rather defensive of those well established in the past for his own system. Thruout his writings on the subject, however, there are many good points that should be considered. Dr. Dewey was such a clear thinker that it is regrettable that he did not bring together his principles in a general statement. This was not done even in the Introduction to the *Decimal Clasification.*

DIESCH, Carl. *Katalogprobleme und Dezimalklassifikation: eine Bibliothekswissenschaftliche Untersuchung und Abwehr.* Leipzig, Harrasowitz, 1929, 66 p. This pamphlet is a trenchant and thorogoing argument against the introduction of the Decimal Classification in European libraries and especially in those of Germany, for use in classified subject-catalogs or otherwise. The lack of scientific and systematic order in the D. C. is regarded as a menace to the systematic organization of the research resources in German libraries. In these pages there are many points of general interest to classifiers; but to those averse to the D. C. Dr. Diesch's criticism will be especially welcome as one of the most powerful that has been brought to bear, tho it is argued with perhaps too much bias.

EDWARDS, Edward. *Memoirs of Libraries,* contains a historic chapter on "Classification Systems" for libraries (Part II, Economy of Libraries, Book III, Chapter II). It outlines leading historic systems.

FOCKE, Rudolf. *Grundlegung zu einer Theorie des systematischen Katalogs:* in *Sammlung bibliothekswissenschaftlicher Arbeiten,* Heft 13, 1900. Also, *Classification: the general theory:* a paper read at the A. L. A. Conference in 1904. These two papers do indeed attempt to lay down general principles of a theory in a rather positive manner, but these are hardly comprehensive, nor altogether valid, nor applicable. Referring especially to the subject-catalog, the principles are extended to bibliographic and to library classification. Dr. Focke advocated a combination of the classified systematic and the alphabetic principles in subject-catalogs. He rightly maintained the importance of grounding library classifications on the system of science and the classifications in the several sciences, while combining these with formal, bibliographic, and literary components.

GJELSNESS, Rudolph H. *Reclassification in Libraries.* This interesting paper in *The Library Journal,* July, 1928, p. 597-600, found considerable reclassification in progress at the time and expects much more to follow. Methods were indicated and economies pointed out. Resulting advantages were considered and the view held that reclassification should be undertaken as conditions permit and increasingly require. Mr. Gjelsness' thoughtful article on *The Classified Catalog vs. The Dictionary Catalog,* in *The Library Journal* for January 1, 1931, p. 18-21, confirms some of my opinions, but it was of subsequent date.

GROLIER, Edmond de. *La Normalisation en matière de Classement systématique et alphabétique,* Conférence faite à la Maison de la Chimie, 1935, and published in *Revue du Livre,* 3. année, 1935, p. 136-140. This masterly article has done much to clarify and encourage thought and purpose in this subject, and in ensuing undertakings. M. and Mme. de Grolier, bibliographers of high reputation in the international circles that have centered about Paris and LaHaye, founders and editors of *La Revue du Livre*, have in several papers and conferences contributed very effectually to the advocacy of a more scientific, efficient, and economical bibliographic classification. They concur with the writer in maintaining that *La Classification Décimale* is disqualified. Their contributions are distinguished by thoro knowledge of the entire field of discussion, penetrating thought, and sound judgment, and by beautiful clarity of exposition.

HULME, E. Wyndham. *Principles of Book Classification.* This series of six brief chapters was published in *The Library Association Record,* October, 1911 to May, 1912. These chapters are thoughtful and attempt to get down to fundamentals, but they are too vague, and the principles on closer scrutiny prove neither valid nor applicable. While Mr. Hulme appreciated the relativity of classes, the principle of collocation, and that of coördination, he failed to recognize the no less important principles of subordination, gradation by speciality, and maximal efficiency. He iterated that principles of classification for libraries had not up to that time been brought out clearly in the discussions, and that the leading systems had not been constructed in consistency with such principles. We agree with him, and we extend the stricture up to this time.

KELLEY, Grace Osgood. *The Classification of Books.* New York, The H. W. Wilson Co., 1937, 200 p. This study was originally a thesis for the degree of Doctor of Philosophy at the University of Chicago, but it has since been expanded and adapted to the broader interests that it now addresses. The book contains seven chapters in 129 pages, followed by a Bibliography of 18 p. and an Appendix of 40 p. (half of them blank) for Problems and questions in detail for students. First "The Reader's Point of View" is considered, then the "Historical Background" in America, again "The Subject-approach," and in Chapter IV thirteen limitations to "the usefulness of classification." After these introductory, implicative, and critical chapters, come two partly statistical investigations: "Investigation Number One, How Systematic Classification Works," which shows that needs "can be met only partially through classification" (p. 127); and "Investigation Number Two, Distribution of Titles under Specific Subjects in the Dictionary Catalog," of which the conclusion was that ". . . of all the material on a subject which is brought out under that subject in a well-made dictionary catalog, one third is shelved under the subject's specific class-number, one third appears in the form of analytical entries shelved with the main series, and one third is shelved elsewhere." (p. 125). These two partly statistical investigations found very inefficient classification in four eminent libraries using the Decimal Classification and that of the Library of Congress.

Impelled by these findings, Dr. Kelley trenchantly questions in the preceding chapters the efficiency of all *specific* classification, by whatever system; and her implications might by the not-too-careful reader be extended to all *subject*-classification, general as well as special. She really does not mean that; but, if she did, the conclusions might be disproved, the writer believes, by her own methods. They have already been anticipated and countervailed by the arguments of this book: that the classifications usually adopted are inefficient because inadequate, unfit, antiquated, and ineptly applied; and that dictionary catalogs are usually equally inefficient, or more so, because they are dispersive, complicated, and cumbersome, that both classifications and catalogs should be more efficient, and that subject-catalogs for large libraries and research libraries should be classified and complemented with subject-indexes.

Regarding Dr. Kelley's first Investigation, intended to show that for special subjects only a part, perhaps only a small percentage, of the resources of a library on that subject, may be found under the special class-mark, too small a sample was chosen, and the subjects were too specific, and in only one library—only three zoölogical subjects: Beaver, Buffalo (or American Bison), and Cormorant. The Schedules of the Library of Congress do not provide for these subjects under those names, but under the taxonomic orders, Rodentia, Ungulata, and Steganopodes. In the University of Chicago Library but little of the material on those subjects (in each case only one book) had been classified under those orders (no wonder), but considerable elsewhere. Other readings, pages, paragraphs, pamphlets, periodical articles, reports, etc. were of course in more comprehensive books, or sets, zoölogical or other. But in the dictionary catalog these titles, together with the analytical entries, had entered under the common names. That is what a subject-index can do. Dictionary catalogs have on principle been developed for specific subjects; classifications *of books* have not, tho schedules *for* very specific details have indeed been elaborated—but not for these specific subjects. Of course, despite the cards in the dictionary catalogs, the actual resources were still dispersed in the libraries. If more general subjects, with distinct class-marks, had been chosen, e.g. Photography, and Wild Flowers, there would have been many books under the class-marks, and classification would have proved as efficient as the dictionary catalog, or more so. These specific taxonomic samples may support Dr. Kelley's arguments, but they should not be mistaken to discredit *all* subject-classification. For from little little can be inferred.

The second Investigation, however, had taken an adequate sample, 70 special subjects in two large libraries using the L. C. schedules, and 54 other subjects in two large libraries using the D. C. But many of the subjects were too special for the classifications as applied in those libraries. It is not surprising that there were no books on Firedamp in the University of Chicago Library, and none on Mites either in Northwestern University or in the Massachusetts State Library; that under Faults, in Geology, there were none in Chicago University, only one in Northwestern University, and only 3 in the Library of Congress; that under Salvage there were only 2 in L. C. and 1 in Chicago University, and that each of these great libraries had only one book classified under Regicides. But for other special subjects in those four libraries that same Table X shows more books and most of them classified under their special class-marks: for Mosses 84 under the class-mark in L. C. and only 9 shelved elsewhere, and 31 analyticals in the catalog, while in Chicago University there were 58 with the class-mark, 12 on other shelves, and only 28 analyticals. For Referendum in Chicago University the respective figures were 34 against 23 and 25; and in L. C. 99 against 58 and 7; and in Northwestern University 28 against 26 and 22. Such subjects show much higher percentages for the classifications as compared with the still higher percentages of the catalogs. Again this investigation is unfair to subject-classification as it *is* — and as it *should be*.

Dr. Kelley's book, however, despite the inconclusiveness of these two "investigations" and despite the perhaps too challenging introductory chapters, which they may have incited, is indeed a very interesting inquiry, thoughtful, comprehensive, well written, and otherwise well documented. Its opinions are based on ample knowledge, wide experience, and thoro scholarship. Its conclusions are mostly valid, even tho some of its implications are not. The chief trouble with it is that it is likely to be mistaken for discredit to all subject-classification in libraries, and that it favors the inefficient dictionary catalog. But Dr. Kelley's study should be studied carefully. It is a valuable contribution to the problems in question.

MANN, Margaret. *Introduction to Cataloging and the Classification of Books. Library Curriculum Studies.* Chicago, American Library Assn., 1930, 424 p. The purposes to furnish an introduction, a text-book, and a study are well justified here and well fulfilled. The book deals with Cataloging more than with Classification, but chapter III gives nine pages to an "Introduction to Classification," then ten pages to a study of a classification of Architecture (as a "type" subject), and the final five pages to statements regarding classifying and making schedules. Then chapters IV and V describe the three leading American systems; and chapter VI is on "Book Numbers and the Shelf-list." Farther on, chapter XII studies "The Classified Catalog." "Cataloging and Classifying History Books" is the subject of the last chapter, XX (ten pages). Appendix III tells how to compute the cost of classifying and cataloging. This is esteemed as a very useful and valuable book, especially in the library schools, for which it has been mainly intended.

MARTEL, Charles. *Classification: a brief conspectus of present-day practice.* This paper, read before The New Zealand Library Association, was published in *The Library Journal*, August, 1911,

p. 410-16. After considering some questions as to the adoption of a classification, it gives a brief historical notice of several older systems, then of Dewey's, of Cutter's, of Brown's, and also of Hartwig's. This is followed by advocacy of the Classification of The Library of Congress. Mr. Martel's tone is fair and restrained; his statements are valid and his principles sound. This article, tho contributing little to theoretical views, is commendable for its informative content and its judicious criticism. An earlier paper of his, read at the A. L. A. Conference in 1904 (*Proceedings*, p. 132-4), is composed similarly of valuable brief comment and fair comparison.

MERRILL, William Stetson. *Code for Classifiers, principles governing the consistent placing of books in a system of classification.* Chicago, American Library Assn. 1928, 128 p. "Code" implies a system of rules approved by authority. This code was issued with the approval of the A. L. A. Committee on Cataloging and Classification. Originally based on the author's rulings in classifying for The Newberry Library, in Chicago, and submitted in 1914 in mimeographed form, for constructive criticism, it has since been expanded in collaboration with Miss Julia Pettee and Miss Grace Osgood Kelley, especially for philosophic and scientific and technological subjects. Tho arranged according to the Decimal Classification, it is applicable, the author says, to any system of library classification. This Code should be useful mainly in supplementing deficiencies of the D. C. The six general "principles" and the ten "Directions applicable to any class of material" seem to this critic less comprehensive than they may have seemed to their author. These (in the front of the book) are followed by seventeen less generally applicable. Some indeed seem less applicable than the alternatives presented, and some are rather gratuitous. Some of the definitions seem good, but others seem out of place. Some of the definitions and rules would be appropriate in a text-book and others would be more useful in schedules of classification. By valid generalization the 300 rules would reduce perhaps to half the number.

PETTEE, Julia. *Factors in Determining Subject Headings*, in *Library Journal*, December, 1929; mentioned on p. 167 *supra*.

PHILLIPS, W. Howard, F.L.A., *A Primer of Book Classification*. London, Association of Assistant Librarians, 1937, 168 p. A concise outline is this of the subject as presented by Brown and by Berwick Sayers, with notices of more recent contributions and some distinctive features of its own. Its purpose is, however, mainly for library-school students and their instructors, especially in preparation for examinations. It seems most interesting in these aspects and is probably better for these purposes than the other books, except Berwick Sayers' *Introduction*. The first fifty pages are descriptive and instructive, the next eighty pages are historical, and the third part, twenty-three pages, is practical and pedagogic. Three interesting appendices follow.

RANGANATHAN, S. R., M.A., L.T., F.L.A. *Prolegomena to Library Classification.* Madras, Madras Library Ass'n, 1937, xvi, 305 p. A theoretical treatment of principles and methods in this book sets forth 28 "Canons" with peculiar but suggestive names, besides other rules and definitions, and elaborates all these with especial reference to the author's *Colon Classification,* published previously, and with detailed comparison with the *Decimal Classification,* the *Subject Classification* of Brown, and the *Library of Congress Classification.* As the writer reviewed the *Prolegomena* more adequately in *The Library Quarterly,* v. 8, p. 299-303 (April, 1938), and as the *Colon Classification* is criticised in a section of this book (p.298-304), it seems needless to notice these interesting books more fully here.

———. *Theory of Library Catalogue.* Madras Library Ass'n, 1938, 393 p. Of this prolific writer's books this is probably the most comprehensive with regard to its subject, and it is penetrating too, as the others have been. It will, we think, reward careful study. The writer welcomes it especially because it strenuously advocates the Classified Subject-catalog. But he repeats the stricture that to effectuate that form of subject-catalog and to render it efficient requires a far simpler notation than that of the *Colon Classification,* or than that of the *Decimal Classification,* or even than that of the Library of Congress. Another welcome confirmation is that "main entries" in the author-catalog should be shorter than in the subject-catalog, where fuller description may be requisite. This means also that the economy of the "unit-card" is uneconomical in the readers' "author-approach."

RICHARDSON, Ernest Cushing. *Classification, theoretical and practical.* New York, 1901; 2nd ed., 1912, 154 p.; 3rd ed., 1930. This little book is so well known as a text and as an annotated bibliographic manual, that it may seem needless here to advise students of library classification regarding it. Simple and elementary, it goes, however, to the roots of the matter. It is replete with wise and witty statements. That it was not very carefully reasoned, written, and printed has been no great detriment, considering its original purpose as elementary lectures for library school classes. Tho used as a text, it is not intrinsically a text-book; it has been much more. It was not intended for scientists and philosophers, nor for classificationists; yet the order of the sciences that it indicated, or advocated, entitle it indeed to its place among the very few that have nearly solved that part of the problem.

SAYERS, W. C. Berwick. *Canons of Classification, applied to "The Subject," "The Expansive," "The Decimal," and "The Library of Congress" Classifications: a study in bibliographical method.* London, 1915-16, 173 p. Mr. Sayers' "canons" are precepts rather than principles or laws drawn from theoretical investigation. They are far from satisfying the quest for fundamentals. The book is valuable chiefly for its descriptive, historical, and critical chapters.

———. *An Introduction to Library Classification, theoretical, historical, and practical, with readings, exercises, and examination papers.* 5th ed., revised, London, Grafton, 1938, xxiv,351 p. Successful thru five editions, this book has received much praise, and has well deserved all praise both for its educational and its literary qualities. It is especially meritorious in its historical, critical, and practical chapters—which is to say virtually thruout its scope. It is more like a text-book than Richardson's and more comprehensive than Margaret Mann's book, cited above, and the recent *Primer* of W. Howard Phillips, also noticed above. The writer has found it more interesting and the reader has probably found it more readable.

———. *A Manual of Classification for Librarians and Bibliographers.* London, Grafton, 1926, 345 p., with illustrations and bibliography. This is the most substantial book of its kind so far published on this subject in English, yet the author modestly says that he wishes it were more so. It is written in an engaging, readable manner, and is graced with a gentle intellectual sincerity. The author expressed fond appreciation for Dr. Richardson's book, which had been a stimulus to his own, which he realized was in some respects inadequate. The materials of Mr. Sayers' preceding books, especially the *Canons,* have been developed, extended, and reorganized in this *Manual.* In its first "Division," called "The Theory of Classification," it goes into logic, tho not too deeply. Its second Division, "History and Description," is, however, especially valuable, as is also the Bibliography in Appendix II. The third division, "The Practical Work of Classification" is informative thruout its ten brief chapters on topics relating to classifying, shelf-listing, cataloging, marking books, filing, etc.

The second edition of this estimable book has been announced by the publishers. The author in correspondence with the writer has intimated that the book will be not only improved but extended. We may indeed expect that its highly valued qualities in the past edition will be much enhanced by new and superior values in the forthcoming edition.

Schneider, Georg. *Handbuch der Bibliographie.* Leipzig, Hiersemann, 3rd ed., 1923, 544 p. This author's comprehensive views on subject-cataloging and classification, and his suggestive animadversions, were less interesting to this reader at the time than his criticism of the Decimal Classification, which is rather trenchant, at least in places. "Viel Irrthum und ein Fünkchen Wahrheit" was the motto he placed under the heading of his critique of the "Brüssler System" (p. 144). The 4th edition differs in extending other parts of the work, while reducing these.

Sharp, Henry A., *Cataloguing, a text-book for use in libraries.* With an Introduction by L. Stanley Jast. 2nd ed., revised and enlarged. London, Grafton, 1937, xxi, 472 p., illustrated. This very good and very complete book contains chapters on "Various Forms of Catalogues and their Purposes," "Cooperative and Centralized Cataloguing," and on "Classification and Cataloging," which are of especial interest to the purposes of our study. Mr. Sharp is fair in estimating the advantages of the classified catalogue over the dictionary form, but one wonders whether he considers the Decimal Classification good enough for that purpose and its lengthy notations short enough for the people to handle, without entanglements. Yet, he says, there is an increasing tendency in England to develop the classified catalogue.

Spofford, Ainsworth Rand. In *A Book for All Readers,* Chapter XXI is on "Classification" (p. 362-72). This is an interesting "back number," written in an interesting style. It has a good grasp of the subject in its practical aspects; and it is still partly right, tho partly wrong. It is right in disapproval of too minute subject classification and too complicated notation. It is wrong in supposing that classification can be practical without being systematic.

Stott, Cecil A., M.A. *Classification and Cataloguing:* Chapter 4 in *A Guide for School Librarians*; issued by The Incorporated Association of Assistant Masters in Secondary Schools. Oxford University Press, 1937. Chapter 4 occupies p. 37-80; section 1, "Classification," p. 37-66; section 2, "Cataloguing," p. 67-80. This chapter is distinctly excellent for intelligent grasp of the subjects, sound judgment, and clear presentation in simplified outlines. The writer admired the clarity with which essentials were epitomized. He is particularly grateful for the comprehension and appreciation of his own system.

Voge, A. Law. *Classification Making.* This was the leading paper in the symposium in the session of the Catalog Section of the A. L. A., June, 1917, (*Papers and Proceedings,* p. 190-5). It is an earnest, thoughtful, and fairly successful attempt to bring forward some fundamentals both theoretic and practical. Some of these are very well stated and all are worthy of careful perusal by those interested in the development of opinion on the subject.

"Es wird nirgends verlangt, dass ein System philosophisch begründet sei; was man aber von einem System verlangen kann und muss, das ist, dass es dem natürlichen Empfinden nicht geradezu ins Gesicht schlägt. Und hierzu ist nur ein natürliches System imstande, das sich der naturgegebenen Ordnung der Dinge zwanglos anpasst. Eine ganz erkünstelte Ordnung, die weder logisch noch alphabetisch noch chronologisch ist, ist eben kein System mehr, sondern ein wirres Durcheinander."

. . . . "Auch das Alphabet ist ja kein logisches, sondern ein rein konventionelles Gebilde, und der alphabetische Sachkatalog, der sogenannte Schlagwortkatalog, entbehrt ja demgemäss auch jeder Logik in der Aufeinanderfolge der Ordnungsworte. . . . . Es ist auch ein durchaus auf mangelnder Kenntnis beruhender Irrtum, wenn man den bekannten natürlichen Systemen logische Überspitzung auf Kosten der praktischen Brauchbarkeit vorwirft."

Carl Diesch.

APPENDIX

THE THEORY OF BIBLIOGRAPHIC CLASSIFICATION SUMMARIZED

Reprinted from the concluding section of a paper presented to the International Federation for Documentation in its XIV Conference, held at Oxford in September, 1938, and printed in the *Transactions*.

A system of classification for such purposes should be *consistent* with the *logical principles* of classification; it should be *logical*. A classification is a system of classes in relations. A class is correlative to its *class-concept*, its definition, and its term, or terms. Classes may be of *real* objects, of *natural kinds* of things, of things *made*, or merely of *conceptual* things. Real and natural classes exist in real and natural *relations*, which also have conceptual correlates. The *objective realities* are correlative to *subjective concepts*, to conceptual subject-matters, to studies, sciences, technologies, and arts. Real and natural classes and relations, however diverse and various, are more *stable* and *permanent* that the conceptual classes and relations, which are more variable, because subjective. In so far as all classes and relations have conceptual correlates, *all* classifications imply conceptual correlation and they may be regarded as *conceptual*. Systems in which most of the classes and relations are natural are called *natural classifications*. They are more stable and permanent than those in which the classes and relations are *selected* and arranged in some subjective interest or purpose but not consistently with the logical principles and with the natural relations and orders. Such are called *arbitrary classifications*. Some of them are philosophic rather than scientific.

A class comprises *all* the individual things defined by its definition and named by its term, or terms. The terms of a classification should be used *consistently*. In these two modes of consistency a classification should be *self-consistent*, as well as consistent with its chosen or determinate *purpose*.

Individuals from several classes may form a *group*; they may come from, and they may enter, other groups. Groups are composite, selective, accidental, local, and temporary; they are not relatively permanent *totalities*, as classes are. But classes likewise may be grouped and re-grouped, and so may subject-matters, studies, and sciences; again so may books, documents, maps, etc. Arbitrary bibliographic classifications differ little from mere groupings of books, etc. Such groups frequently need to be re-grouped for uses, as interests require. But by logical and natural classifications such grouping is facilitated and economized.

A class may be divided into *sub-classes of specific characteristics and differences*; and these sub-classes may be subdivided again and again more and more specifically. The sub-classes of any class are more closely related to one an- and its subdivisions as *ramifications*. In each division the more specific sub-classes are *subordinate* to the more generic classes, in graded *subordination*, in *gradation by speciality*. *Generic* and *specific* are relative terms. Classes, or sub-classes, of the same order, or grade, are *coördinate*. The sub-classes of a single class may be regarded as its branches other than to those of other classes. Sub-classes chosen singly from successive grades may form a *scalar series*. In branching, ramifying, and scalar classifications subordination and coördination are thus relative and coherent. This is logical and systematic classification as distinct from arbitrary grouping.

By consistent logical *subordination* of the specific to the relevant or comprehensive generic classes, by *synthesis* and by *collocation* of *coördinate* classes and sub-classes, with regard to intrinsic likenesses, characteristics, and relations and to convenience in access and use, a synthetic and systematic bibliographic classification becomes most efficient in its various services—as efficient as the conditions permit. Such *maximal efficiency* depends moreover on consistency with the special classifications in the sciences, technologies, industries, and arts, and in the educational studies and the humanities, and generally on consistency with the comprehensive organization of knowledge established in the consensus of scientists and educators.

Logical, natural, and scientific classifications prove not only more efficient but more *stable and permanent* than philosophic and arbitrary classifications, the more so in their *natural* classes and their *general* classes, because these are more *comprehensive, adaptive,* and *developmental.* Moreover in their special details they tend to become more *stable* and *permanent* as the relevant theories become better verified and the knowledge comprised in them becomes more definitely organized in coherence with the comprehensive organization of knowledge. This stability depends on the *constancy of the order of nature,* on the reality of the relations comprised, and on the correlation of the knowledge to the verified realities. Such a comprehensive classification is adaptable and serviceable to many interests and purposes.

This logical, consistent, scientific, comprehensive, stable, and adaptable classification is also *systematic* and *synthetic.* In adaptation to bibliographic classification it should be furthermore systematic. The logical relations of subordination and coördination result in series of coördinate series, or *schedules.* The subordination of these coördinate series may be indicated by *indention,* or by secondary and tertiary columns, etc., that is, *tabular* classification. A tabular classification, or *table,* is convertible into a serial classification, or *schedule*; and the converse is true. Preceding the schedule, a condensed table, or *synopsis,* should show the logical and scientific relations. For each main class there should be a *class-synopsis,* and for the entire classification a general synopsis. Complex branching classifications, subclassifications, and cross-classifications may likewise be reduced to schedules. Thus a bibliographic classification, while consistent with the organization of knowledge, may itself be consistently systematic.

To adapt this system to the several more important views that are not too inconsistent with it, *alternative locations* should be provided and should be indicated in the schedules. *Details* in the schedules should also be alterable as need requires. Some less closely related subjects, not collocated in the classification, should be referred to in the schedules, and also in the shelf-labels, as in subject-catalogs. The system should be *expansible* by further subdivision, and it should be adaptive to insertion of new terms, or new specifications. It should moreover provide for *reclassification,* and should economize this. The classification should be adapted to the *plan of the building* and its furniture and equipment, or better, these should be adapted to the classification.

Notation is correlative to and *subsidiary* to classification, and it should be *readjustable.* It should be as simple and short as possible, should avoid *complex combinations,* and should have sufficient *capacity*; its *base* should equal, or exceed, the number of main classes, and it should be *expansible* correlatively to the classification. It should not exceed the *economic limit* of four or five factors for *class-marks* and four or five factors suffixed for the *internal notation.* Where it is mnemonic it should not distort the classification.

Auxiliary schedules for recurrent or common subdivisions or specifications by *forms,* methods, aspects, relations, languages, countries, cities, historical periods, etc. should systemize and economize the compilation, printing, and use of the schedules. Where two or more of these specifications are combined in *complex* or *composite* classification, the schedules should show which should *precede,* or they should present the alternatives.

For such systematic auxiliary schedules the notation may be partly *mnemonic,* but it should be as brief as possible and should avoid *confusing complexities.* It should not have too many composite orders, or complex *devices,* or symbolic suffixes. It should not be misconceived as mnemonic "*short-hand*" for the terms of the specifications. Nor should complex notation attempt to comprise all conceivable composite relations, aspects, and analytical contents of subject-matters or of resources. Such particulars and variations may be serviceable to *documentation* in its more intricate extensions, and to records and expressions of thought and discussion, but for bibliography they are too indefinite, and in the resources they are too intricate, and too complicated. They are accessible less effectually in bibliographic classification than in subject-cataloging and indexing; they are attainable in terms and definitions rather than in bibliographic classes. Thoughts and the relations of ideas, and their linguistic, literary, and artistic expressions and records may be rendered symbolically, but the symbolism of mnemonic notation for bibliography is limited by the simplicity and conciseness requisite for its uses.

An alphabetic *index* should locate all the terms of the classification, and also the customary synonyms, by means of the notation. The index should be more *specific* and *analytic* than the schedules in referring terms to the classification. It may moreover be *indirectly synthetic* in subordinating specific and topical sub-headings under certain of its general headings, or in merely referring from specific to general subjects; for analysis and synthesis are thus converse.

A systematic bibliographic classification consistent with the logical principles of correlation, subordination, and coördination, and with the synthetic principles of comprehension and collocation under general classes, may be consistent moreover with the comprehensive organization of knowledge maintained in the consensus of scientists and educators, and self-consistent in its terms and notations, and in the development of its schedules. In alternative locations and methods and in expansion of schedules and readjustment of notations it may become adaptively available for various applications and uses, especially for collections of books and documents and for their subject-catalogs, for bibliographies and for documentation. In *systematic schedules* it should economize *recurrent* specifications or *common subdivisions* and it may provide *systematically* for *composite relations* that can not economically be detailed in schedules. Such a system will prove not only functionally more efficient but structurally more stable and permanent than arbitrary and inadaptive classifications or groupings. Such a system should be coöperatively compiled, revised, and standardized by a representative international institution or association.

For special interests, institutions, sciences, technologies, industries, etc. special classifications, or expansions, should be coöperatively compiled and institutionally standardized. They should be consistent with the comprehensive standard, availing of alternative locations and methods, omitting irrelevant parts, readjusting or reapportioning the notations, or even adapting a different notation. For the different national requirements there should be similar adaptations, especially for histories and for literatures; and they should be institutionally developed and standardized also. Thus a plurality of classifications, special and national, may be consistent with and coherent and unitary in a comprehensive, standardized, international classification and system of standardization.

INDEX

NOTE

Adequacy, convenience, and economy here require subordination, inversion, concision, and abbreviation. Indention indicates subordination under the leading term,* but it also often implies a following term or phrase, e.g. Alternative methods / indicated. Inversions too imply subordination, placing the generic term ahead of the specific or modifying terms, or phrases, as Notation, / mnemonic, / schedules for. These have initial capitals only where they are names of persons or subjects or are distinctively name-like, for example Schedules, / Systematic. Some special subjects are, however, entered by their more specific terms, because distinctive, for instance, Collocation. References to *see* and *see also* are inserted where likely to avail. *See also* references under a subordinate term, or phrase, usually refer to another item under it, and so they need not express the more generic term. Adjective modifiers are used as shorter than their abstract nouns, where clear enough to specify, e.g. Classes, adaptive. But one must discern whether the adjective specifies, as in Notation, / mnemonic; or predicates, as in Notation, / letters, / mnemonic; or negates, as in numerals / not mnemonic. The few abbreviations that are not customary are recurrent and obvious.

INDEX